Alfred Williams Momerie

Defects of Modern Christianity and Other Sermons

Preached in St. Peter's, Cranley Gardens

Alfred Williams Momerie

Defects of Modern Christianity and Other Sermons
Preached in St. Peter's, Cranley Gardens

ISBN/EAN: 9783337077235

Printed in Europe, USA, Canada, Australia, Japan

Cover: Foto ©Lupo / pixelio.de

More available books at **www.hansebooks.com**

DEFECTS

OF

MODERN CHRISTIANITY

AND OTHER SERMONS

Preached in St Peter's, Cranley Gardens

BY

ALFRED WILLIAMS MOMERIE

M.A., D.SC., LL.D.

LATE FELLOW OF ST JOHN'S COLLEGE, CAMBRIDGE;
PROFESSOR OF LOGIC AND METAPHYSICS
IN KING'S COLLEGE, LONDON

FOURTH EDITION, REVISED

WILLIAM BLACKWOOD AND SONS
EDINBURGH AND LONDON
MDCCCXC

CONTENTS.

	PAGE
DEFECTS OF MODERN CHRISTIANITY—	
I. RADICAL MISCONCEPTION AS TO THE NATURE OF CHRISTIANITY, . .	1
II. WANT OF ENTHUSIASM, . . .	12
III. MISDIRECTED ENTHUSIASM, . . .	23
IV. WANT OF PROGRESS (I.) . . .	35
V. WANT OF PROGRESS (II.) . . .	47
VI. WANT OF DEVOTION TO CHRIST, . .	61
JOB—	
I. INTRODUCTORY, ...	73
II. CHAPTERS I.-III., . . .	83
III. CHAPTERS IV.-X., ...	97
IV. CHAPTERS XI.-XVII., ...	108
V. CHAPTERS XVIII.-XXI., . . .	120
VI. CHAPTERS XXII.-XXVIII., . . .	132
VII. CHAPTERS XXIX.-XXXI., . .	144
VIII. CHAPTERS XXXVIII.-XLII., . . .	156

ELIHU'S SPEECH—

  JOB XXXII.-XXXVII., ... 171

CHRISTIANITY AND PRE-CHRISTIAN RELIGION—

 I. PRE-CHRISTIAN RELIGION, . . . 182
 II. THE INCARNATION, ... 198
 III. THE ATONEMENT, ... 213
 IV. REDEMPTION, ... 226

CHRISTMAS-DAY, ... 239
THE REST OF FAITH, ... 251
AGAINST CENSORIOUSNESS, ... 265
THE GREATNESS OF MAN, ... 276
PUNISHMENT, ... 291
THE GIFTS OF THE SPIRIT, ... 305
THE TRIUNE GOD, ... 317

THE CONNECTION BETWEEN REASON AND FAITH—

 I. THE RELIGIOUS USE OF REASON, . . 330
 II. THE LIMITATIONS OF KNOWLEDGE, . . 343
 III. THE FUNCTION OF FAITH, . . . 355

Defects of Modern Christianity.

I.

RADICAL MISCONCEPTION AS TO THE NATURE OF CHRISTIANITY.

"Not every one that saith unto me, Lord, Lord, shall enter into the kingdom of heaven; but he that doeth the will of my Father."—MATTHEW vii. 21.

WE are, in a sense, too familiar with the Bible. No doubt the fact that its words have fallen upon our ears from our earliest childhood, has connected them in our minds with a number of associations which are of great, and almost priceless, value. But on the other hand, the very same repetition which tends to produce and increase these associations, tends at the same time to obscure the full and exact meaning of the words themselves. The New Testament abounds in expressions which would startle us if we were to hear them now for the first time; but as it is, they have little or no effect. We have heard them so often that we think we must understand them, and therefore we never attempt to fathom their significance. Take, for example, such sentences as these: "Labour not for the meat which perisheth." "Lay not up for yourselves treasures upon earth." "Seek ye first the kingdom of God." "He that taketh not his cross and followeth after me is not worthy of me." "Except ye eat the flesh of the Son of man and drink His blood, ye have no life in you." "If any man come to me, and hate not his father and mother, yea, and his own life also, he cannot be my disciple." "Whosoever he be of you that forsaketh not all that he hath, he cannot be my disciple."

I propose to speak to you this Lent about some of the defects of modern Christianity. I want you to contrast the Christianity of Christ with the Christianity of Christendom, Christianity as it is with Christianity as it should be, Christianity as it is frequently misrepresented and misunderstood with Christianity as it is described in the words of its divine Founder.

It is manifest, of course, that everything which

calls itself Christianity cannot be legitimately entitled to the name, for we find the most antithetical and contradictory systems laying claim to the same designation. One sect, for example, tells us that God loves all men, and wishes them to be saved; another says that, with a few exceptions, He hates them all, and has determined they shall be damned. One sect says that the disciple of Christ is bound to set an example of good conduct; another says that it does not in the least matter whether his conduct be good, bad, or indifferent.[1] This diversity in so-called Christian sects existed from the very first. St John found it necessary to exhort his readers to exercise a thoughtful discrimination. "Believe not every spirit," he said, "but try the spirits whether they are of God; because many false prophets are gone out into the world."

Iniquities have been perpetrated by professed Christians, and even in the sacred name of Christ Himself—iniquities as grievous and abominable as ever disgraced the most benighted

---

[1] One of my reviewers thinks there is no such sect. But the above clause expresses precisely the doctrine of the extreme High Calvinists, who hold that an elect person does not sin, even when he commits actions which are in themselves wicked. Whittier speaks of
"Antinomians free from law,
Whose very sins are holy."

paganism. And the antagonists of Christianity often take advantage of these enormities, and urge them as arguments why a right-minded man must refuse to call himself a Christian. "To so many evils has religion persuaded men," exclaimed Lucretius and the old opponents of religion. "To so many evils has Christianity persuaded men," say the modern opponents of Christianity. This is a rhetorical device of which Swinburne has been fond of availing himself. But I was pleased to notice the other day—I daresay you noticed it too—in his sonnet published in the newspapers upon the persecution of the Jews, he rightly distinguishes the Christianity of Christ from the Christianity of Christendom. He does Jesus the justice to exculpate Him from the crimes which His professed followers have committed. He closes the sonnet with the following apostrophe:—

> "Face loved of little children long ago!
> Head hated of the priests and rulers then!
> Say, was not this Thy passion to foreknow,
> In Thy death's hour, the works of Christian men?"

I do not intend, however, now to dwell upon flagrant and atrocious violations of Christian principle. I wish to criticise rather, respectable, mediocre Christianity. I wish to speak of that kind of Christian (so called) who seems as innocent of doing anything very bad as he is of doing anything very good. By the expression "defects of modern Christianity," I do not mean, of course, to imply that all the defects to which I shall allude characterise, in their extremest form, *all* modern Christianity. God forbid! I only mean to say, that they are characteristic of large classes of men and women who are wont to call themselves Christians. Friedrich von Logau once said—" The Lutherans, the Papists, the Calvinists, are extant and flourishing, but where is Christianity?" There was this much truth in the sarcasm, that if we compare the members of these or any other denominations with the standard of excellence set up by Christ, we shall be compelled to acknowledge that some fall sadly short of that standard, and that others bear to it not the remotest resemblance.

To-day I wish to call your attention to a very common, but a very fatal, misconception as to what Christianity really is. The misconception to which I refer consists in regarding Christ's religion as a creed to be believed rather than a life to be lived. Christianity, of course, like every other religious system, does imply and require the acceptance of a creed. But it implies and requires infinitely more. Of two men who believe, or believe that they believe, identically the same creed, one may be a Christian and the other a pagan. And yet the Christian life is often represented as consisting simply in the adoption of a certain belief. The scheme of salvation has frequently been regarded as a device (kindly meant on the part of God, perhaps, but singularly ungodlike)—a device for making things comfortable to us, for saving us *in* our sins, for taking us to heaven with any amount of guilt and pollution we may choose to carry there. The man who has intellectually assented to the proposition that Christ died for him, or at any rate the man who has experienced some sort of moral spasm, which is dignified with the name of faith,—that man may dispense altogether with any attempt at right conduct. For him all good works are works of supererogation. He may not, perhaps, be any the worse for a few of them, but they are as unnecessary to his salvation as proficiency in the fine arts.

It is seldom, however, believers in this doctrine can be brought to admit that they really hold it. When it is stated to them in plain English, they generally say that they believe something else. And no doubt there is a modified, and less offensive, form of the belief, which is not uncommonly adopted. Many persons, for instance, put it in this way. They say that Christ's first and chief purpose was to procure our admittance into heaven; but they admit that He had also a subsidiary and less important purpose—viz., to teach us to act rightly here. Now this doctrine is *precisely the reverse* of that which the Saviour taught. He was always reiterating to His disciples the truth that their conduct *here* was of paramount importance, since it was that which would determine their condition hereafter. The future reward or punishment He represents as the direct consequence of conduct. "Come, ye blessed of my Father, inherit the kingdom prepared for you: *for* I was an hungered, and ye gave me meat: I was thirsty, and ye gave me drink.—Depart from me, ye cursed, into everlasting fire: *for* I was an hungered, and ye gave me no meat: I was thirsty, and ye gave me no drink."

In no religion is so much stress laid upon right conduct, in none is so much right conduct required, as in the religion of Christ. "He tightened," says the author of 'Ecce Homo,' "in an incredible degree all the obligations of morality. He rejected, as utterly insufficient, what had been regarded by the Jews as the highest moral attainments. It is useless, He said, to refrain from injuring your neighbour, if, notwithstanding, you have the wish, the impulse, to injure him. The movement of hatred is, according to Christ, morally equivalent to a murder. And even if you have no such immoral impulses, yet if your disposition towards your fellow-creatures be purely negative, if you are not actuated by an enthusiastic love and benevolence towards all mankind, you are morally good for nothing. Christ was not content, like the earlier moralists, with prohibitions, with condemning those who did wrong. He condemns those who have not done good. The sinner whom Christ habitually denounces is he who has done nothing. This character comes repeatedly forward in His parables. It is the priest and the Levite who pass by on the other side. It is Dives, of whom no ill is recorded, except that a beggar lay at his gates unrelieved. It is the servant who hid in a napkin the talent committed to him. It is the unprofitable servant who has merely done what it was his duty to do. And Christ not only raised the standard of morality to the highest possible point; but further, He insisted far more vehemently than previous moralists had done, upon the necessity of attaining the standard. He does not say—This is morality, but, as it is difficult of attainment, God will forgive your shortcomings. On the contrary, He says —To be moral in this high sense is life and peace; not to be so is death and eternal damnation. "Every one that heareth these sayings of mine, and *doeth them not*, shall be likened unto a foolish man, which built his house upon the sand; . . . and it fell; and great was the fall of it."

To say, then, that right-doing is unimportant for the Christian, or of secondary importance, is to give a flat contradiction to the words of Christ. He has never been more horribly blasphemed than by those professed disciples who insinuate that His gospel is not a gospel of right-doing. "The gospel," says Ruskin, "'let His life rule your lives,' is eternally true and salutary. The gospel, 'let His life be instead of your lives,' is eternally false and damnatory." Ruskin is right. The one is the gospel of Christ, the other is the gospel of the devil. They are as opposite as light and darkness; and yet, unhappily, the one is sometimes mistaken for the other. It is an appalling fact (unfortunately so common that we sometimes forget its deadly significance) that a sermon which aims at exhorting men to right-doing, would be characterised by some professing Christians as not a Gospel sermon. Not a Gospel sermon! Then Christ did not preach the Gospel, did not even comprehend it. He must have been sent into the world too soon. If He had but enjoyed the advantage of listening to these enlightened critics, they would have instructed Him in the way of salvation! In the Sermon on the Mount, Christ does not tell His hearers that He is going to do everything for them, and that they may sit still and take their ease. No! He gives His benediction to those who hunger and thirst after righteousness. "Except your righteousness," He warns them, "shall exceed the righteousness of the scribes and Pharisees, ye shall in no case enter into the kingdom of heaven." He exhorts them to let their light shine, so that men may see their good works. He commands them to avoid even an angry thought, or an unkind word, or a wanton look, and to be perfect even as their Father in heaven. "Every tree," He assures them, "which bringeth not forth good fruit, is hewn down and cast into the fire." "Many will say to me in that day, Lord, Lord, have we not prophesied in Thy name? and in Thy name have cast out devils? and in Thy name done many wonderful works? And then will I profess unto them, I never knew you: depart from me, ye that work iniquity." "Not every one that saith unto me, Lord, Lord, shall enter into the kingdom of heaven; but he that *doeth* the will of my Father."[1]

[1] See also the sermons on "The Gospel" and on "The Practical Nature of Christianity" in my 'Preaching and Hearing.'

Defects of Modern Christianity.

II.

WANT OF ENTHUSIASM.

" Whosoever he be of you that forsaketh not all that he hath, he cannot be my disciple."—LUKE xiv. 33.

THERE are many persons in the present day who never manifest enthusiasm about any thing. The *nil admirari* theory of life, suggested formerly by Horace, and reiterated by the love-sick hero of Tennyson's 'Maud,' is one of the gospels of the age. "Not bad" is about the highest praise which some persons would think it *respectable* to bestow. They consider enthusiasm to be a sign of under-breeding, or at any rate of ignorance. They imagine it shows wisdom to seem bored, to appear "used up" in the fruitless endeavour to discover something that has anything in it. They remind one of the lady of whom Steele said that she was much too "nice" to be quite alive. When the eccentric leader of one of the new cliques in English society tells us that there is nothing worth seeing in Switzerland, and that he considers the Atlantic a failure, he speaks not for himself alone, but for a large class of which he is the representative, and which forms his *raison d'être*. Strong feeling, energetic action, earnestness, zeal, devotion, self-abandonment, all this is considered by many quite unsuitable for the upper classes. Just as Lord Chesterfield would have us never laugh, for fear of distorting our countenances, so we are often forbidden to be enthusiastic, for fear of disturbing the calm dignity of a monotonous existence.

In religion the absence of enthusiasm is especially remarkable. There are, I fear, large classes of men and women who call themselves Christians, and who do not take the slightest interest in the religion of Christ. They profess Christianity merely because it is the correct thing to profess it. A few years ago, just before the mathematical tripos at Cambridge, a newspaper reporter called to interview the man who was expected to be senior, and asked him among other things what was his religion. "Oh," said the mathematician, " you had better put me down as an atheist." " But," urged the reporter, " that will not sound well. May I not say that you are of the same religion as your father ? " "Certainly," he replied, " by all means. Call me a member of the Church of England." There are a great many persons who are members of the Church of England on the same principle, because they think it would not sound well to be members of anything else. If Episcopalianism became unfashionable, they would discard it as ruthlessly as a worn-out garment. If religion were to be blotted out of human life, they would not miss it—or rather, they would agreeably miss it. The tiresome social duty of going to church would be at an end for them; and they would be saved a certain amount of expense— viz., the guinea or two they pay for their seat, and the threepenny-pieces they are obliged to put into the bag. They much begrudge this money; but as things are, they feel that they gain by the transaction.—And these people, who are only dishonest pagans, have the audacity to call themselves Christians!

The common misrepresentation of Christianity, to which I called your attention in the last sermon, has tended to prevent men from recognising the extreme importance which attaches to enthusiasm in the Christian system. If Christ's religion consisted in the mere acceptance of a creed respecting future destiny, it could never excite in us any strong or continued emotion. It would be easier to feel enthusiasm about the multiplication-table. That does lie at the basis of our daily transactions. But a future life, disconnected from the present, could never permanently affect men's hearts. The man for whom the only difference between Christ and Mohammed amounts to this, that if he believes in the one, he will be by-and-by, in theological language, saved; and if he believes in the other, he will be by-and-by lost,—such a man can never believe in Christ at all, except in a cold, matter-of-fact fashion which is *the very opposite* of Christian faith. If Christ's sole work is to take us to heaven, then we shall be satisfied, naturally and justly satisfied, with the smallest quantity of belief which will suffice for that purpose. Those who regard the plan of salvation as merely a device for escaping hell, need not feel at all insulted if the sarcastic language of Bailey's "Festus" is applied to them:—

> "Ye think ye never can be bad enough,
> And as ye sink in sin ye rise in hope.
> And let the worst come to the worst, ye say,
> There always will be time to turn ourselves
> And cry for half an hour or so to God.
> Salvation sure is not so very hard;
> It need not take one long; and half an hour
> Is quite as much as we can spare for it."

But Christ's religion is no mere creed about the future. It is a life to be lived in the present. And no life can be well lived without enthusiasm. Do you suppose you would succeed in the army or at the bar if you were satisfied with passively believing that they were a good sort of institution—if you contented yourself with appearing at certain stated times on parade or in the law courts? No indeed! You cannot be successful without hard study, strict discipline, and persevering effort, through which nothing but enthusiasm can carry you triumphantly. And if enthusiasm be necessary to live worthily the life of a soldier or a barrister, still more essential is it for him who would live the life of a Christian. Nothing else can possibly enable us to fulfil the requirements of Christ.

Let us see what these requirements originally were, and let us inquire how far they are the same for ourselves. To the young man who asked what he must do to inherit eternal life,

Christ replied that he must sell all that he had and give the proceeds to the poor. Another who professed himself ready to follow Christ, but asked permission first to attend his father's funeral, was curtly told to leave the dead to bury their dead. And a third was informed that if he really wished to become a disciple, he must not even go back to bid his relations farewell. "If any man come to me," said Christ, "and hate not his father, and mother, and wife and children, and brethren, and sisters, yea, and his own life also, he cannot be my disciple. . . . Which of you, intending to build a tower, sitteth not down first and counteth the cost, whether he have sufficient to finish it? Lest haply, after he hath laid the foundation, and is not able to finish it, all that behold it begin to mock him, saying, This man began to build, and was not able to finish. . . . So likewise, whosoever he be of you that forsaketh not all that he hath, he cannot be my disciple."

These are hard sayings. What are we to understand by them? He could not possibly have intended that they were to be always *literally* obeyed. He could not possibly have meant, for example, to ignore or deprecate the family affections as such. The very essence of Christianity is to show love and kindliness to all men. Christ could not, therefore, intend that those who had the strongest claims upon us should be treated with harshness and discourtesy. What He wished to teach was, that the family affections must be subordinate to the religious. When a man could not be loyal to an earthly love without being disloyal to Christ, then the earthly love must be suppressed. This explanation will help us, I think, to understand all similar injunctions. Christ spoke vehemently in order to startle men into attention. He was determined to be followed only by enthusiasts—by men who were prepared, if need be, to sacrifice everything for His sake. Commands and exhortations, like those I have quoted, constituted His winnowing-fan, with which He got rid of half-hearted followers. At one time He was enormously popular. It was when He was being followed by a large multitude, that He insisted on the necessity of their counting the cost, before making any profession of discipleship. No one, he intimated, need attempt to follow Him who would be unwilling, if occasion arose, to forsake all that he had. The true disciple must love his Master so much that, *in comparison* with this enthusiastic devotion, all other affections would appear but as hatred.

But what is the significance *for us* of these and similar words? The Dean of St Paul's, in his valuable lectures on the 'Gifts of Civilisation,' says that they meant more for those days than for ours. I would rather prefer to put it in this way: not that they meant more, but that they were oftener susceptible of a literal obedience. They seem to me only strong and passionate modes of enjoining men to seek first the kingdom of God; and this injunction is as binding to-day as ever. Christ requires of His followers now, as then, a willingness to give up whatever clashes with His claims on them. The only difference is, that formerly they had more frequently to prove this willingness by the *actual* forsaking of everything. To be a Christian then, was to put one's self in opposition to society and to the State. Christianity could only be procured a footing in the world by the fidelity, even unto death, of large numbers of its early propagators. The call of Christ, which always demands the same spirit of self-denial, involved then as a rule severer actual sacrifices. His religion would have died almost as soon as it was born, but for the sufferings and martyrdoms of its evangelists, which proved its power by showing what it was capable of helping men to endure. "The blood of the martyrs is the seed of the Church." Had His disciples been destitute of enthusiasm the name of Jesus of Nazareth would have been unknown to-day, or known only to the curious student of Jewish antiquities. At the present time, Christian missionaries are the only persons who occupy the same kind of position as the early disciples. Missionaries frequently have, in the most literal sense, to forsake everything out of regard for their work. We cannot, however, all be missionaries. It is not desirable that we should. And therefore the need is not likely to arise in our case of forsaking everything for Christ. But the need is certain to arise of forsaking much. Nay, more,—Christ requires even from us the willingness, *if need be*, to forsake all. Unless we feel for Him an enthusiasm sufficient to give Him the first place in our hearts, we cannot, He says, be His disciples, and we have no business to make any profession of Christianity.

And enthusiasm, which is thus requisite to start us on the Christian career, is needed throughout the whole of its course. For

Christian morality is not merely negative, it is positive in the highest degree. You will see better what I mean if you contrast Christianity with Judaism. A man did not require enthusiasm to make him a good Jew. There was enthusiasm, doubtless, among the psalmists and prophets, among the wiser and nobler members of the nation, as there always is among the good and great. But this was not necessary to make them Judaically religious. The requirements of Judaism were few and simple: they consisted merely in abstaining from certain clearly defined sins, and offering certain clearly defined sacrifices. But Christ's redeeming work is something very different. It consisted in the creation within His disciples of a passionate devotedness to the welfare of their fellow-men.[1] The ideal Jew is the man who never injures his neighbours. The ideal Christian is the man who is always doing them good. And for this, what but enthusiasm can suffice? It would be easier for an imbecile to become a philosopher, than for a cold-hearted man to live the Christian life. "If," says the author of 'Ecce Homo,' "there sometimes appear in the history of the Church instances of a tone which is pure and high without being enthusi-

[1] See sermon on Redemption.

astic, it will probably be found that all that is respectable in such a mood is but the slowly subsiding movement of an earlier enthusiasm, and all that is produced by the lukewarmness itself is hypocrisy and corrupt conventionalism. Christianity is an enthusiasm, or it is nothing."

It behoves us, therefore, to ask ourselves, Does Christ stand first in our affections? Are we *enthusiastically* endeavouring to live the Christian life? Are we, for example, more anxious about the Christ-likeness of our character than we are about our dividends or about our personal appearance? You remember some lines of Manrique's, which have been translated by Longfellow :—

> "Could we new charms to age impart,
> And fashion with a cunning art
>   The human face,
> As we can clothe the soul with light,
> And make the glorious spirit bright,
>   With heavenly grace,—
>
> How busily each passing hour
> Should we exert that magic power!
>   What ardour show!
>   .   .   .   .   .
> Yet leave the free-born soul within
>   In weeds of woe."

Should we? God forbid!

Defects of Modern Christianity.

III

MISDIRECTED ENTHUSIASM.

"The Samaritans did not receive Him, because His face was as though He would go to Jerusalem. And when His disciples James and John saw this, they said, Lord, wilt Thou that we command fire to come down from heaven, and consume them, even as Elias did? But He turned and rebuked them, and said, Ye know not what manner of spirit ye are of."—LUKE ix. 53-55.

IN the last sermon, I drew your attention to the want of enthusiasm, which is too often apparent in modern Christianity. Now let me ask you to consider the misdirected enthusiasm which frequently characterises it. The next worst thing to being destitute of enthusiasm altogether, is to expend it on the wrong objects.

The words I have read as a text afford a very suggestive example of my subject. "Shall we command fire to come down from heaven, and consume them?" Here was enthusiasm, and enthusiasm for Christ; but it was expending itself in unchristian, and even anti-Christian, channels. "He turned and rebuked them, and said, Ye know not what manner of spirit ye are of." Ye think that ye are Christians, but as yet ye are not. Ye do not even know why I am come into the world. "The Son of man is not come to destroy men's lives, but to save them."

We are constantly meeting in our everyday experience with instances of misdirected enthusiasm. For example, there are persons who will shed floods of tears over the imaginary griefs depicted in a novel or on the stage, who are hardness itself to the real sufferings around them in actual life. Their entire stock of sympathy is expended on fictitious objects. They have none left for practical life. There are persons, again, who feel the greatest interest in morality,—but unfortunately it is in the morality of other people. They never tire of pointing out defects in their neighbours' characters, but they take no pains to discover any in their own. And there are others who waste all their enthusiasm upon trifles. A great national calamity fails to move them; but if anybody utters a syllable derogatory to their own personal dignity, they are beside themselves with excitement.

Now, in every case in which enthusiasm is misdirected, it is worse than wasted. For its expenditure in the wrong direction necessarily involves its absence in the right. If it is wasted upon trifles, there will be none left to bestow upon matters of real importance. Like all the other forces with which our nature has been endowed, our power of enthusiasm is a strictly limited quantity. It may be diminished by carelessness; it may be increased by care; but it is at the best incapable of anything approaching to indefinite expansion. How important, then, that it be always wisely and justly bestowed! The very meaning of the word suggests that enthusiasm should not be given to anything and everything, but that it demands a worthy object. It signifies, etymologically, to be full of the Deity —to be, as we say, inspired. The term "enthusiasm" has been used, I know, by Locke, Isaac Taylor and others, in a bad sense — for the working of a diseased imagination, or for the stupidity of an unreasoning prejudice. But in modern English and in common speech, we signify by enthusiasm the taking a deep and ardent interest in any object or pursuit. And truly there is no power possessed by man so deserving of being called divine, as the power of becoming in this sense enthusiastic. Without it, as I pointed out in the last sermon, no life can be successful. With it, if duly applied, no life can be altogether a failure. But alas for the man who *wastes* the inspiration, which he needs to bring him triumphantly through the great struggles and conflicts of his career!

There are three cases, it seems to me, in which the enthusiasm of Christians—many of them good and earnest Christians—has been misdirected; I refer to what may be called the Puritanical, the Theological, and the Ritualistic enthusiasms.

By the Puritanical enthusiasm, I mean the giving up and anathematising certain practices and amusements, not on the ground that they are wrong, but on the ground that they are "worldly." This is the result of a mistake regarding a passage in St John's Epistle. "If any man love the world," he says, "the love of the Father is not in him." Now it is often forgotten that, in the very same Epistle, "the world" is defined as "that which lieth in wickedness." Nothing, then, can be legitimately called worldly, in the bad sense of the term, merely because it is fashionable or common. It is as absurd to suppose that everything fashionable is bad, as it would be to suppose that everything unfashionable is good. The Bible has nothing to say against the world except in so far as it is wicked. "I pray not," said our Lord, "that Thou shouldest take them out of the world, but that Thou shouldest keep them from the evil." So that the worldliness which is to be avoided by the Christian, is only another name for evil. Much mischief has arisen from supposing that it was something else. Classing together things which differ, always leads to great confusion, and in moral matters often ends in great sin. To believe in the wickedness of what is essentially harmless is to make a most fatal mistake. Those who exhaust their enthusiasm in hating what is *not* wrong, will have little—if any—left for hating what *is*. There are persons who think it more wrong to play a game of chance than to do a mean or ungenerous action. They must not be surprised at the accusation urged against them by Butler in his 'Hudibras':—

> "They *compound* for sins they are inclined to,
> By damning those they have no mind to."

And even less extreme cases of misdirected enthusiasm will have a very injurious effect upon the young. If they are taught that it is wrong to break the Commandments, *and* that it is wrong to play at certain harmless games, what is the result? Why, this: when they come to discover that the games *are* harmless, and cannot therefore be sinful, they begin to doubt whether the importance of the Commandments has not been equally overrated. Their notions about right and wrong become hopelessly disturbed, and not unfrequently they end in believing that there is nothing wrong in anything. I have known cases—you have known cases—where young lives have been shipwrecked by the severity of their puritanical training. The parents thought they were driving their children to heaven, when all the time they were really driving them in the opposite direction. Enthusiasm—like some powerful physical force—if it be exercised at random, is dangerous in proportion to its strength.

Then, secondly, there is what may be called the Theological waste of enthusiasm—manifested by persons who bestow on theology an amount of ardour which ought only to be given to religion. Theology and religion are sometimes supposed to be one and the same thing; but there are no two things in the universe more different. Theology is a collection of facts, or supposed facts, scientifically arranged and formulated. Religion is a state of heart and a mode of life. A theologian is not necessarily religious, any more than a physiologist or an astronomer. There is no more connection between the knowledge of theology and the practice of religion, than between the knowledge of geography and the possession of a landed estate. Theology, at best, is but theory. Indeed it has not unfrequently happened that those whose business it has been to teach the theory, have been in their lives conspicuously unchristian. The theologians have disagreed, and terrible has been the hatred, grievous has been the bloodshed, that have followed their disagreement. Instead of letting their enthusiasm go forth in the direction of doing all possible good to all men, they have too often wasted it in seeking to do all possible harm to those who hold different opinions from themselves. You remember the scene in 'Bleak House,' where poor Jo is dying. He is asked if he ever knew a prayer, to which he gives his usual answer that he " never knowed nothink." And then he goes on to explain that city missionaries had often come into the wretched alley where he lodged, but that they had been mostly occupied in pointing out each other's errors to their benighted congregations. "Different times," he said, "there was genelmen come down Tom-All-Alone's a-prayin', but they all mostly said as t'other ones prayed wrong." Alas! alas! how often the devil's purposes are effected in the Saviour's name! Our world would be infinitely better than it is if but a tithe of the enthusiasm, now expended on theology, were devoted to the task of living a religious life. Men are so busy shouting their party shibboleths, which Christ once and for ever condemned, that they have neither time nor heart to do the one sole work which He intrusted to their hands. They have been so anxious to be orthodox that they have forgotten to be good.

And once more, there is, as it seems to me, a Ritualistic waste of enthusiasm. I have nothing to say against ceremonies and vestments as such. Personally I do not care to see them multiplied; but that, of course, is no argument against them. What I do very strongly deprecate, however, is that so much enthusiasm should be expended on these matters. They have simply nothing to do with Christianity as Christ understood it. There is a pious sound about the word "vestment"; but, after all, it is only the Latin equivalent for what, in common speech, we call clothes. Just try and imagine, if you can, Christ delivering a discourse, or the apostles engaged in a discussion, as to the garments in which they should proceed to convert the world. And yet the question of clothes has destroyed the unity of the English Church.

I shall be told, of course, that the Ritualists are not fighting merely for vestments, but for principles. It was ingeniously suggested, some time ago, that they were in reality carrying on the designs of the Reformation, inasmuch as they were fighting for freedom—freedom against the tyranny of the bishops and the State. Very well. But even so, I ask, is it worth while? This alleged tyranny is only exercised in regard to what Christ at any rate would have considered minor matters.

I admit, of course, that at present there is a discrepancy between the Prayer-book and Lord Penzance, which common-sense demands that we should annul. What is called the "ornaments rubric" says that officiating clergymen are to wear the vestments worn in the reign of Edward the Sixth. These are the very vestments which the unfortunate Ritualists are prosecuted for wearing. Lord Penzance has decided—on what grounds I do not know—that this rubric is no longer legal. Now no one can suppose that either the rubric or Lord Penzance is divinely inspired. Therefore, since we cannot obey both, why should we not obey whichever will lead to peace? You say this is mean. I say it is not. The rubric, you observe, is called the *ornaments* rubric. To seek peace by discarding ornaments is not mean. To seek war by retaining ornaments is not noble. If a particular vestment be distasteful to my parishioners,—why, in the name of peace and quietness, can I not be content without it? "If it make my brother to offend, I will not wear it while the world standeth, lest I make my brother to offend."

But there is another side to this question. While I cannot understand the ritualistic enthusiasm *for* vestments, still less can I understand the anti-ritualistic enthusiasm *against* them. There cannot be anything more un-Christian in a berretta than in a college-cap. Why, then, while the one is considered harmless, should the other be subjected to such fierce hatred? The stole is an illegal vestment; and yet you find it even in churches where the sermon is preached in a black gown. I am wearing one at this moment. It never seems to excite anybody's ire; and yet the sight of some equally innocent ecclesiastical garment will rouse many Churchmen to fury. The enthusiasm expended by the Church Association and its friends, in hunting up or creating aggrieved parishioners, and otherwise persecuting the Ritualists—all such enthusiasm seems to me even more misplaced than that of the Ritualists themselves. In some recent prosecutions, the vestments worn by the clergymen were not distasteful to his congregation. Yet meddlesome outsiders must step in, persuade three parishioners to declare themselves aggrieved, and so try to get the pastor removed from people who were devoted to him. Surely this is the very prostitution of enthusiasm.

I have been obliged this morning to tread on delicate ground. You may not all agree with me. But that is a matter of small importance. I am not here to give you opinions. You are not here to receive opinions from me. We are met rather, I take it, to think things over together. And even if, in the end, we must agree to differ, it does not necessarily follow that our thinking will have been in vain. The important thing for you and for me, is to do our best to discover Christ's idea of Christianity, and to let our enthusiasm go forth into the same channels in which His was wont to flow. If this be our earnest and constant endeavour, then, although we may sometimes make mistakes, although we may, like the Boanerges, incur the rebuke, "Ye know not what manner of spirit ye are of," it will be a *gentle* rebuke— one of pity rather than of condemnation.

Defects of Modern Christianity.

IV.

WANT OF PROGRESS (I.)

"I have yet many things to say unto you, but ye cannot bear them now. Howbeit when He, the Spirit of truth, is come, He will guide you into all truth."—JOHN xvi. 12, 13.

"He that believeth on me, the works that I do shall he do also; and greater works than these shall he do."—JOHN xiv. 12.

DWARFS—that is to say, people who have never grown—are much more common in the moral than in the physical sphere. To be a dwarf is with some the very ideal of moral perfection. The notion of progress is repugnant to them. It reminds them of earthquakes, and revolutions, and everything that is disagreeable. Happiness and monotony are, in their estimation, synonyms. They are content to be everlastingly thinking the same thoughts, reading the same books, and engaged in the same pursuits, which they have been accustomed to think and read and engage in as long as they can remember. They live in a state of the most perfect complacency regarding themselves and their ancestors. There could not, they believe, be wiser or better people; and consequently they consider it impossible to improve on the institutions and modes of life and forms of thought which have been patronised, and are still being patronised, by such worthy gentlemen. If one attempts to point out to them defects in anything they have adopted, from theology down to sanitary arrangements, they have one invariable reply—that what was good enough for their forefathers is good enough for them. There, perhaps, they are right. For such people it is probably too good. Even if they could be brought to see that any improvement was theoretically desirable, nothing would ever induce them to effect it. Change is so fatiguing. The game, they fancy, would not be worth the candle. They would rather die under bad arrangements of their ancestors, than live under improved arrangements of their own.

To such persons the idea of progress in religious matters is peculiarly abhorrent. They justify their spiritual stagnation by asserting that progress in religion is tantamount to scepticism, irreverence, and what not. The people who never think always have a pious horror of those who do. The human mind they seem to regard as an invention of the devil's, for they take special pride in living as if they did not possess one. Their conception of the Christian religion is, that it consists in the blind acceptance of *some one else's* creed. When they have accomplished this feat, they imagine themselves relieved from all further responsibility. They will have no deeper insight into Christianity at sixty years of age than they had at six. But they do not want it. They have a pleasing assurance that when they learnt the Catechism they mastered Truth. The portion of their creed which they most thoroughly comprehend and value is the doctrine that Christ did everything. From this they proceed to draw the comforting corollary that they need do nothing; and to give them their due, they act up to this corollary with marvellous consistency.

Now this state of spiritual coma, which dares to call itself Christianity, is the very opposite of the religion of Christ. Our Lord's belief in progress is strikingly illustrated by His treatment of the Bible. He acknowledged the inspiration of the Scriptures. "He always spoke of them," says the author of 'Ecce Homo,' "with the utmost reverence, and He seems never to have called in question the Jewish idea that they were the infallible oracles of God. Yet He regarded them in a sense critically, and introduced canons of interpretation which by their boldness must have astonished the religious men of the day. He regarded the laws of Moses, though divine, as capable of becoming obsolete, and also as incomplete. On the question of divorce, He declared the Mosaic arrangement to have been well suited to the hard-heartedness of a semi-barbarous age, but to be no longer justifiable in the advanced condition of morals. So too in the matter of oaths, the permission of private revenge, and other points in which the Mosaic legislation had necessarily something of a barbaric character, He unhesitatingly repealed the acts of the lawgiver and introduced new provisions. But not only did He find the Mosaic code in part obsolete; He found it throughout utterly meagre and imperfect. And this was inevitable. Between the rude clans that had listened to Moses in the Arabian desert, and the Jews who in the reign of Tiberius visited the Temple courts, there was a great gulf. The hard-heartedness of the primitive nation had given way under the gradual influence of law, and peace, and trade, and literature. Laws which in the earlier time the best men had probably found it hard to keep, could now serve only as a curb upon the worst. The disciples of Moses were subject to lawless passions which they could not control, and the fiercest ebullitions of which seemed to them venial misfortunes rather than crimes. Self-restraint of any kind was to them a new and hard lesson. They listened with awe to the inspired teacher who told them not to covet their neighbour's wife or property; and when they were commanded not to murder, they wondered doubtless by what art or contrivance it might be possible to put a bridle on the thing called anger. But how much all this was afterwards changed! If one like Paul had gone to a Christian teacher, after the new enthusiasm of humanity had been excited in him, and asked for instruction in morality, would it have satisfied him to be told that he must abstain from committing murder and robbery? These laws, to be sure, were not obsolete (like those about divorce and revenge), but the better class of men had been raised to an elevation of goodness, at which they were absolutely unassailable by temptations to break them. Their moral sense required a different training—far more advanced instruction."

Now Christ expressly and plainly declared He was labouring under the same kind of disadvantage as Moses, and that therefore His own teaching must also be limited and elementary. "I have yet many things to say unto you, but ye cannot bear them now." The Jews had made great moral advances since the days of Sinai, but they were still incapable of comprehending the deepest truths of Christianity. They were not, however, always to remain in the intellectual and moral condition in which Christ found them. He seemed able to do but little for them during His lifetime. But He Himself declared that their progress was to continue long after He had passed away. He promised them the inspiration of the Spirit of God to carry them forward, far beyond the point to which He Himself was able to lead them. "When the Spirit of truth is come," Christ said to them, "He will guide you into all truth." The same idea of the progressiveness of Christianity is even more strikingly suggested by the second part of our text. "He that believeth on me, the works that I do shall he do also; and greater works than these shall he do." Mark you, Christ asserts this not only of those immediately around them, but of every one who should hereafter become a disciple. The expression is perfectly general,—" he that believeth on me." This assertion of our Lord's may sound somewhat startling, and yet it was but the simple truth. The explanation of it was given by Christ Himself. " Greater works than these shall he do; because I go unto my Father." Christ had to die before it was possible for the mighty achievements to be accomplished, which Christianity was ultimately destined to effect. Just think how little Christ was able to make of His disciples while He was alive. They were always misunderstanding Him and His work: wanting to call down fire from heaven; wanting Him to declare Himself king of the Jews; wanting to sit on His right hand and on His left hand in His kingdom; wanting Him to show them the Father—to make God visible to their bodily eyes; wanting to censure a man for doing good, because, as they put it, "he followeth not us"; wanting their Master to live and not to die, when life would have meant the most ignominious failure and death was the sublimest victory; wanting Him to do, and wanting to do themselves, anything and everything that was incompatible with His great plan. This was how they treated Him until the end. When that came, they all forsook Him and fled. And these were the most devoted of Christ's followers. No wonder, then, that He said, "He that believeth on me, the works that I do shall he do also; and greater works than these shall he do." There are in the world to-day a vast number of men and women—the converts, it may be, of very mediocre teaching and preaching—who understand Christianity far more clearly, and work for it far more wisely, than did the best of the disciples during the lifetime of the Saviour.

Let me entreat you to ponder over the fact that Christ, as plainly as words can do it, has declared progress to be an essential element in His system. Both by precept and example He condemned the worship of the past,—that most foolish and pestilent of all idolatries.

To any one who thinks at all it is a self-evident truth that as the world grows older it must, or at any rate it ought, to grow wiser. But, curiously enough, the converse has been more generally assumed as axiomatic, viz., that it was wisest—as wise as it could be—in its childhood. If men had held this creed at the beginning, they would never have emerged from their primeval barbarism. If the primitive savage had thought himself omniscient, the world would have been even now uncivilised. But savage though he was he knew a good deal better than that. And as time goes on and men grow really wiser, they become more and more dissatisfied with their present achievements. Our ancestors tried like freemen to make advances upon *their* ancestors. Alas for the heritage they have bequeathed us, if we have been transformed thereby into slaves!

In physical science we do not hesitate to assert our own rights. *There* we demand the liberty of making progress. And why should we not do so in theology? If any one supposes that inspiration makes a difference and renders progress impossible, I reply that it does make a difference, but that it renders progress imperative. The greater the inspiration which is claimed for the Scriptures, the greater becomes the opportunity and necessity for progress in the study of them. If they are really worthy of being called divine, it is not surely to be imagined that their full significance for all time will be discovered on a single careless reading.

Men can only see in the Bible, as in any other book, what they bring with them the power of seeing; and their faculty of spiritual vision should be continually gaining strength. But, for some unaccountable reason, this faculty is frequently supposed to have been steadily deteriorating, since the time of what are technically called the Fathers. There are many persons who have the greatest contempt for *modern* theology—who believe, in fact, that all theology, properly so called, must be of necessity ancient. Any one who expresses an original opinion is at once extinguished by them with the assertion that he is no theologian. They imagine that the farther they go back, the more likely they are to get at the mind of Christ—always provided that they do not go quite to His own words, but stop at the interpretation put upon them by some primitive expositor. Of all curious delusions this is perhaps the most singular. In the spiritual world, as in the natural, every age should make new discoveries—discoveries which may, or may not, be inconsistent with the older views, but which in all cases amount to a fuller, clearer, deeper insight into the truth of God.

"Fresh notions," says Walter Savage Landor,

"are as disagreeable to some as fresh air is to others; but the inability to bear them is equally a symptom of disease." The healthy mind is not concerned with the oldness or newness of a doctrine, but simply and solely with its truth. We owe a debt of gratitude to all the thinkers of the past. But we do not compliment them, we insult them, by acquiescing in their ideas as final. This you may say is quite self-evident. What is the good of insisting on it at such length? I have insisted on it for this reason: it is not every one who sees its applicability to spiritual truth. Many who admit we are under no obligation to square our opinions with those of Aristotle, hesitate to apply the same rule to St Augustine. And therefore I ask once more, if we make progress in our study of nature, shall we make no progress in our study of God? Year after year we learn to know something more of the material world beneath us; and shall we be content with what we already know, or think we know, of the Divine Spirit above us? If any one says that theology should not be progressive, that it is a perfected science and must therefore be stationary, he is guilty, however unintentionally, of the grossest blasphemy. For he virtually asserts that God is the one

Being in the universe who can be easily and completely fathomed.[1]

> "Do not crouch to-day and worship
>   The old Past, whose life is fled;
> Hush your voice to tender reverence—
>   Crowned he lies, but cold and dead.
>
> For the Present reigns our monarch,
>   With an added weight of hours;
> Honour her, for she is mighty—
>   Honour her, for she is ours.
>
> She inherits all his treasures,
>   She is heir to all his fame,
> And the light that lightens round her
>   Is the lustre of his name.
>
> She is wise with all his wisdom;
>   Living on his grave she stands;
> On her brow she wears his laurels,
>   And his harvest in her hands.
>
> Noble things the great Past promised,
>   Holy dreams both strange and new;
> But the Present shall fulfil them:
>   What he promised she shall do."

---

[1] See also sermons on "Truth" and "Right Thinking" in my 'Origin of Evil'; sermons on "Bigotry," and paper on "Dogma and Philosophy" in my 'Preaching and Hearing.'

Defects of Modern Christianity.

V.

WANT OF PROGRESS (II.)

"I have yet many things to say unto you, but ye cannot bear them now. Howbeit when He, the Spirit of truth, is come, He will guide you into all truth."—JOHN xvi. 12, 13.

"He that believeth on me, the works that I do shall he do also; and greater works than these shall he do."—JOHN xiv. 12.

WE have seen already how strikingly these passages illustrate the fact that progress is an essential feature of the Christian religion. In the last sermon, I spoke about progress in knowledge. I pointed out the absurdity of supposing that either we or our ancestors knew all that was to be known about God and His truth. Even in nature men are always making fresh discoveries. And if, as we believe, the Bible is a yet higher revelation, it is simply impossible that its significance can have been completely fathomed.

But growth in knowledge is not the only development which vital Christianity will display. Freshness of ideas is good, but it is not everything. There should be a corresponding advance in wisdom—wisdom being applied knowledge, or knowledge put into practice. The practical habits and modes of action of Christians in the nineteenth century, instead of being far behind, as is too frequently the case, should be far in advance of those which belonged to Christians in the first century.

No religion is capable of undergoing such changes as Christianity, which is proved by those which it has already actually undergone. Since the Saviour's time, it has been subjected to one transformation at any rate so thorough and complete, that a superficial observer might fancy it had been altogether destroyed. This change is due to the fact that formerly Christ's Gospel was opposed, whereas now it is supported, by the State; formerly it was despised by the upper classes in society, whereas now it has become a recognised part of the social system. Nearly all Christ's precepts and exhortations were given to men who were about to live in the midst of hardship, penury and persecution, with the possible climax of a martyr's death.

Yet to-day it is only in very exceptional cases that any of these sufferings are experienced by the followers of Jesus in virtue of their discipleship. Nearly everything that Christ said was uttered on the supposition, that those to whom He spoke would have to give up all connection with the world—all interest in its commerce, its professions, its amusements, and its various pursuits. But you, who profess and call yourselves Christians, do not so understand your Christian duty.

There is, of course, a ridiculous sense in which the term "world" is sometimes used, as representing some half-dozen amusements for which the persons who abuse them do not happen to care, and which, on this account, they imagine must be pre-eminently sinful. But of the world, in that sense, the Bible says nothing. St John uses the term as a synonym for wickedness, and in this sense his commandment applies to all nations and to all times. "The world which lieth in wickedness," the world as far as it is wicked, *the sin of the world*, we are bound as Christians to hate.

As regards the world in the ordinary sense of the term, according to which it stands for human life with its varied interests and pursuits, there is an enormous difference between our position and that of the first disciples. By them these interests and pursuits had to be given up, by us they have not. You all believe this. At least you all act as if you did. You do not give up the common interests of life. You are engaged during the week in purely secular pursuits; you pay calls and give parties; you eat and drink and pass your time, pretty much in the main as other persons do who make no profession of Christianity. But not so the early disciples. Such a state of things was then impossible. At first a profession of Christianity was absolutely incompatible with a comfortable or even tolerable life. And this arose not so much from anything peculiar in Christianity, as from the peculiar opposition with which it met. While this opposition lasted the profession of Christianity inevitably entailed physical disaster and social ruin.

But it was not desirable that this state of things should last for ever. On the contrary, the full benefits of Christianity could only come to men after the opposition had passed away. Christ said nothing to His disciples about their participating in the world's occupations and pursuits; and yet this participation, since it has proved itself legitimately practicable, is manifestly an advance upon the isolation of the early Church. It would not surely be for the good of the human race, that Christianity should always be in antagonism to civil law and to the refined and cultured classes. Manifestly it must be better for it to acquire, as it has actually done, an influence in the State and in society, that thereby the State and society may be regenerated. It came into collision with them in the first instance, not for the sake of collision, but for the sake of ultimate harmony. "Society," says Dean Church, " as well as religion, is God's creation and work. If we have anything to guide us as to God's will in the facts of the world, if we see His providence in the tendencies and conditions amid which we live, and feel that in them He is our teacher and interpreter,—we must believe social order, with its laws, its necessary incidents and pursuits, is God's will for this present life. He meant us to live in the world; and for the world, what we call society—the rule of law, the employment of business, the increase of wealth, the embodiment of public force and power, the cultivation of our infinite resources, the continued improvement of social arrangements—all this is indispensable. There is no standing still in these matters; the only other alternative is drifting back into confusion and violence. If the necessities of our condition, with all the light thrown upon them by long experience, are no evidence of God's purposes, we are indeed in darkness; if they are, it is plain that man, both the individual and the race, has a *career* here—that he has been furnished for it, I need not say how amply, and was meant to fulfil it." In spite of the early collisions between society and the Gospel, it soon became evident that there was nothing necessarily antagonistic between them, and at the same time it appeared that Christianity was intended for a wider purpose than had been disclosed at first. "Even war and riches, even the Babel life of our great cities, even the high places of ambition and earthly honour, have been touched by Christ's spirit, have found how to become Christian." And Christianity has been transformed, no less than society, by this change in their mutual relations—transformed, not indeed in its essential character of self-denial, but in the manner in which this self-denial is manifested. Thank God, there are other, and in some respects higher, ways in which self-denial may be exhibited than by martyrdom.

But now that physical suffering has ceased to be the necessary concomitant of the profession of Christianity, the outward aspects of that religion have assumed a totally different form. And so remarkable a change, the occurrence of which cannot possibly be denied, should lead us to expect other important modifications and developments. Doubtless as time goes on there must be many such.

In one sense the morality which Christ taught was perfect and complete. It was so in its fundamental principles. The golden rule, as far as we can see, is final and unalterable—equally adapted for the nineteenth century as for the first, as obligatory in heaven as upon earth. We cannot conceive of any collection of sentient and intelligent beings, for whom it would not be well if one and all of them observed this law. But our *method* of observing it, the particular actions which we perform in obedience to it, should be more or less different from time to time, since in every succeeding age men should attain to a higher ideal of life. Christ gave His disciples certain suggestions for carrying out in detail the new commandment. But a literal adherence to these suggestions is by no means the whole of our Christian duty.

We may succeed in accomplishing much more than it was possible for the original disciples even to imagine. Hence, to be acting in strict harmony with the letter of the Gospel precepts, will often amount to being altogether out of harmony with their spirit. Let me explain. Christ was always insisting, in the strongest terms, upon the paramount duty of relieving the distresses of our suffering fellow-creatures. He said little or nothing about the necessity of preventing these distresses. The latter was a problem which for many reasons the disciples were then incapable of comprehending. But it is with the latter that we to-day should chiefly concern ourselves. "No man," says the author of 'Ecce Homo,' "who loves his kind, can in these days rest content with waiting as a servant upon human misery, when it is, in so many cases, possible to anticipate and avert it. Prevention is better than cure; and it is now clear to all that a large part of human suffering is preventible by improved social arrangements. Charity will now, if it be genuine, fix upon this enterprise as greater, more widely permanent and beneficial, and therefore more Christian, than the other. It will not, indeed, neglect the lower task of relieving and consoling those who have actually fallen into calamity. But when it has done all that the New Testament enjoins, it will feel that its task is not half fulfilled. When the starving man has been relieved, modern charity inquires whether any fault in the social system deprived him of his proper share in nature's bounty. When the sick man has been visited, and everything done which skill and assiduity can do to cure him, modern charity will go on to consider the causes of his malady—what noxious influence besetting his life, what contempt of the laws of health in his diet and habits, may have caused it; and then inquire whether others incur the same danger and may be warned in time."

Similarly in regard to another important problem of the age,—the problem viz., as to how we may elevate the tastes and brighten the lives of the lower classes. We are only now beginning to recognise the important part played by recreation in the proper development of the race. And it is our duty to apply this new knowledge, so far as we possibly can, to the amelioration of the lives of our poorer brethren. We owe a debt of gratitude to Mr Besant for the valuable suggestions and the healthy stimulus contained in his 'All Sorts and Conditions of

Men.' That book, as you know, has already led to the formation of Toynbee Hall and the People's Palace. And undertakings of this kind, though quite foreign to the spirit of the first century, though they never entered—never could have entered—into the minds of the early disciples, are nevertheless part of our present Christian duty.

It is but seldom, however, that these larger views have obtained as to the scope of the Gospel of Christ. There is no doubt a great deal of reflective and scientific philanthropy now in existence, but it would not generally be regarded as forming an essential portion of the Church's work. Philanthropy is too often supposed to be something different from Christianity. It certainly is not the whole of Christ's religion, but just as certainly it is a part. It is true that the Church has to care for the spirits of men, but it is not less true that she has also to care for their bodies. It is true that she must endeavour to make men better, but it is not less true that she must also endeavour to make them happier. That this is her duty, according to Christ's conception, no one who honestly reads his New Testament can possibly doubt. All vital Christianity therefore—every

Church, in so far as it is alive—will take the utmost pains to discover new and better expedients for the diminution and prevention of all the ills to which flesh has hitherto been heir, but from which it may be conceivably relieved. This should be as much the recognised duty of the Church to-day, as was that "relief of widows in the daily ministrations" which is mentioned in the Acts of the Apostles.

Those for whom Christianity means the acceptance of a creed will of course deny this. The business of religion, as they understand it, is to take themselves—and perhaps a few others—to heaven. Philanthropy, they imagine, lies altogether outside its sphere. They don't trouble themselves much in relieving actual distress; and as for making systematic efforts to prevent it, as for trying to increase the happiness of men here on earth,—all this they look upon as a sort of foible, with which those who are sure of heaven need not in the least concern themselves. Yet, strange to say,—I know nothing stranger in the history of human error,—they seem to think that they are disciples of Christ.

Lastly, and in a word, let me call your attention to the want of progress *in character* which is too often apparent among modern Christians.

Though the outward aspects of Christianity may change, though in one age it may be associated with suffering and distress and in another with prosperity and comfort,—the Christian life has an unfailing characteristic, it is always governed by the law of progress. As time passes on, it should be evident that we are becoming better men and women, as well as wiser. Otherwise, it is but a mockery for us to pray the prayer, "Thy kingdom come." If we are in a lethargic and stagnant state, we are ourselves insuperable obstacles to the prayer being answered. Christ's kingdom can never come in its full glory while a single unperfected member remains. But how many there are who make no serious effort after moral perfection! Not to speak of those who, as they grow older, distinctly deteriorate, who become more grossly selfish, more fussily thoughtful for their own comfort and more rudely neglectful of other people's, more troublesome and exasperating to all who have the misfortune to live in the same house with them,—not to speak of such as these, who have no right to the name of Christain, how many there are who have really felt an affection for Christ, and who endeavour, fitfully and feebly, to serve Him, who are yet quite contented to remain year after year and decade after decade in the same spiritual state —in Christ indeed, but merely babes in Christ! Let us see to it that this be not our condition. Let us see to it that we *grow* in grace. Let us remember, in regard to moral as in regard to mental acquirements, that we have not already attained neither are already perfect. "Let us forget the things that are behind, and reach forth unto those that are before; let us run with patience the race set before us in the Gospel; let us press toward the mark, for the prize of our high calling"—for that perfected character which should eventually be ours.

But we shall not attain it without steady, patient, and unceasing effort. No one ever did. In the words of the poet who has just passed away:[1]—

> "The heights by great men reached and kept
> Were not attained by sudden flight;
> But they, while their companions slept,
> Were toiling upward in the night."

Such toil, however, is far sweeter than ignoble rest. There is no higher joy than the consciousness that all the capabilities of our nature are being steadily developed. You who are

[1] Longfellow.

living thoughtful, serious, progressive lives, have often, I daresay, been shocked at meeting again, after a few years' interval, some friend of your boyhood or girlhood. He was then your equal in attainments, if not your superior. But now you seem to be separated from him by an infinite gulf. He has the old thoughts and aims and sympathies and conversation, which were once yours also but which now you have completely outgrown. The contrast between your present self and him is so great, that you can hardly believe you ever lived on so low a level. How sorry you feel for him! And truly he deserves your pity He has but one use, and that is to serve as a warning. If ever you are tempted to relax in your efforts for personal progress and for the progress of the world; if ever you are wearily inclined to let the world take its chance, and not to trouble yourself any more about your own development,—think of your poor stagnant friend, and your flagging energies will be revived. You will feel that you would rather do anything, and bear anything, than allow yourself, even for a moment, to play such a contemptible part.

Defects of Modern Christianity.

VI.

WANT OF DEVOTION TO CHRIST.

"Except ye eat the flesh of the Son of man, and drink His blood, ye have no life in you."—JOHN vi. 53.

THE Saviour intended that affection, passionate affection for Himself, should be the motive power in His followers' lives.[1] He knew that no other influence would be strong enough to comform them to His own perfection. He repeatedly insisted upon it as being absolutely essential to the true disciple. And yet in the present day personal devotion to Christ is conspicuous, in the majority of professing Christians, either by its absence or at any rate by its extreme feebleness. There are many who pride themselves on their orthodoxy, who talk glibly

---

[1] See sermon on Redemption, p. 224.

about the divinity of Christ, who worship Him at stated intervals with their lips, but who in their hearts are utterly indifferent to Him. Notwithstanding all they say, they have never felt for Him the slightest gratitude or sympathy or affection.

And even of His genuine followers, there are but few nowadays who love Him as did the first disciples or their immediate successors. "The prevalent feeling towards Him among religious men is an awful fear of His supernatural greatness, and a disposition to obey His commands, arising partly from dread of future punishment and hope of reward for doing right, and partly from a nobler feeling of loyalty, which however is inspired rather by His office than by His person. Beyond this we may discern in them an unceasing conviction that He requires more personal devotion, which leads them to spasmodic efforts to kindle the feeling by means of violent raptures of panegyric, and by repeating over and getting by rote the ardent expressions of those who really had it. That is wanting for the most part which Christ held to be all in all, — spontaneous, free, genuine devotion."

Now, why is it that men love Christ less in

the nineteenth century than they did in the first? One, perhaps the chief, reason is the undue influence which has been exerted by theology, and the undue importance which has been attributed to it. In a previous sermon,[1] I pointed out to you that there was no necessary connection between theology and religion; that the former was of comparatively small, the latter of the greatest possible moment; and that enthusiasm was wasted when bestowed upon theology to an extent which religion alone deserved. In no case may the bad effects of such misspent energy be seen more strikingly, than in the personal relation which too frequently subsists between Christ and His professed disciples. They have substituted belief for affection, dogma for devotion. I will not say that those who are strongest in theology are, as a rule, weakest in religion. But whatever may have been the result of their labours upon the theologians themselves, there can be little doubt that the effect of these labours upon the world in general has been to obscure, rather than elucidate, the real Christ. Homoousianists and Homoiousianists, Arians and Athanasians, Docetæ and Apthardocetæ, Sabellians and So-

[1] P. 29.

cinians, Ebionites, Monarchians, Patripassians, Theopaschites, Manicheans, Nestorians, Monophysites, Agnoetæ and Aktistetæ, Ktistolatræ and Phthartolatræ, Monothelites and Dyothelites, Nominalists and Realists, and a host of others, orthodox, heterodox, and doubtful, have all been hotly engaged in metaphysical discussions as to Christ's nature and essence; but the chief effect of their cloudy logomachies has been to *conceal* the beauty of His character and the charm of His life. Had there been less theology in the world there would have been more religion. It was not for profound and diversified knowledge, it was not for scientific classifications and formulæ, that Christ asked, but for love. His chief strength lay, as He Himself knew full well, in his power over the human heart. But the multiplication of theological discussions and controversies has diminished this power, and made Him less attractive than of yore. He is too frequently regarded as a subject for curious speculation, rather than as a Being to be loved. He has been transformed from a man into a dogma. And however much hatred dogma is capable of inspiring, it is quite incapable of exciting any love.

This leads me to suggest a second reason

why Christ is less loved now than He once was. Various causes have tended to throw His humanity into the background, whereas He Himself always brought it into prominence. Strongly as He insisted upon His divinity, the title by which He most frequently called Himself was the Son of man. But how difficult we find it now to feel that He really was bone of our bone and flesh of our flesh, in all things made like unto His brethren! "Many calling themselves Christians," says Dr Abbott, "and being in a certain sense Christians, have passed through life worshipping Christ as God, but have never even for an instant realised the fact that He actually sorrowed, pitied, was tempted—much less that He grew in wisdom and learned obedience by the things which He suffered. How few believe, at least in their hearts as well as with their lips, that He was a perfect man, endowed with human motives as well as human flesh! Are there not some of us who might confess, if we searched our hearts, that we have been more touched by the story of the death of Socrates, more thrilled by the familiar and fictitious miseries of King Lear, than by the narrative of the sorrows of Jesus of Nazareth? And why? Why, but because our hearts have not yet realised that He, being man, endured for us the mental and spiritual sufferings of humanity, as well as the mere bodily agonies of human flesh?"

Did you ever see the Passion-play at Ober Ammergau? If not, you will probably imagine that it must be irreverent and repulsive. But if you have, you will, I think, agree with me in believing that it serves a legitimate and highly useful purpose. It enables the spectator, for once in his life, vividly to realise the humanity of the Redeemer. It is the simplest and most effectual method of instructing the minds and touching the hearts of the ignorant Bavarian peasants. And it releases for a time the educated visitor from the deadening effect of custom; it revivifies for him the Gospel narrative, and makes him feel that the earthly life of the Man of Sorrows is no mere dogma, but a fact. And you need not be afraid that a vivid realisation of Christ's humanity will necessarily make you sceptical about His divinity. On the contrary, it is in the superhuman beauty of His human life that we have the strongest, the only thoroughly convincing and irrefutable, proof of the fact that in a very special and unique sense He came forth from God. It is not by reading disquisitions upon His divinity that we best see the God-likeness of Christ. It is rather by studying His human life as it is unfolded in the Gospels, and in one or two books which have succeeded in catching the spirit of the Gospels. It seems to me that a simple work like 'Philochristus' will have an effect in drawing men to Christ, which could not be attained by ten thousand volumes of systematic theology. His divinity will never be proved by reasoning. It can be seen only in Himself. That is a beautiful idea, and a true one, which Dr Abbott puts into the mouth of Philochristus, the imaginary disciple whose autobiography he is writing: "It seemed not to us as if we honoured Jesus by calling Him God; but it seemed rather as though we were striving to honour God by saying that He was one with Jesus, for saying this seemed the same as saying that God was Love."

There is a third cause which may have contributed to the coldness of heart so frequently manifested by professed disciples of Christ—viz, a misunderstanding of the word of belief. There are a goodly number of foolish persons who never think or even read for themselves, and who therefore really do not know that they ought to love Christ. They have heard the words, "God so loved the world that He gave His only begotten Son, that whosoever believeth in Him should not perish but have everlasting life." They seize upon the word "belief" and apply it to their own case. They do not disbelieve in Christ: therefore they believe in him; therefore they are heirs of eternal life, and have done everything which is required of them according to the divine scheme of salvation. They do not know, or they never remember, that this belief was explained by Christ to consist in eating the flesh and drinking the blood of the Son of man, —than which anything more different from their own spiritual condition could not possibly be conceived. There are, in fact, two totally distinct kinds of belief. There is one which *does not*, and there is one which *does*, affect conduct. There is one which is merely intellectual, and consists in understanding the terms of a proposition and assenting to it, or not denying it; and there is another which is emotional, and necessarily passes into action. There is one which produces no perceptible change in a man's life; and there is another which effects in it a complete revolution. Let me illustrate this. You believe in Mohammed and you believe in your wife. The first belief simply means, that you have been given to understand that a certain man, named Mohammed, was the founder of a certain religion, called Mohammedanism. You may take an antiquarian interest in this religion; but it does not and cannot have the slightest effect upon your thoughts or feelings or actions. If by some curious accident you had never heard of Mohammed at all, your lives would not be thereby in the slightest degree affected. But does your belief in your wife merely amount to a piece of historical information that there is such a person? For good, or for bad, it must be something very different from that. If for good—if your marriage is at all an ideal one—you and she form, as it were, a "two-celled heart beating with one full stroke." She has given a new direction to your thoughts, a new motive to your energies, a new stimulus to your ambition. You have been transformed by your love for her into a different man, into a superior being. Life without her, you feel, would be but a protracted death. She is your "other dearer life in life," "your own self's better part." *All that* is implied in your belief in her, and would pass through your mind if the belief were ever called in question.

This simple illustration will suffice to show that there is the greatest conceivable difference between the active belief which is embodied in life, and the passive belief which is not. Unfortunately, it has been very common in Christendom to suppose, that faith in Christ consists merely in giving a mental assent to certain propositions regarding Him. And so a most unchristian Christianity has been invented, in which the acquiescence of the intellect is substituted for the outgoings of the heart. To every adherent of this spurious Christianity belongs the reproach, which was once addressed to the Church at Sardis: "Thou hast a name that thou livest, *but thou art dead.*" The justness of this accusation can only be denied by giving the lie to Christ. "Except," said He, "ye eat the flesh of the Son of man and drink His blood, ye have no life in you." No words could express a closer or more absolute union. They imply that the nature and characteristics of the Master are "to pass into and become" the nature and characteristics of the disciples. And there was a time when some of his followers actually experienced this strange transformation, when some of them were able to say: "For me to live is Christ. It is not I who live, but Christ who liveth in me."

How many are there, I wonder, in Christendom to-day, who could honestly say the same?

If you do not love Him, it must be because you do not know Him. Either he is seldom in your thoughts, or you think of Him as a dogma rather than a person. Try and picture Him to yourself as of old He lived, and talked, and worked in Palestine. Remember how wonderfully, like no one before or since, He combined all conceivable excellences. He had the tenderness of the most womanly woman, and at the same time the strength of the manliest man. Though invincible by the temptations which assailed Himself, He was always ready to make the most generous allowance for those who failed and fell. He lived much with God, but this seemed to bring Him only nearer to man. He delighted in solitary communion with the Father, but He was fond also of mingling with His neighbours at their social meetings and festivities. He was keenly alive to the paramount importance of the Spirit and eternity; and yet no one was ever so thoughtfully considerate for men's temporal and bodily welfare,—He ministered to them in their bereavements and in their diseases, He was not unmindful even of their hunger and thirst. He had the most sensitive nature, which yearned inexpressibly for sympathy, and yet He never, for the sake of sympathy, swerved from the path of duty. Though all His followers deserted Him, under the conviction that their confidence had been misplaced, He persevered unto the end. He avoided no effort, He shirked no sacrifice, He shrank from no anguish, by which He might serve the race in revealing God and reconciling man. Think of this and much more in that sad, beautiful, sublime career. Think of Him till you love Him and your love has made you like Him. Nothing short of this will make you what Christ would call a Christian. "Except ye eat the flesh and drink the blood of the Son of man, ye have no life in you."

Job.

I.

INTRODUCTORY.

THE Book of Job is one of the least read books in the Bible; but at the same time, there are few more worthy of our serious attention. If justice is to be done to it, it must be studied as a whole; and when so examined, it will be seen to stand, both as a work of art and as a book of spiritual instruction, upon the very highest level. In regard to this matter all competent critics are agreed. "I call that book," said Thomas Carlyle, "apart from all theories about it, one of the grandest things ever written with the pen. There is nothing, either in the Bible or out of it, of equal literary merit." Similar testimony is borne by Mr Froude. "It is a book," he declares, "of which it is to say little that it is unequalled of its kind. One day, perhaps, when it is allowed to stand on its own merits, it will be seen towering up alone above all the poetry of the world."

With regard to its date, there has been great diversity of opinion. Some have held that it was of pre-Mosaic origin, written in the age of the patriarchs. For this view there are no good grounds. The hero, it is true, is represented as having lived in that period, but there is nothing to suggest that the book was written contemporaneously. It has also been placed in the Mosaic period: and, according to a Jewish tradition, had Moses himself for its author. This view has little to support it except some trifling affinities to the style of the Pentateuch, and the fact that its writer, in common with Moses, evidently had a considerable acquaintance with Egypt and Arabia.

That the book was not written *before* the time of Solomon is sufficiently proved by one characteristic alone—viz., its catholicity of spirit. Such a spirit did not exist among the Jews until that date. It seems to have been the result of the new and wider relation into which they had begun to enter with the more cultivated nations of antiquity. The aim of the Solomonic literature was, as Godet says, to find something deeper than Judaism, to discover the man beneath the Israelite, and to discourse of that Eternal Wisdom whose delight is in *all* the children of men. This is very strikingly illustrated in Job. Neither the hero nor any of the subordinate characters are Jews; the place where the events are said to have occurred is out of Palestine; the worship described in it, consisting of sacrifices offered by the father of the family, was common among the Gentiles; and from beginning to end there is no allusion to Jewish history or institutions. "Such a noble universality," says Carlyle, "reigns through the book, that one feels as if it were not Hebrew. It is all men's book." Delitzsch and others assign the Book of Job to the Solomonic era, when this spirit of catholicity at first arose.

There has long, however, been a tendency among scholars to refer it to a much later date. Ewald thinks that it belongs to the great prophetic period, and that its author was contemporary with Jeremiah. To this Mr Froude objects that the prophetic period was an era of decrepitude, dissolution, sin and shame. The energies of the prophets were devoted to rebukes and warnings and exhortations. In such a time men would be too absorbed with the present for searching, like the writer of Job, into the deepest mysteries of existence. On the other hand, Dr Samuel Davidson says, it is not likely that the problem of misery would have forced itself upon men's attention during the prosperity of the Solomonic age. He considers Job to have been the outcome, directly or indirectly, of some great national calamity. The literature called Chokmah or Wisdom,—which sprang up in the time of Solomon and continued to flourish for many centuries afterwards,—Dr Davidson divides into three periods: (1) The period of principles, to which belongs the Book of Proverbs; (2) The period of problems, when Psalms xxxvii., xlix., and lxxiii. were written; and (3) The period of exhaustion, when men had given up all attempt to solve the mysteries of existence. To the last division belongs the Book of Ecclesiastes. Job, says Dr Davidson, was certainly not produced in this period. And he also thinks that it cannot be placed in the first, because the doctrine of evil belonging to that period is the doctrine of the friends, a view from which this book signalises the final departure. The spirit of Job is that of the Psalms above mentioned and of the prophets; and it must therefore, he thinks, have been written between the seventh and fifth centuries B.C.

In regard to the subject-matter of the book, there has been no less diversity of opinion than in regard to its date. Some have thought that it was in the strictest sense historical. This was the ancient opinion both among Jews and Christians. Those who credited Moses with its authorship said that he wrote the opening and closing chapters and compiled the dialogues, from MSS. which he met with during his residence in Midian, in which MSS. the various speeches were supposed to be reported accurately and *verbatim*. This view, so far as I am aware, has at present no eminent supporter. Others have regarded the book as purely a work of imagination, having no foundation in fact. In the Talmud, for example, we read, "Job did not exist. He was not a man but a parable." The fact of his existence, however, seems to be assumed by the sacred writers Ezekiel and St James. Further, as Ewald justly remarks, the invention of a story without foundation in facts —the creation of a person who had no real historical existence—is wholly alien to the spirit of antiquity. And again it is hardly likely that in any era, however catholic, a Jew would have taken a Gentile to represent the most perfect of men, had the representation been purely fictitious.

The truth probably here, as elsewhere, lies between the two extreme theories. The book is neither altogether historical nor altogether imaginary. The main facts of the story were literally true, and they happened in the patriarchal age. Job's history was handed down traditionally from generation to generation, growing in volume and beauty, till it was taken up by a post-Solomonic poet and worked into its present exquisite form. This was Luther's opinion. "I look upon the Book of Job," he said, "as a true history; yet I do not believe that all took place as it is written there, but that a pious and learned man of genius brought it into it its present form." But who that man of genius was, the world will never know.

Now let us inquire for a moment into the purpose of the book. This is generally inadequately, not to say incorrectly, conceived. According to the popular notion, the writer merely wished to refute the common theory that good men were necessarily prosperous. On the contrary, it seems to me that this theory is rather confirmed than refuted. It is indeed shown that the merited prosperity may not come at once. But Job is declared *in the end* to have become twice as prosperous as ever.

Again, many critics suppose that the chief intention of the book is to prove the power of an unselfish love for God. "Hast thou considered my servant Job," says Jehovah to Satan, "that there is none like him in the earth, a perfect and an upright man, one that feareth God, and escheweth evil?" To which Satan replies: "Doth Job fear God for nought? Hast not Thou made an hedge about him, and about his house, and about all that he hath on every side? Thou hast blessed the work of his hands, and his substance is increased in the land; but put forth Thine hand now, and touch all that he hath, . . . put forth Thine hand now, and touch his bone and his flesh, and he will curse Thee to Thy face." The book was written, say certain critics, to refute this cynical supposition. But inasmuch as the supposition is never mentioned after the second chapter, it can hardly be supposed that the whole poem was written to refute it. In fact no poem, worthy of the name, was ever written to prove or disprove anything. Art cares nothing for demonstration.

The purpose of the book is something far

higher than to refute any definite theory or teach any definite doctrine. It is the history of a soul in its struggle after God. The scene of the drama is the heart of Job. Here is a man who by his losses, his bereavements, his horrible disease, and above all by the ill-advised conversation of his friends, is driven to the very verge of madness. He had been a good man—the best of men. He had been pious and devout, not merely in outward conduct, but he had lived, as he thought, in filial communion with God. Now, however, it was as if the great Father were dead. Surely He would not otherwise be deaf to such passionate entreaties. Perhaps, after all, he had been but worshipping a phantom of his own imagination; or worse, perhaps the powerful Being, in whom he had believed as a loving God, was but a malignant fiend who took pleasure in insulting him—who had once made him glad only to increase his present anguish. But no! when he remembers his past experience, there was something too real, too beautiful in it, to admit of this supposition. He will still trust. Perchance the old blessedness may return. And yet, and yet,—and so he goes through all transitions of despair and hope; "now praying and trusting; now utterly cast down; now quiet and submissive; now violent, and ready even to blaspheme; and at last rising suddenly to a height of rapture in which everything disappears in a beatific vision of God."

To follow him in his spiritual experience will be for us a matter not merely of speculative interest, but of real practical value. Job was assailed by no fiercer doubts than may come to us. At any time we may be overtaken by the most terrible calamity. And if not, unless we be very thoughtless, our spirits will sometimes be weighed down by an oppressive sense of the mystery of existence. The waste and cruelty so apparent throughout nature; the deadly regularity of law going on its relentless course, in spite of the entreaties and groans of the myriads whom it tortures and prematurely slays; the necessity of believing, if we are to believe at all, not only without seeing, but even in opposition to what we seem to see; the consciousness that we have sought for God and found Him not, so that there is nothing for it but to say with Job, "Behold I go forward, but He is not there; and backward, but I cannot perceive Him: on the left hand, where He doth work, but I cannot behold Him; He hideth Himself on the right hand, that I cannot see Him;"—such feelings as these may at times weigh upon our spirits like a nightmare, and lead us to exclaim with the poet:—

> "Who shall read us the riddle of life?
> The continual sequence of pain,
> The perpetual triumph of wrong,
> The whole creation in travail to make
> A victory for the strong?
>
> How are we fettered and caged,
> Within our dark prison-house here!
> We are made to look for a loving plan;
> We find everywhere sorrow and fear.
> We look for the triumph of Good;
> And from all the wide world around,
> The lives that are spent cry upward to heaven
> From the slaughter-house of the ground,
> Till we feel that Evil is Lord.
>
> And yet we are bound to believe,—
> Because all our nature is so,—
> In a Ruler touched by an infinite ruth
> For all His creatures below.
> Bound, though a mocking fiend point
> To the waste and ruin and pain;
> Bound, though our souls should be bowed in despair;
> Bound, though wrong triumph again and again,
> And we cannot answer a word."

The study of Job may help us. He who had fathomed to its deepest depth and its blackest darkness the abyss of despairing scepticism, attained eventually to the joy of joys—the happiness of a calm and unwavering faith. And so, God helping us, may we.

Job.

II.

CHAPTERS I.-III.

THE Book of Job naturally divides itself into seven parts. I. The prologue, contained in the first and second chapters, setting forth the early history and circumstances of the hero, and explaining the origin of that terrible mental conflict which it is the chief business of the poem to portray. II. Job's curse, contained in the third chapter. III. A discussion, extending from the 4th to the 25th chapter, as to the connection between suffering and sin. This discussion, as we shall see, is not introduced for its own sake. It is no mere piece of intellectual gymnastic. Its purpose is to unfold and explain the struggle which is going on in the heart of Job. IV. Job's soliloquy in chapters

26-31. V. (Chapters 32-37 are an interpolation.) The discourse of Jehovah in chapters 38-41. VI. Job's final confession of faith, in the first six verses of the last chapter. VII. The epilogue in the remaining verses.

The prologue and the epilogue are but the setting of the poem. They describe the temporal circumstances of the man with whose spiritual experiences the poem itself is concerned. They are written in prose—in order, as I imagine, that they may not be confused with the main action of the drama, which lies in the heart of Job. Many parts of the prologue are fully as dramatic and imaginative and poetical in spirit as anything that follows. But had the poetical form been adopted, it would have interfered with the essential unity of the drama as conceived by the author. He intended it to describe the progress of a soul from darkness to light, from scepticism to faith. And to this purpose everything is subordinated.

We are introduced in the outset to a highly prosperous and a truly good man. He had property which, estimated at the present value of money, must have made him what we should call a millionaire. He had, we are told, seven sons and three daughters. Large families in those days were peculiarly prized, and sons were more valued than daughters: girls, I am sorry to say, were not thought of much account. He was no less good than prosperous: he was a "perfect and an upright man, fearing God and eschewing evil." One characteristic feature of his religious life is mentioned in particular. It seems that his sons were in the habit of holding festive gatherings periodically at each other's houses. There could have been no harm, no impropriety, in the festivals, for their sisters were always invited to join them. But when the feast-days were over, Job offered up sacrifices on behalf of his children. "It may be," he said to himself, "that my sons have abandoned God in their hearts." He was afraid that they might have been led, by their very happiness, into forgetfulness of God. In a word, for prosperity he was the "greatest man in all the East," and for goodness "there was none like him on the earth."

Now it was such a man as this that, according to the old tradition, had once been overtaken by the direst calamities with which ever mortal was afflicted. Tradition gave the facts, but it was puzzled by them; for up to the time when this book was written, suffering was regarded as invariably retributive. The poet wishes to intimate, at the outset, that suffering may have a far higher—viz., a didactic—purpose. It may teach lessons which there are no other means of learning. Job's sufferings, for example, and the way in which he bears them, go far to prove that men are capable of an unselfish love for God. With a view of suggesting to us the didactic use of suffering, the poet introduces us into the court of heaven. The Ministers of State—" the sons of God," as they are here called—are represented as coming to report themselves, and with them comes a being called in Hebrew the Adversary and in our authorised version Satan. Herder, Eichhorn and others say that he is intended for a divinely commissioned recording angel. It seems pretty evident however, that he had not received his commission, like the rest, from the hands of the Lord, for he is asked, "Whence comest thou?" His is a self-appointed task. He goes about misrepresenting goodness, and trying to make out that it is merely a form of evil. He is the impersonation of cynicism. We do not unfortunately need to go out of the world to find his like. Literature abounds in definitions like the following: Pity is the consciousness that the same calamity might happen to ourselves. Love is our belief that we need the beloved object. Liberality is the vanity of giving. Friendship is a mere traffic, in which self-love always proposes to be the gainer. Gratitude is a lively sense of favours to come. Virtue is doing right according to the will of God for the sake of happiness. All these definitions imply that human beings, during their progress from the cradle to the grave, are incapable of a single unselfish thought, of a single generous emotion, and that the best of men are but hypocrites skilfully acting a part,—

> " Who, trimmed in forms and visages of duty,
> Keep yet their hearts attending on themselves."

On the same principle Satan, when Job is mentioned to him as a man whom even he would be unable to traduce, throws out the suggestion that the person in question was religious only because he found it paid, that he served God merely for what was to be got out of Him. "Do you think so?" says Jehovah; "try him and see." And he tries him. The arch-cynic is here represented as being almost omnipotent for mischief. On one day Job loses all his property and all his children. But he does not curse God as Satan had predicted. He falls on his face and worships. "The Lord gave," he said, "and the Lord hath taken away; blessed be the name of the Lord."

The Adversary, however, does not consider himself beaten. With diabolical evil-mindedness he suggests, that the loss of Job's children was nothing to him so long as his own health was spared: let that be touched and he would appear in his true colours—selfish to the core. Again Jehovah replies, "Try him and see." And now the ruined, childless man is struck with elephantiasis—the worst form of leprosy—the loathsomeness of which it is impossible for me here to describe. Job, when he feels himself smitten, goes and sits down on the *mezbele*,—"among the ashes" as we have it in our version. This was a heap of refuse lying outside a town or village. It was usually burnt once a-month, and so became a firm, compact mass. It was the regular resort of the homeless and destitute, and of those who were afflicted with any contagious disease which prevented their being admitted into the society of their fellows.

His wife[1] finds him in this position,—the

---

[1] The commentators have generally treated Job's wife with great unfairness.

greatest man of the East sitting beside outcast beggars! Poor woman! she could bear it no longer. She had not uttered a complaint at their loss of property; she had been silent when her children died; but this more immediately concerned her husband, and therefore, like a true woman, she felt it more acutely. She, for her part, now comes to the conclusion that religion is a mistake. "Curse God, and die," she says. "It will be a relief to curse Him. He can but kill you for your pains; and then at any rate you will have done with this terrible Enemy." Or she may have meant to be even more sarcastic in her expostulation; for curiously enough in Hebrew the same word, derived from a root meaning to kneel, signifies both to curse and to bless. She may therefore have intended to say, "Bless Him again, and you can only expect to lose your life. You blessed Him once, and He took away all your possessions; you blessed Him a second time, and He gave you the worst of all possible diseases; try it once more, and He will kill you for your pains."

But Job holds on his way unmoved. The God whom he had loved was, even yet, dearer to him than aught beside. He could have said with Xavier:—

> " My God, I love Thee not because
>   I hope for heaven thereby,
> Nor yet because who love Thee not
>   Must burn eternally :
> Not with the hope of gaining aught
>   Nor seeking a reward,
> But as Thyself hast lovèd me,
>   O ever-loving Lord."

As yet Job utters no word of complaint. He even attempts, as best he can, to justify the Almighty. "Shall we receive good," he asks, "at the hand of God, and shall we not receive evil?" Evidently then Job's previous religiousness had not been mere self-seeking; for now he had nothing, less than nothing, yet he still continued to worship. The author's purpose in this part of the prologue is to suggest to us that he knows the assertion of the adversary to be false. He wishes us to understand that he assumes the possibility of an unselfish piety. Worship, he thinks, should be independent of rewards and punishments. He is possessed and inspired by the idea that God is worthy of being served for nought.

Job appears to be fully conscious of the depth of his misery only after the arrival of his friends, who came according to etiquette to pay him a visit of condolence. His affliction and his disease have made such havoc that at first they do not recognise him. The only real kindness in their power was to mourn with him in silence, and this for a time they did. "They sat round the ash-heap for seven days and seven nights; and none spake a word unto him; for they saw that his grief was very great." All this time Job remained brooding over his woe. At last a change comes over him; his patience gives way; he is calm no longer, but breaks forth into a passionate malediction. This is the beginning of the poem.—

Perish the day wherein I was born. Let it be turned into darkness. Let not God regard it. Let those who decide what days are to be unlucky join me in cursing it. Let it be a day of blackness and terror and grief, nay, let it pass out of the calendar and be altogether forgotten, because it allowed me to be born.

If it was necessary that I should come into the world at all, why did I not forthwith expire? I should now have been sleeping quietly with kings and princes, in that happy spot where all are equal and all are at peace; where the prisoner is at liberty and the slave is free; where the wicked cease from troubling and the weary are at rest.

Or if I could not die as soon as I was born,

why was I not allowed to expire when life became unbearable? As it is, sighs and groans are my only food. My worst fears, since I became afflicted, have been more than realised. Trouble cometh upon trouble. Death I regard as the most precious treasure. To the grave I look forward as to a happy home. Why is life forced upon me?

This brings us to the discussion between Job and his friends. Eliphaz was probably the oldest of the three, for in the East the greatest respect was paid to age, and he always speaks first. He was decidedly the wisest and the best of them,—a more original thinker, a more gentlemanly controversialist, and a more sympathetic, or rather a less unsympathetic, friend. He had something of "the vision and the faculty divine." He had heard voices and talked with spirits from the unseen world; and it is on this experience that he now bases his argument. Bildad has nothing of his own to bring into the discussion, but he is great in proverbs and in the opinions of the Fathers. He thinks as he does because his reading has shown him that such were the views of his ancestors. Zophar is neither a thinker nor a scholar. He is an ignorant and vulgar bigot. He could hardly say when or how his opinions first came into his head; he has never asked himself *why* he believed anything. The fact that his ideas are his own is their all-sufficient justification. A man so pleased with himself is naturally very hard upon others. Accordingly we find Zophar more cruel in his treatment of Job than either of the other two.

The discussion consists of three parts. The friends speak in each part, and are separately answered by Job, except on the last occasion, when Zophar, with more sense than we should have been inclined to credit him, holds his tongue.[1] The discussion springs out of Job's malediction, which has aroused their orthodox zeal. According to their view of matters, he ought to have been confessing his sins instead of cursing his fate. "A little sympathy on such an occasion would have been worth a good deal of theology." But theology was their strong point, and so they begin to talk it. Their speeches are throughout based on the assumption, that rewards and punishments—of a physical and palpable nature[2]—are meted out strictly according to moral

---

[1] See note, p. 139.
[2] As to other rewards and punishments, see a sermon on "Retribution" in my 'Origin of Evil.'

desert, that none but the wicked suffer, and that their sufferings are in exact proportion to the magnitude of their sins. This assumption in the old oriental theology is, if you come to think of it, very curious and suggestive. One would have imagined it a most patent truth that, so far at least as superficial observation can detect, men are *not* dealt with according to their deserts. No doubt violations of natural law are followed by disastrous physical consequences; and so, if detected, are violations of social law. But with moral offences it is different: there is no visible punishment which invariably follows them. Nature, moreover, often destroys the innocent, and society frequently persecutes its benefactors. Since the world began, the best men, to all outward appearance, have often been the most unfortunate, and the worst men the most successful. The manifest *want of adjustment* between men's deserts and their external circumstances is, with our modern theologians, one of the strongest arguments for a future life. But formerly, it had been assumed that the adjustment was absolutely perfect. The facts, numerous enough and striking enough, which contradicted the assumption, the older theologians never seemed to see. " Experience," says Mr Froude, " when it contradicts our cherished convictions, is like water dropping on the rock, which it wears away indeed, but only after thousands of years." This theory, as to the exclusively retributive nature of suffering, had formed part of Job's own theology; and, as we shall see, the difficulty, or rather the impossibility, of reconciling it with his own experience was one great source of his mental distress. His friends were quite sure he deserved his afflictions. Men are generally very sceptical as to the merits of their neighbours. They were also sure that he should have endured them with patience. Other people's troubles are so easily borne. They begin by hinting vaguely that he must have been guilty of some heinous crime, and they exhort him to repentance, in order that he may be forgiven and restored to his former prosperity. But afterwards, when he has indignantly denied their accusations and in the bitterness of his spirit accused God of injustice, they no longer content themselves with hints, but make definite charges against him, anything serving their purpose that happens to suggest itself in the excitement of the moment. His anger cools as theirs gets hotter. At first, when their insinuations were vague, he was half afraid lest his friends might be right; but afterwards the accusations lose all force by their very definiteness, and he becomes quite sure that they must be wrong. He no longer troubles himself about them. They have put themselves beyond the pale of controversy. Though at first they angered him, they have on the whole been leading him to the attainment of peace. Eliphaz by his misinterpreted visions, Bildad by his misapplied quotations, Zophar by his self-complacent stupidity, have been driving him nearer to God. The want of human sympathy has been helping him to believe that God, though more just than man, is at the same time infinitely more merciful. As Faber has beautifully expressed it:—

> "There is no place where earth's sorrows
>   Are more felt than up in heaven;
> There is no place where earth's failings
>   Have such kindly judgment given.
>
> But we make His love too narrow
>   By false limits of our own;
> And we magnify His strictness
>   With a zeal He will not own.
>
> For the love of God is broader
>   Than the measure of man's mind;
> And the Heart of the Eternal
>   Is most wonderfully kind."

Job.

III.

CHAPTERS IV.-X.

I HAVE already given you a general idea of the discussion which extends from the 4th to the 25th chapters of the Book of Job. We must now look at this discussion a little more in detail.

It is opened by Eliphaz. He acknowledges Job's previous piety, but at the same time suggests to him that suffering can only result from sin. He then exhorts him to repent and to become pious again, assuring him on these terms of a brilliant future. He begins apologetically—

My conscience compels me to say something to you. Might I venture to speak without your being vexed? How is it that you, who have so often comforted the distressed, are dismayed as soon as calamity comes upon yourself? Instead of despair-

ing, you should remember that the innocent never perish. It is only the wicked who are consumed.

You need not be ashamed to own your sin, for all of us are sinners. This was revealed to me once in a vision. In the darkness of the night, when deep sleep falls upon men, a fear came upon me and trembling, a wind swept over my face, and there stood before me a Presence, whose form I could not discern. It spoke in a clear, soft voice, and asked, "Shall mortal man, who is sooner crushed than the moth, be pure in the sight of God his Maker, who chargeth even the angels with folly? It cannot be." Ask any of the holy ones themselves, and they will confirm my doctrine.

I have watched the wicked, and always found it ill with them. Their property is enjoyed by robbers. Their children ruin themselves with lawsuits. They themselves prematurely pass away. But this suffering is no accident; it is the punishment of sin. And since all men are sinners, suffering must come, more or less, to all. Man is born to trouble as the sparks fly upward. Your grief is but an extreme illustration of the common rule. Were I in your place, I would have recourse to God. Forgiveness and happiness may seem more than you can hope for; but God is always doing great things past finding out. He is continually exalting those that are cast down. Happy is the man whom God correcteth. Despise not His chastening. It is for your good. His purpose is to make you reflect. God only bruises in order that He may heal. Return to Him, and your prosperity will be restored—nay, increased. In famine He will sustain you. In war He will protect you. You will laugh at all forms of danger. Wild beasts will never hurt you. Even the stones of the field will be in league with you, and, instead of obstructing your crops, will give them a more luxuriant growth. Your children will be multiplied as the very grass of the land. You shall go down to the tomb in a ripe old age, like a shock of corn fully ripe. This, Job, is my experience. Hear it and learn it for your good.

Such is the gist of the speech of Eliphaz, as contained in the 4th and 5th chapters. If he must preach rather than sympathise, he could not well have preached a better sermon. The harshness of the insinuation that affliction was a judgment, he delicately tempered, by suggesting that suffering was common to man, and by assuring Job of a happy future if he would but repent. Still it was evident that he had not realised the greatness of the sufferer's grief.

Had he done so, he would never have attempted to assuage it by theology.

In the 6th and 7th chapters we have Job's reply. He begins with upbraiding Eliphaz, and ends with upbraiding God. *True, I have been passionate, but my passion is as nothing if compared to my grief, which is heavier than the sands of the sea. The poisoned arrows of the Almighty are rankling in my soul. You might have guessed what I was suffering when you heard my complaint. Not even a brute cries out without cause; still less would a rational man. Your moralisings are insipid and disgusting to me. You threaten me with death, if I do not confess that I am guilty. Death is the very thing that I desire. I am not afraid to die, for I have never broken the commandments of the Holy One. Oh that God would crush me out and out, instead of preserving me for this lingering torture! I would dance for joy under any pain that might speedily end in death. You promise me a happy future, if I do confess. But there can be no future for me. It is too late to hope for restored health. I am not made of stone or brass. It is the part of friendship to show pity, otherwise the afflicted may be led into despair and atheism. My brethren have deceived me. They are like a brook,* which in the winter-time, when it is not wanted, rolls along in a full, turbid stream; but in the summer, when the parched and thirsty caravans are in need of water, it has dried up. If I had asked you to give me anything, to help me in any difficulty or danger, I should not have been surprised at your refusing. I never expected your friendship to be good for as much as that. But I only asked for pity, and even this you refuse. You tell me I have sinned, but you do not tell me how. As for the bitter language of my curse, any one but a monster would make allowance for the frenzy of despair. And what I said about my innocence was quite true. I can repeat it in perfect calmness. I would not lie to your face. Do you suppose I have lost all sense of the difference between right and wrong?

You have drawn a pretty picture of a divine Father; but it would have been truer to the facts if you had talked about a divine taskmaster. Man has a hard service to perform upon earth. As a slave pants for the shadow of night, which will release him from his work, so man pants for death, when his misery will end. As for me, I have been allotted days of vanity and nights of weariness. And there is no prospect of any compensation. For this life of ours is but a breath;

it has no sooner come, than it has gone from us for ever. Man goes down to Hades, and returns nevermore. He vanishes like a cloud that is dissolved. He will never again see good.   O God, why dost Thou torture me thus? Is it because Thou art afraid of me? Can such a poor, worn-out wreck as I, be an object of terror, like an ocean or a sea that needs to be restrained? Let me alone. My days are but a vapour at the best. Why must I be harassed throughout my little span? Why shouldst Thou give Thyself so much trouble about such a pitiful creature as man? Is it worth Thy while to come inspecting me morning by morning, putting me to the proof moment by moment, scaring me with dreams, terrifying me with visions, making my life a burden too heavy to be borne? Wilt Thou never take Thine eyes off me, Thou spy upon men? Perhaps I HAVE sinned, but what harm have I done to Thee? If my sin is so distasteful to Thee, why couldst Thou not pardon it, and cause it to pass away?
As for me, I must soon lay me down and mingle with the dust.

Job has no sooner ceased than Bildad comes forward, "with a little store of maxims preaching down the sufferer's heart." He makes no apology for venturing to speak, but bluntly begins with a rebuke. *How long will you continue to rage? Do you suppose God is unjust? He would not have killed your children unless they had been grievous sinners. To you an opportunity of repentance has been granted, inasmuch as He has spared your life. If you will but become again pure and upright, He will make you more prosperous than ever. Mark me, I do not offer this as my own private opinion. I am but of yesterday and know nothing. What I am teaching you has been handed down to us from antiquity, where all wisdom is to be found. The ancients tell us that a man who forgets God can no more prosper than a tree can live without water. They tell us that the hope of the wicked is doomed to disappointment, its foundation being as frail as a spider's web. They tell us that the wicked will perish like a plant growing in stony soil, which is soon destroyed, and leaves no trace of its existence behind. Such is the sinner's* JOYFUL *career! But if you will turn to God, your mouth may even yet be filled with laughter.*

In chapters ix. and x. Job speaks again. He points out that omnipotence is no proof of justice. He tries to show that God is in actual fact unjust; and he concludes by passionately expostulating with the Almighty.

You say God rewards the good. Well, I know He does; at least He rewards those whom He chooses to consider good. But how is an innocent man to establish his innocence, if God refuses to acknowledge it? He is an almighty Adversary. Look at His action in the world around us. He causes earthquakes and eclipses and tempests, out of mere capricious fury. And not content with devastating nature, He must now be crossing MY *path,—at least so it seems by the disasters that have been happening to me. He has seized upon my property and my children and my health, and I am powerless to resist Him. I cannot even say to Him, What doest Thou? I am so weak that I dare not complain. I can only supplicate my Adversary for mercy. If I ventured to call Him to account, and He were to appear in answer to my summons, I should have no hope that He would listen to me. He would but redouble my sufferings. He would take away my breath, so that I should be speechless. He would ask me ironically, "Have you summoned me to a trial of strength? If so, I am ready for you. Or is it a trial of right that you want? What can be the good of impeaching me?" I should be so confused and terrified that, however innocent I knew myself to be, I should declare that I was* guilty, though I should despise myself for doing so all the while.

It is all one to me whether I live or die; so I may as well speak out my mind. This talk of yours about His punishing the guilty is nonsense. He destroys the guilty and the guiltless alike. If there is any difference, the guilty have the best of it. The earth seems to be given over into the hands of the wicked. At the calamities of the righteous, God only laughs. My days are swifter than a courier, and they will soon be over; so that there will be no time for compensation. Besides, I know Thou wilt not clear me. Well, if I must be guilty, I must be. Thou hast determined to have it so. Were I to wash myself in snow-water and cleanse my hands in potash, Thou wouldst thrust me into a ditch, and make me so foul that my very garments would shrink from contact with me. I am helpless. He says I am guilty, and I cannot disprove it; for He is God, and I am only man. There is no arbiter to come between us, no mediator to reconcile us and explain us to one another. If there were, I would speak and not be afraid: for I am innocent; I know no cause for fear. And speak I will, even as it is. I can but lose the life which I loathe. In the bitterness of my soul I will say *unto God, Show me wherefore Thou contendest with me. Is it becoming in Thee to oppress the weak, to give prosperity to the wicked, to despise the very work of Thine own hands? Can it be that Thou hast only human eyesight, that Thou hast been misled as to my real character? Or is it that Thy days are numbered, and that Thou hastenest to glut Thine anger before Thou art no more? Thou knowest I am not guilty, yet Thou inventest sins of which to accuse me. Thy hands fashioned me, yet now Thou art destroying me. Oh remember how soon I must return to dust! Once thou didst grant me favour. Once Thou didst watch over me and guard me. But Thou must have been hiding malice in Thine heart all the time. Thou wast preserving me only to amuse Thyself with my anguish. That this was Thy purpose, I know. It mattered not whether I was innocent or guilty. Had I done wickedly, Thou wouldst have taken vengeance on me. Had I been righteous, Thou wouldst have been doubly angry. Thou wouldst not have permitted me to hold up my head; Thou wouldst have suborned witnesses to convict me; Thou wouldst have proved Thyself omnipotent for my discomfiture. Oh to be as though I had not been! Would that I had been carried from the womb to the grave! But as it is, forbear! Get Thee gone! Leave me alone, that I may know some little comfort, before I go away into the land from which there is no return—that land of disorder and of gloom, where the very light is darkness.*

In this state of mind we must leave him for the present. The burden of his complaint, you will have noticed, has been twofold. He laments, first, that God, by so grievously afflicting him, has virtually declared him to be pre-eminently sinful; and secondly, that his little span of life is being wasted in anguish, when it is the only life he will have. He has spoken words which fall little, if at all, short of blasphemy. But these words were the natural product of his creed. The theology in which he and his three friends had been instructed, contained at least two seriously erroneous doctrines. It taught that suffering was an invariable proof of the divine displeasure; and it also taught that human life ended with the grave. It is in the light, or rather in the darkness, of these doctrines, that Job has hitherto been studying his experience. No wonder he despairs.

Job.

IV.

CHAPTERS XI.-XVII.

IT is now Zophar's turn to speak. He has only the same doctrine to preach as Eliphaz and Bildad, and he is a vastly inferior preacher. But, with the self-conceit natural to an ignorant man, he seems to think that he alone can satisfactorily answer Job's arguments.

Your boastful babblings about your purity shall not go unanswered. Would that God might appear to you as you have wished! He would soon make you conscious of your guilt. You would then see that your punishment was less than you deserved. What do you know about God? Are you acquainted with the heights and depths and lengths and breadths of the divine perfection? Iniquity cannot be hid from Him, and nothing can hinder Him from punishing it. He sees evil even when He seems to see it not. A man may be as stupid and intractable as a wild ass's colt, but God can make him wise. Do you, therefore, draw near to God, having first put away your iniquity. Then you will once more be able to hold up your head. The light of prosperity will dawn upon you, and become brighter than the glory of noon. Peace and hope and safety will be yours, and many will pay court to you. But as for the wicked, they shall perish. Their hope is as fleeting as the sigh of an expiring man.

Job in his reply gives a long harangue on the power of God. He wishes his friends to see that he can be as eloquent on this subject as they can; but in opposition to them he maintains that Providence, so far from being strictly retributive, is arbitrary, or at any rate inexplicable, in its action. He declares that he will summon his divine Adversary to a formal trial; and, as though the trial had been already instituted, he demands to be informed of what he is accused. But failing to elicit any response, he relapses again into his old despondency. For a moment it occurs to him that there may be a future life: but he dismisses the thought as a vain delusion.

No doubt but ye are the people, and wisdom will die with you. Why, you have been uttering truisms. I know these things, and every one knows them as well as you.
To think that I should have become a laughing-stock to my friends,—I, the just, the innocent, the religious man, a laughing-stock! It is the way of the world to treat the unfortunate with contempt.
But as for the wicked, they are never unfortunate. Tranquil are the tents of the spoilers. Those who recognise no God but their fist are always prosperous. What you say about the power of God is true enough, but not original. Any one may see the hand of Jehovah in bird and beast and fish, no less than in the human race. From Him every creature derives its breath. You have been quoting proverbs, but proverbs are not to be accepted indiscriminately. We must inquire if they agree with facts. No doubt wisdom is to be looked for in the aged, but in its perfection it exists only in God. If we would be wise, we must examine His ways for ourselves; and when we examine them, what do we find? Why this, that they are altogether inexplicable. What He destroys is never

repaired. From His prison-house there is no deliverance. He sends on men now a deluge, and now a drought. With Him undoubtedly is wisdom and strength; but that is all we can say. We cannot see the reason of His actions. Men are deceived, and deceive one another, because He will have it so. Kings and priests, senators and judges, He carries away into captivity. The strong He makes weak, the wise foolish, the eloquent speechless; upon the nobles He pours contempt; the most cherished secrets He brings to light. At one time He exalts a nation; at another time He destroys it. At one time He makes it prosperous; at another He plunges it into adversity. The leaders of the people He deprives of their leadership, and they find themselves wandering in a pathless waste, groping about in darkness, staggering like drunken men. This is the result of my experience.

You have only been patching up old saws; and a bungling piece of patchwork you have made of it! The wisest thing you could do would be to hold your tongue. My answer to you is this: You do not believe what you say. You say it because you think it is the correct thing to say. You have been telling lies for God. You have been playing the part of sycophants. But He will not be imposed on by your flattering speeches.

He does not want your dishonest support. He will only punish you for your pains. You have threatened ME with His appearing. But what if He appears against YOU? Your old saws will not avail you then. Be silent.

Come what will, I am determined to speak out. He may slay me—He very likely will, but I will defend myself. This surely should speak for my acquittal. A sinner would not dare to come before Him. I am ready to begin pleading. I have set my cause in order. I know that I have right on my side. Where is the man that can bring any accusation against me? There is no such man. If there were, I should die of shame. But Thou must grant me two conditions, O God, or the trial will not be a fair one. Remove my pain, so that I may think; and divest Thyself of Thy Majesty, so that I be not affrighted. Then I am ready to be either plaintiff or defendant. Do Thou accuse, and I will answer. Or let me speak, and do Thou respond. Art Thou silent? Then I must open the case for myself. How many are my iniquities? Show me my transgressions.

Thou makest no reply? Why dost Thou hide Thy face and treat me as a foe? Is Thy conduct worthy of Thee? I am feeble as a driven leaf. Why dost Thou hunt me? The sins that I committed in my early years, when I knew no better, have been long since put aside. And yet Thou dost punish me for them with this bitter punishment, confining me to the ash-heap, where I lie wasting away. And mine is no isolated case. Man that is born of woman inherits all her frailty. He lives but a few days, and even those are full of trouble. He is fragile as a flower, and fleeting as a shadow. Can it be right that a creature so frail and evanescent, so loaded with sorrows, should be dogged with an incessant and suspicious vigilance, and called to a stern, judicial account? Canst Thou expect a clean thing to come out of an unclean? Thou hast ordained man's days to be few and evil. Thou hast given him but a paltry nature, of which but little can be made. Canst Thou not let him alone in his misery, till the days of his servitude are over? Man is the most miserable object in the world. Even a tree may hope to renew its life from time to time; but man giveth up the ghost, and where is he? When he lieth down, he riseth nevermore.

But may it not be that man shall rise again? Oh that Thou wouldst keep me in the under-world until Thy wrath be past! Perchance man may live even after he has died. Oh that Thou wouldst appoint some time in that future life for the res-

H

toration of Thy favour! If only I had such a hope, I would wait patiently all through the days of my servitude. Surely it will be so. Thou must yearn towards the work of Thine own hands. But no; instead of this yearning towards me, Thou art dogging my steps, watching eagerly to catch me in sin, treasuring up against me my every slip. As water wears down the stone, as floods wash away the soil, as everything in nature changes and passes away, so dost Thou destroy the hope of man. Thou prevailest against him, and disfigurest him. Thou bringest him into such a condition that he cares no longer for his nearest kin. He can think only of himself and of his pain.

So ends the first part of the discussion. In the second, the friends no longer try to prove that the good always receive good from God, They content themselves with reaffirming that the evil always receive evil. They begin to treat Job as a hardened sinner for whom there can be no hope. They do not now urge him to repent. Job, on the contrary, is making progress faith-wards. At times he is as sad as ever, as impatient of the truisms of his friends, as fierce in resenting the wrong done him by God and man. But on the whole he is calmer than before: he begins to hope; sometimes he does more than hope—he feels certain that all will by-and-by be well. Of this we shall meet a remarkable illustration in the next sermon.

Eliphaz opens the second part of the discussion as he did the first. He is still less inconsiderate than the other two. But even he is by this time very wroth. He tells Job that he is self-condemned—condemned by his own impious language; and then he paints a sombre picture of the doom that awaits the wicked. Having no more visions to relate, he now falls back, like Bildad, upon tradition.

You say you are as wise as we are; but you do not talk like a wise man. Your arguments prove nothing. Your words are as meaningless as the wind. When a man, once noted for piety like yourself, behaves in this way, he brings religion into contempt. Your own mouth convicts you, for you say that God is unjust. Pray, are you the oldest member of the human race? Do you belong to the Privy Council of the Almighty? Has no one any wisdom but yourself? What do you know that we do not know? Why, on our side are hoary-headed men, older than your father. With delicacy and consideration we have offered you the consolations of God, but you have spurned them. How is it that you are so carried away with passion as to speak blasphemy? You talk about your sinlessness. Why, the very angels are not faultless; the heavens are impure in the sight of God: how, then, can man be pure? Man drinketh in iniquity like water; he is altogether loathsome and unclean. Listen to me, and I will give you the result of my experience. What I tell you is supported by the authority of my ancestors, who were never corrupted by heathen superstitions. As long as the wicked lives, he suffers torment and is in slavery. Terrible sounds are ever in his ear. Even in times of peace the spoiler falls upon him. He is marked out for the sword. He cannot tell where he may find bread to eat. He is in constant dread, until at last he is destroyed. He set himself against God, and proudly dared the Almighty's curse: but he shall never be rich. Any wealth he may acquire soon passes away. He has no hope of ever escaping from the darkness that envelops him; nay, he knows that a yet darker day is coming. The only light he will ever see is the fire that shall consume his children. He himself will be destroyed by the breath of God's mouth. Fool that he is, let him expect nothing but evil as a reward for his deeds! He shall die prematurely, his children having perished before him. The punishment of his doings is mischief, disappointment, ruin.

Job begins to reply to Eliphaz with a few sarcastic personalities, but soon turns to God in a passionate utterance of mingled complaint and entreaty, interspersed by occasional flashes of hope.

You are miserable comforters, all of you, with your empty truisms. What can induce you to talk as you do? Suppose you were in my place, and I were to string together maxims against you, and shake my head in disapproval of you, and offer to console you with heartless words, how would you like it? But ah me! neither speech nor silence can make much difference to my grief. My strength is exhausted. I am shrivelled up. My emaciation is a witness against me. God, like a beast of prey, is pursuing me with glaring eyes and gnashing teeth. My friends are at His heels, ready to devour me. He seizes me by the throat, He shakes me and rends me in His fury, and then flings me to the yelping pack. He has set me up as a target: His arrows are flying all about me; they pierce to my inmost soul. He has stormed me like a fortress, and laid me low in the very dust. My eyes are red with weeping. The shadows of death are gathering about me. And all this when I have done no iniquity, when I have been a sincere worshipper of God. O earth, earth, that refuseth to drink the blood of the innocent, let my blood lie on thy breast, crying out in my behalf until I be avenged! I feel that I have a witness in heaven. I will turn from the friends who mock me, and look up beseechingly unto God. Though He is my Adversary, I will ask Him to be my Arbiter—to right me even though He condemn Himself—to declare me innocent before my fellows. But it must be quickly done; for in a few short years I shall have reached the end of that path along which no traveller returns. My life is fast ebbing away. There remains for me nothing but the grave and the mockers who perpetually provoke me. O God, wilt Thou not give me some present pledge of my future justification? Wilt Thou not bind Thyself to appear for me? They are so heartless and foolish, Thou wilt never give the victory to them! They have been untrue to the duties of friendship; and they or their children must suffer for it. As for me, I am become a byword, an object of scorn, among men. My eye is dim with grief. My limbs are wasted into shadows. Good men are astonished and indignant at the treatment I am receiving. Nevertheless I am righteous. I will hold on my way, and in the end I shall find support. Do not go away, my friends. Return to your arguments. I am ready for you. There is not a wise man among you. My days are run out, my most cherished purposes are frustrated. You would try and persuade me that light may arise out of darkness. But it cannot be. If I have any hope, it is to reach my home in Hades. I have grown so familiar with the thought of death, that I say to the grave, Thou art my father; and to the worms, Ye are my sisters. Death is my only hope; and it will be realised when I mingle with the dust.

Once again we must leave Job in the very depths of his divine despair. But it *is*, you will observe, a *divine* despair. It is caused by the conviction that some unaccountable misunderstanding has arisen between himself and God. Acutely as he feels his sufferings, he declares that he could bear them all with patience, if only he had the most distant hope of this misunderstanding being removed. Even when his words come nearest to blasphemy, we can detect in his heart the unspoken cry,—" Whom have I in heaven but Thee? and there is none upon earth that I desire besides Thee."

Job.

V.

CHAPTERS XVIII.-XXI.

WE have now reached Bildad's second speech. He gives a graphic account of the punishment which overtakes the sinner, working into his description, with cruel ingenuity, some of the very calamities which had fallen upon Job.

How long will you continue to speak without having anything to say? What business have you to treat us as though we were unreasoning brutes? You talk of God rending you in His anger, but it is you who are rending yourself with your furious passion. What is the good of it? The divine laws are unalterable. Do you suppose they are going to be set aside, that you may escape the punishment of your sins? The prosperity of the wicked does not last. His ambitious schemes only end in ruin. He is taken in his own snares. His footsteps are dogged by alarms. Destruction lies in wait, ready to devour him. Leprosy, the first-born of death, eats away his limbs. He is torn from his home and dragged before the King of Terrors. He is hunted out of the world and thrust into darkness. Strangers dwell in his tent. His children are destroyed by brimstone. He leaves no survivors behind him. His very name is forgotten in the land; or, if remembered, it will only be with horror and disgust. Such is the doom of him who knows not God.

Job in his next speech declares, more emphatically than ever, that his sufferings are not reconcilable with any known principle of divine government. He makes one final appeal to his listener's pity—an appeal of heartrending pathos. But they offer no response. As they sit beside him in grim silence, he feels more keenly than ever his loneliness and misery. It was well that they did not respond; for only after their persistent cruelty had made him supremely conscious of the magnitude of his woe, did he gain a belief in the resurrection of the dead. He once dismissed the idea of a future life as a delusion. But at last he sees it in a new light; it appears to him to be a necessary truth. He, sitting there on his ash-heap, rotting away in agony; his friends, whose lives had certainly not been better than his own, looking down upon him with self-complacency and contempt,—what possible justification, what conceivable explanation of this could there be, but the fact that there was another life, in which such inequalities would be corrected? So certain does he now feel in regard to the resurrection, that, before declaring his belief in it, he calls special attention to what he is about to say, implying that it is not the transitory feeling of the moment, but a profound and unalterable conviction.

How long will you rack my soul with your words? You have shamelessly overwhelmed me with reproaches. You have exhausted every form of insult. If I had sinned, you need not have troubled yourselves, for you would not be answerable for it. But if you must meddle with me, let me tell you, I have NOT *sinned. I have not brought my misery on myself, like your "wicked man." I am not taken in my own snares. It is God who has flung His net about me; and in doing so, He has treated me wrongfully. I protest against the wrong, but I am not answered. I cry aloud, but I get no justice. He has blocked up my way so* that I cannot pass. He has surrounded me with darkness. He has stripped me of my honour, and taken the crown from my head. All is over. Even of my hope He has bereft me. He is so enraged that He is sending forth His troops in battle array against me. He has made me such an object of loathing and contempt that my neighbours will have nothing to do with me. My kinsmen stand aloof from me. My acquaintance have forgotten me. My servants treat me as a stranger, and will neither obey my commands nor listen to my entreaties. I am become offensive even to my wife. The very children despise and ridicule me. My bosom friends abhor me. Those whom I loved are turned against me. All that I had has been taken away. I am reduced to the shadow of my former self. Have pity on me, have pity on me, O ye my friends, for the hand of God hath smitten me! Are you not satisfied with what I am already suffering? Why must you join with God in persecuting me?

But stop. I see a great light. I should like what I am about to say to be written down, to be graven on the eternal rocks. I know that there lives for me an Avenger, and that He will by-and-by stand over my grave, and pronounce my cause just. My body will be destroyed, but without it

I shall see God. Yes, I myself shall see Him. Come, happy day!   As for you, if you persist in persecuting me, beware of the sword of my Avenger.

Zophar now speaks again. To a man like him there is no sin so heinous as that of heresy. Job had by this time clearly proved himself heterodox. He did not receive the accepted notions about suffering, and he was full of new-fangled ideas of his own—as, for example, this theory about a resurrection. And such a heretic had ventured to threaten him—Zophar —with the divine disapproval. No wonder the foolish man was angry. And he thought, of course, that he did well to be angry. "His wrath was but the resentment of wounded pride, but he mistook it for the inspiration of religious zeal." The wicked man whom he *now* describes, in whose portrait he intends that Job should see himself, is no ordinary sinner, but a very monster of iniquity. The penalties attached to such extravagant wickedness Zophar proceeds to enumerate, in language the coarseness of which I shall be obliged to do him the injustice of somewhat toning down. He begins in a confused sort of way. He feels he must say something, but he hardly knows what.

I am burning to reply. I am ashamed at having been subjected to such reproaches. I have an answer in my head, if I could only bring it out.

Do not you know that from the beginning of the world, the triumph of the wicked has only endured but for a moment? Though in his pride he exalts himself to the very heavens, he shall be cast aside like the vilest refuse. He shall pass away like a dream, perishing completely as if he had never been. He will be compelled to restore his ill-gotten gains. His children will have to beg from those whom he once impoverished. He shall go to the grave in his youthful vigour. As a gourmand dallies with a dainty morsel, which when it is swallowed turns to poison within him, so he voluptuously lingers over his sin, which in its effects will be gall and wormwood. The days of his luxury will come to an end. His dishonest gains he will have to disgorge. He ill-treated and despoiled the poor; his greed knew no bounds; nothing was safe from it. But his enjoyment shall not endure. In the fulness of his abundance he shall be straitened. Everything that can make a man wretched shall come upon him. In the midst of his gluttonous feasting he shall find himself surfeited—surfeited with fire and brimstone from God. If he escapes one danger, it shall only be to fall into another. He lives in constant dread. His treasures are doomed to destruction. Fire from above shall devour everything that he hath. Heaven and earth shall unite to reveal his iniquity and to ensure his ruin. He and his children shall be utterly destroyed. This is the portion appointed for the wicked by the Lord.

Job in his reply follows Zophar's speech almost point by point, and shows that, generally speaking, the wicked are not visited by any of the punishments which Zophar has mentioned.

Let me at least have the consolation of answering you. Give me a fair hearing; and after that, if you are not convinced, you may mock me as much as you please. My complaint is against God, and I have good ground to make it. If you would but look at me, you must be struck dumb with astonishment. Even as I think of it I tremble. Why is it that the wicked live on to old age and acquire power? Their homes are free from fear. Their children are established prosperously around them. They are visited by no chastisement from God. Their flocks thrive and multiply. Their children may be seen in troops, dancing for joy. Their days pass away in mirth. Even when death comes, it comes kindly and suddenly. Yet they have been saying all their lives, "*Depart from us, O God, for we do not care to know Thee; what is the use of serving the Almighty?*" Their prosperity comes I know not whence; but however it comes, I would have none of it. Far from me be the devices of the wicked. How seldom is the prosperity of the wicked cut short! How seldom does God apportion them any calamity! How seldom does He blast them with the destruction they deserve. God, you will say, punishes the children for the iniquities of the fathers. But that is no punishment at all. It is the sinner himself, and not his children, who should drink the wrath of the Almighty. What cares the wicked man for his posterity, so long as he is allowed to live out his time in peace? In setting up your own opinions against facts, you are virtually sitting in judgment upon God. You say that retribution should be exacted; but it is not, not even in death. Death is as unequal as life. One man dies after years of prosperity; another in bitterness of soul before he has ever tasted good. They lie down side by side in the dust, and the worms do their work upon them both. I know what you are hinting at, when you say that the wicked are destroyed. But it is not true. It may have been so in your small experience. But ask those who *have travelled, ask those who have seen more of the world, and they will tell you a different story. They will tell you that many a proud and cruel despot has altogether escaped calamity. He is so powerful that no one dares accuse him, that no one can retaliate on him. He is carried to the tomb in pomp. A monument is erected in his honour. The clods of the valley lie softly upon him. His success induces many to follow him along the same flowery, well-trodden path of sin.*

Your arguments are fallacious, and your consolations are just as worthless.

So ends the second part of the discussion. The more the friends persist in asserting their doctrine that the wicked only suffer, and that they suffer in proportion to their wickedness, the clearer does it become to Job that the doctrine is contradicted by experience. But they remain blind to the contradiction. In most debates three out of four debaters argue, not for truth, but for victory. So it was here. How completely the minds of the three were closed against new ideas, is curiously illustrated by the fact that they take no notice of Job's assertion regarding a future life. They pass it by as unworthy of comment. They had never before heard any mention of such a doctrine; and to minds so constituted it would therefore seem but the wandering of a diseased imagination.

I had better, perhaps, ask you specially to notice exactly what it was that Job said upon this subject. The passage in our Authorised Version is very much mistranslated. In my paraphrase of his speech I gave you his meaning in modern English. A more literal translation of the Hebrew would be this: "I know that my Avenger liveth, and He will stand at last over my dust; yea, after my skin, when my body is destroyed, without my flesh I shall see Him. I shall see Him for myself, through my own eyes and not through those of another. For that my heart pines away within me." A Hebrew would understand by the Avenger the nearest relative of the deceased, whose business it was to take cognisance of any wrongs that had been done to his departed kinsman. Job's idea then is, that there will come a time when God, who seems now to have forsaken him, will act the part of this avenging friend—that the Almighty will one day stand solemnly over his grave and conclusively vindicate his character. Further, Job believes that he himself will be then alive: though his flesh will have seen corruption, yet with the eyes of a spiritual body he

I

will behold his divine Avenger. It was a marvellous anticipation of St Paul's teaching, that the death of the natural, is the birth of the spiritual, body. "Flesh and blood cannot inherit the kingdom of God." "Thou sowest not the body that shall be. . . . It is sown a natural body, it is raised a spiritual body." "We know that if our earthly house of this tabernacle [our physical body] were dissolved, we have a building of God, an house not made with hands [a spiritual body], eternal in the heavens."

While, then, the friends are gaining nothing by the discussion, Job has already gained much; he has won in fact "the blessed hope of everlasting life." His experience, so far, is beautifully expressed by some lines of Mr Greg's:—

> "Around my path life's mysteries
>   Their deepening shadows throw;
> And as I gaze and ponder,
>   They dark and darker grow.
>
> Yet still, amid the darkness,
>   I feel the light is near;
> And in the awful silence
>   God's voice I seem to hear.
>
> But I hear it as the thunder,
>   Or the murmuring of the sea;
> The secret it is telling,—
>   But it tells it not to me.

Then I ask the wise and learned
  If they the thing can show;
But the longer they discourse thereon,
    The less I seem to know.

So I seek again the silence,
    And the lonely darkness too;
They teach me deeper lessons
    Of the Holy, Vast, and True.

And I hear a voice above me
    Which says,—'Wait, trust, and pray;
The night will soon be over,
    And light will come with day.'

To Him I yield my spirit,
    On Him I lay my load:
Fear ends with death; beyond it
    I nothing see but God."

Job.

VI.

CHAPTERS XXII.-XXVIII.

WE have now reached the third and last part of the discussion. Eliphaz is by this time so very angry as to be scarcely distinguishable from poor Zophar. He accuses his suffering friend of the most vulgar and brutal crimes. At the close of his speech, however, he seems to feel some little compunction, for he once more promises the divine forgiveness to Job if only he will repent.

God gains nothing by the goodness of the good. He loses nothing by the badness of the bad. His motives in punishing men must be disinterested, and therefore just. You have summoned Him to your bar but He will not condescend to argue with you. Nor is there any need. Your iniquities are great and endless. You have distrained the poor, when you yourself were well off. You have stripped the beggar of his raiment. You have withheld bread from the famishing, and water from the faint. You have acted as if no one but your strong proud self had any business in the land. You gave no assistance to the widow; and you wrested from the orphans their means of support. This is why you are beset with dangers and alarms. This is the cause of the mental darkness which envelops you, and the flood of misery which is overwhelming you. Do you think God is so exalted that He cannot see men's doings? Do you suppose that, as He dwells above the clouds, the sinner is hidden from His view? It is an ancient path you are treading,—the path of the men of sin who were swept away prematurely by the Deluge. This was their punishment for saying, "What is the use of serving the Almighty?" Suddenly their firm foundation became a flowing stream. They had been for a time in great prosperity;—but far from me be the devices by which such prosperity is attained! We righteous rejoice when we see the discomfiture of our adversaries—the wicked. We laugh when they and their substance are destroyed.

Make friends now with God, and then peace

and prosperity will return to you. Listen to His precepts, and cherish them in your heart. Give up your sin, and you will be restored. Learn to regard gold as dross, and God will become your treasure. You will be able to hold up your head before the Almighty. He will no longer be deaf to your prayers. Your enterprises will all be attended with success. Your votive offerings will be accepted. The light of prosperity will ever shine upon your path. Nay, you will be able, by quoting from your own experience, to cheer those who are cast down. Your prayer will prevail, even for those who are not without sin.

Job in his reply complains that God is hiding Himself from him—that he hides Himself from the race. He points out how large classes of men live, through no fault of their own, in the most abject misery and servitude, while their oppressors have a good time of it and go down to the grave in peace. Yet God never interferes. So far from retribution being regular, as the friends say, it would seem as if there were no such thing as Providence.

I will still persist in my complaint. Loud and bitter as it is, it does not express my anguish. Oh that I knew where I might find Him! I would press even to His throne. I would lay my case before Him, and pour out argument upon argument; and then I should hear what He had to say against me. Instead of contending with me in the greatness of His strength, He would listen to me; and, as I am upright, I should be acquitted once for all by my Judge. But I do not know where to find Him. Behold, I go towards the east, but He is not there; and westward, but I cannot perceive Him: towards the north, where He is working, but I cannot see Him; and southwards He concealeth Himself, so that I cannot find Him. If He would try me, I should come forth as gold. I have walked, God knows, in His way. I have obeyed His commandments. I have preferred His will to my own. But He is not to be turned from His purpose. What He has decreed for me He will carry out. It is His usual way. Therefore I am troubled at His presence. When I think of His decrees, I am afraid. I am unmanned and rendered speechless, not by my sufferings, but by the thought that they have been inflicted on me by God. It is He who has filled me with confusion.

Why does not God appoint days of judgment, so that those who believe in Him might SEE something of His providence? The wicked steal their neighbours' possessions, and rob even the widow

and the fatherless, reducing them to such poverty
that they have to eat roots and herbs, like the wild
asses of the desert. Or if they are taken on to the
estates as serfs, not so much as clothes and shelter
are given them for wages; and they are drenched
by the winter storm, unless they can find a cleft of
the rock in which to hide themselves. The oppressors will steal the very infant at the breast and sell
it into slavery. There is none so poor as not to be
robbed by them. Their slaves carry their corn, but
are left to hunger; and tread the wine-vats, but die
of thirst. The cities too, like the country, are full
of groaning slaves; and mingled with their groans,
you may hear the cry of wounded soldiers, whose
lives the oppressors have flung away. Yet God
heedeth not their wrongs! Then there is another
class of evil-doers, such as the murderer, the thief,
the adulterer. To all of these the light is hateful.
They shut themselves up in the daytime, but come
forth in the dark to their housebreaking work.
Night has no terrors for them, but they are as
frightened of the dawn as of the shadow of death.
It may be that the heritage of such men is cursed,
but they themselves glide quietly down the stream
of life. They have passed away before the curse
comes into effect. They are cut off by no terrible
catastrophe. Death removes them in as gentle a

manner as the snow is melted by the sun. They plundered the very widows, and God saw them doing it, but none the less He sustained and protected them. They lived in ease, they were fortunate, they died in a ripe old age. Which of you can say that this is not so?

Bildad's third and last speech is perhaps his best. It is the least unkind, the least irrelevant, and the shortest. He no longer attempts to prove his old thesis. He no longer recriminates his friend. He merely restates a doctrine frequently mentioned by Eliphaz—the doctrine, viz., of the infinite distance between God and man, and the consequent impurity of the latter. This has, of course, nothing to do with the main argument, as to whether great suffering be a sign of great sin. But it is relevant to Job's assertion that he is sure of a complete acquittal.

With God is absolute dominion. He ruleth the multitude of the heavenly host; and by His rule they have peace. His glory shines through them all. Even the moon's silver sheen appears soiled in His eyes. The very stars to Him seem impure. How, then, can that worm—man—be pure?

The awesomeness of the divine Majesty, upon which Bildad has thus briefly touched, has a fascination for Job in his present mood; and so, after a few personalities, he begins to discourse upon it himself.

I am weak and in need of help; but do you suppose that your speeches are any good to me? You have poured out a flood of words; but do you think they contain instruction? You give forth your commonplaces as if they had come to you by special revelation. As for the majesty of God, yes, even in the under-world His presence is felt. The very shades of the dead writhe with fear when He looks at them. He stretched out the vault of the heavens, and poised the earth in space. He restrains the waters in clouds as it were in vessels; but these very clouds hide His throne from our view. He has surrounded the earth by an ocean, which extends to the confines of darkness. The mountains are convulsed by His anger, and they quake. He rouses the sea into a storm; and when it is fiercely raging, He smites it, in its pride, into a calm. When the dragon swallows up the sun and so causes an eclipse, God drives him away, and the heavens again become bright. And these are BUT PARTS *of His ways. He reveals Himself to us in nature gently, as by a zephyr. But the thunder of His omnipotence, deafening by excess of sound, who can hear?*

There the formal discussion may be said to end. Chapters xxvii. to xxxi. constitute what is generally called Job's soliloquy. He now rises into a higher style of speech, called in the English version parable, or, as it should rather be, strain. This term is never used except for discourse of a peculiarly elevated type. He begins by modifying some of his previous statements. He found, on reflection, that he had not done sufficient justice to the arguments of his friends, and that he had pushed the facts which he adduced in opposition further than they would legitimately go. He now admits that, as a rule or at any rate very frequently, the wicked are punished.[1] But he feels this will not explain the mystery of his own suffering. Great though his anguish be, it is not the anguish of the wicked, for he can still cling to God. The fact is, as he proceeds to show in

[1] Many critics say that verses 13-23 were really uttered by Zophar. But they are not at all in Zophar's style. And it seems more likely the poet would represent Job as admitting, after he became calmer, that very often the wicked *are* overtaken by visible punishments. You will observe, however, that "the wicked" are here described as being altogether, hopelessly destroyed, in contrast to Job himself, who has a hope after death (v. 8), and who is able, even in the midst of his trouble, to call upon God and confidently invoke Him for justice (9 and 10).

chapter xxviii., they had all been attempting to solve an insoluble problem. *Why* he has been called upon to suffer was, and must continue, a mystery. He points out the limitation of human faculties, and maintains that while man is capable of marvellous attainments, there are yet many matters of which he must always remain ignorant. Men's achievements in mining operations seem to have struck him as the most stupendous proof of human power. He gives, therefore, an eloquent account of the miner's work; and then goes on to contrast man's knowledge in such matters with his ignorance in regard to the purposes of God. We may dig into the earth, he says in effect, and abstract its hidden treasure, but we cannot penetrate into the heart of God. "His ways are past finding out."

As God liveth, though He hath denied me justice and embittered my soul, while I live I will never speak the thing that is not true. Far be it from me to allow that your charges against me are just. Till my last expiring breath I will maintain that I am innocent. My conscience does not reproach me. It is not I who am wicked, but my foes. Wretched as is my lot, it is not the lot of a sinner. However prosperous he may be in life, he has nothing to hope for after death, as I now have. He does not, as I do, delight himself in God, and confidently invoke Him for justice. God does not hear his prayer as He will hear mine. I will explain to you how the hand of God is manifested upon the wicked; and yet you have seen it for yourselves, so that there is no excuse for your foolish speaking. This is the doom of the wicked. He may have many children, but they shall perish by the sword or by famine; and if any survive, they shall be destroyed by a pestilence —by a pestilence so dreadful that not even their widows will follow them to the grave. He may amass gold as though it were but dust, and raiment as though it were of no more value than mire, but eventually his property shall all be enjoyed by the righteous. The house which he builds himself is fragile and destructible as the moth's. His riches vanish in a moment; and in the twinkling of an eye he himself is no more. Terrors overtake him like a flood. Death shall carry him away suddenly like a whirlwind. God shall shower evils upon him without sparing, and men shall regard his discomfiture with scornful derision.

The cause of my suffering cannot be discovered. It is one of the unsearchable secrets of God. Man has found the veins of silver and the places where gold-dust may be washed out. He has discovered the iron-mines, and the rocks which contain copper. In his mining operations he invades the kingdom of darkness; and, passing through the subterranean rocks, penetrates, as it were, into the very blackness of death. He sinks his shafts deep down below all human habitations, and carries on his work far away from the sound of human footsteps. The under parts of the earth he blasts by fire, in order to reach the precious stones and the nuggets of gold. The path thither neither the eagle nor the hawk have seen, neither the lion nor the tiger have trodden. This is man's prerogative. No difficulty can stop him. He assaults the granite rock, and uproots the mountain from its base. He dams up the waters, and turns them into channels of his own contriving. But what of wisdom? what of the understanding which comprehends the divine procedure? That is beyond man's faculties. He knows not her abode. She is not to be found with mortals. The sea saith, She is not with me. The abysmal depth which feeds the sea replies, Nor with me. Neither silver nor gold can buy her. Corals and crystal are not to be mentioned in comparison with her. The topaz of Ethiopia is inferior to her. The price of wisdom is beyond pearls. Where, then, does wisdom dwell, and how shall she be obtained? Her abode is hidden from every living eye, yea, even from the fowls of heaven with all their powers of divination. Hades and death, which reveal so many secrets, have to confess that they have heard but the vaguest rumours of her. He only who can look to the ends of the earth, who can observe all that is under heaven, God alone, has seen the abode of wisdom. When He was weighing out the winds and measuring the waters, giving a law to the rain and tracing a path for the lightning, then He saw her and gave her a place in His creation. But He perceived that she was beyond the reach of human faculties. Man can never comprehend things as God comprehends them. We may attain to perfect goodness, but not to perfect knowledge. To man, therefore, He said,— "The fear of the Lord is the beginning of wisdom, and to depart from evil is understanding."

Job.

VII.

CHAPTERS XXIX.-XXXI.

IN the last sermon, we broke off in the middle of Job's soliloquy. Having summed up the debate, he now falls into a less argumentative and a more pensive mood. He gives a pathetic description of his former prosperity, full "of the tender grace of a day that is dead." We learn that he was the sheikh, not of a nomadic, but of a settled clan; that his estate was situated in the suburbs of a well-ordered city; that he had held the office of a judge, and had been universally respected and beloved. After reviewing his former life, he passes on to contrast with it his present position. Instead of being reverenced by the highest, he was now despised by the lowest. The base-born churls, to whom he refers as the most virulent of his insulters, were probably the aborigines of the Hauran, conquered and dispossessed by the superior race of which Job was chief. They would no doubt be glad of an opportunity for revenging themselves, such as was afforded by his present misery and helplessness. Job brings his soliloquy to a conclusion by reasserting his uprightness, and giving a minute description of the innocency of his past life. His conduct, we shall see, had fallen little, if at all, short of that inculcated by the Sermon on the Mount.

Oh that I were as in months of old, in the days when God kept guard over me, when I walked in the light of prosperity, which He caused to shine about me,—in those golden days of the autumn of my manhood, when the Almighty dwelt as a friend in my tent, when my children were yet around me, and nature showered her choicest blessings on me with unstinted prodigality! If I went into the city, and sat in its gate as a judge, young men withdrew as being unworthy even to salute me, and the grey-headed arose and remained standing. Princes and nobles were silent when I wished to speak. All who had ever seen me or heard of me, had something to say in my praise. For I rescued the helpless out of their troubles, I filled

K

the widow's heart with joy, and I saved many who were on the point of perishing. I was so upright a judge, that I seemed as it were to be clothed with righteousness and crowned with equity. I was eyes to the blind, and feet to the lame, and a father to the poor. I pleaded the cause of the alien for whom no one cared, and I took the prey out of the very teeth of the oppressor. So I thought to myself, I shall lengthen out my days like the phœnix, and when death comes at last, it will find me still in my happy home. I thought that I was like a tree abundantly nourished by water and by dew, and that my glory and strength would be perennial. Men waited for my advice, and never gainsaid it. My discourse seemed to them as refreshing as harvest-showers. However despondent they were, my smile was able to revive them. I sat among them as their leader, as their king, as one who comforteth the mourners.

But now, instead of the old respect, they that are younger than I insult me. The fathers of those who mock me were thievish outcasts, whom I would not have trusted as I did my dogs. And they themselves are enervated creatures, having not strength enough to perform any decent work. They are lean from famine; their only bread is what they can find in the desert-wastes. They

gnaw wild roots like beasts. They have been
driven away from human society like the thieves
that they are. Base-born wretches, they were
hounded out of the land. They dwell in gloomy
caverns, or herd together among the bushes. The
jargon that they talk sounds like the braying of
an ass. These are the men to whom I have become a by-word—a theme for their comic songs!
They shun me, and hold themselves aloof; or if
by accident they come near me, they do not hesitate to spit in my face. They insult me without
restraint. They set themselves studiously to destroy
me. They bring accusations against me—me, who
was once their judge! They press upon me like
besieging troops, this rabble of outcasts, so helpless
but for evil. They cast up their works against
me; they make wide breaches in my ramparts;
they pour in through the ruins they have effected.
I am terrified at their violence. And
so my pristine honour is driven away, like a cloud
before the blast of the storm.

My soul is dissolved in complaint. Days of
misery hold me in their power, and will not depart. In the night my bones are pierced with
anguish, and my gnawing pains never sleep. My
torture clings to me like a closely fitting garment.
Thou hast humbled me to the dust. I cry to

Thee, and Thou answerest me not. I stand up to attract Thy attention, and Thou wilt not look at me. Thou art changed. Thou hast become very cruel to me, and dost press me hard in Thine omnipotence. Thou dost cause me to vanish like a cloud before the storm. I know that Thou hast determined to bring me to the grave—the house of assembly for all living. It is no good praying when He raises His hand against one. And yet I cannot help crying out, useless as my cry may be. What am I the better for having sympathised with the unfortunate? Instead of the bright prosperity which I expected, the blackness of adversity has come upon me. This is why my heart is so indignant.

My skin is blackened by the fever of my leprosy; it burns into my very bones. The shrieks that I utter are shrill as those of a jackal. The melody of my life has been changed into grievous discord.

I was chaste even in my very looks; for I knew that God beheld all my ways, and would bring calamity upon the sinner. If I have ever turned aside from the paths of rectitude at the bidding of evil inclinations, if there is any stain of sin upon my character, then let my harvests fail and let the fruit of my labours be enjoyed by others. Were

God only to weigh me in an even balance, He would discover my integrity. If my heart has ever been ensnared by my neighbour's wife, then may my own wife become another's slave. It would have been in me an infamous crime; I should never have prospered; it would have been my ruin. If I had ever refused justice to my servants, I should not be now demanding it before the bar of God: for are we not the children of the same Father? If I have been unmindful of the necessities of the poor; if I have increased the widow's sorrow, instead of helping her in her distress, as it was my lifelong practice to do; if I have neglected the fatherless, instead of treating him as a son; if I have seen any perish for lack of clothing, instead of warming them with the fleece of my own flock; if I have used my judicial authority to the detriment of the orphan,—then may my shoulder fall from its socket, and may my arm be broken at the joint. I could not have done such things, for the fear of the Lord was ever before me. If I have set my affections upon gold, and exulted in the greatness of my wealth; if I have dishonoured God by kissing my hand to the sun or to the moon; if I have cursed my enemies, or even rejoiced in their adversity; if I have not opened my doors to all comers;—the men of my household will testify to *my hospitality; if, like so many, I have been guilty of sins which I kept secret, for fear of losing the esteem of my inferiors and my peers:——Oh that there was one who would hear me! I present my written vindication to my Almighty Adversary. Oh that He, in return, would write out my indictment! I would not conceal it, for there would be no fear of its revealing my shame. I would wear it as a badge of honour, as a symbol of victory. I would tell Him all my doings. I would hide nothing from Him. I would come before Him, not as a guilty sinner, but with the pride and dignity of a prince:——If I have been guilty of any grievous sin; if, for example, my land cries out against me that I have wrongfully possessed myself of it, if it weeps for its rightful lord, if its fruits have come to me by robbery or murder,—then in future let thistles spring up instead of wheat, and instead of barley noisome weeds.*

So ends the soliloquy. Here follows in our version, the speech of Elihu. But those best able to judge are agreed, that this speech did not belong to the Book of Job as it came from the hands of the author. The chief arguments against its genuineness are the following. 1. Elihu's speech destroys the connection between Job's last remarks in the soliloquy and the speech of Jehovah. The latter is introduced with the words,—"The Lord answered Job," and this implies that Job had just been speaking. 2. Elihu's speech weakens the speech of Jehovah, inasmuch as it anticipates the appeal to the divine power and wisdom, upon which so much stress is there laid. 3. It is inconsistent with the speech of Jehovah, for it professes to give a *logical* solution of the mystery of suffering. 4. The language and style of Elihu's speech differ greatly from those which we find in the rest of the poem. It must have been written, according to Dr Samuel Davidson—who is perhaps the highest authority on the subject—at least a hundred years later than the original work.

The Rev. Samuel Cox, to whose book I am indebted for many useful suggestions in the preparation of these sermons, has made an eloquent defence of the speech. His strongest reason, however, for believing in its genuineness is, that "it adds something to the argument of the poem; that it meets and refutes the main positions taken up by Job." But as I endeavoured to show you in my introductory remarks, and as we shall see more clearly still in the next sermon, the poem is not an argument at all. It is the history of a soul's experience. The long discussion which Job is represented as carrying on with his friends, is only introduced for the sake of unfolding and explaining the various stages of doubt and despair through which the sufferer passed. Elihu's discourse, on the contrary, completely destroys the unity of the poem. He had attained, no doubt, to somewhat clearer views, as to the meaning of suffering and the dealings of God with man, than were possessed by the afflicted patriarch.[1] But just for that very reason, we may be sure, such a speaker would never have been introduced by the author of the poem, who was an artist of the very highest type. A true poet does not, of course, work in everything that he knows, but only such portions of his knowledge as will conduce to the perfecting of his poem. The fact that the author of the Book of Job *could* have thrown light upon some of Job's difficulties, was no sort of reason for his doing so. He conceived of Job as a man in whose mental experience these difficulties had never been logically answered. In the poem therefore, which is devoted to describing Job's experiences, logic would be out of place. If argument had been the poet's aim, there surely

[1] See pp. 171-181.

would have been a splendid display of it in the climax of the poem—viz., in Jehovah's speech. But there is none. That speech is not an argument at all, but a mere outburst of feeling. It is an appeal to the emotional side of Job's nature, not to the intellectual. But the copyist who interpolated Elihu's speech did not see the purport of the poem. Though strong in logic, he was weak in art. He imagined that the author's chief purpose was the discussion of mental difficulties, not the description of mental experience. He was probably, like the character whom he interpolated, a young man, full of the impetuosity and conceit from which very few young men are altogether free. As he read the poem, he was astonished to find that his own pet ideas had not been introduced. Feeling that he had it in his power to answer some of Job's objections, and to set the three friends right, he could not bear that this ability should be wasted. As the discussion goes, in his view of it, limping along, he feels constrained to interfere. He fancied he was coming to the assistance of the poet by strengthening his argument, when in reality he was only spoiling his poem.

In the original poem then, Job's soliloquy, which finished in chapter xxxi., was immediately followed by Jehovah's speech, which begins in chapter xxxviii. This speech we shall have next to consider. In the meantime, let us just notice the state of mind in which Job at present finds himself. He is now comparatively calm. He has attained to a belief in the resurrection of the dead, and therefore his affliction can never again appear to him so desperate as it did, when he supposed that *his little all of life* was being swallowed up in calamity. But the most fervent faith in *another* world will never make it agreeable to suffer in *this*. He is still as much puzzled as ever in regard to the why and wherefore of his afflictions. He knows of no other meaning in suffering than punishment; and punishment, he is sure, he has done nothing to deserve. He longs as much as ever for an explanation. He has found out that the solution of the problem is beyond the reach of human faculties. But he wants a special revelation. He would like to hear an explanation from the lips of God Himself. He no longer gives vent to blasphemous recriminations against God. He no longer explicitly accuses the Almighty of injustice and tyranny and cruelty; but he is, nevertheless, quietly, despondently sceptical. God, at any rate, he feels, must have forgotten him. There is a verse in Austin's "Human Tragedy" which exactly expresses his mental condition. We have all, I suppose, at times felt constrained to ejaculate the same bitter cry :—

> "Stupendous Power! that, secret and afar,
>   Sitt'st on Thy throne, where none may come to Thee,
> O fling the gates of heaven ajar,
>   That for one moment suffering flesh may see
> Thy face, and what Thy darkened judgments are!
>   Are war and sin and sorrow Thy decree?
> Is Fate our Father? Thou art supremely strong,
> And we so weak! How long? O Lord, how long?"

Job.

VIII.

CHAPTERS XXXVIII.-XLII.

WE have now come to the speech of Jehovah. "The Lord answered him out of the whirlwind." This is the oriental way of saying that it was the sight of a storm, which led Job into some such train of thought as that which follows. Generally speaking, men see God most distinctly in what is strange and appalling. In Longfellow's "Evangeline" we read for example:

"Keenly the lightning flashed, and the voice of the echoing thunder
Told her that God was in heaven and governed the world He created."

The same truth is asserted by the falling dew. But for one who will observe God speaking in the still small voice, there are—even in the nineteenth century—thousands who will hear Him in the thunder-peal. And the ancients were even less affected than we are by any natural phenomenon which was quiet and commonplace. This was the reason why the poet adopted a storm as the vehicle of the divine suggestions. Jehovah's speech is somewhat as follows:—

Who is this that obscures the ways of Providence by his foolish words? Prepare now for the contest with me which thou hast desired. I will question thee, and answer me if thou canst. Where wast thou when I founded the earth? Tell me, how was it done? Who determined its measurements? and on what were its foundations laid? Did you hear God's elder children rejoicing over this new creation? Who was it, at the birth of the sea, made clouds into garments for it, and mists into swaddling-clothes? Who was it that restrained the ocean as by bars and gates, and said to it, "Hitherto shalt thou come, but here shall the pride of thy waves be stayed"? Hast thou ever commanded it to be night, or taught the dawn when it was to appear and disperse the works of darkness? —How wonderful is the dawn! All the features of the landscape stand out in relief, and the earth decks herself with her gayest colours. Night is the sinner's day, but with the dawn his fell purposes are stopped.—Hast thou gone to the sources of the sea, or traversed the abysses of the ocean? Have the gates of death been opened for thee? Tell me, dost thou know the earth in all its length and breadth? Where does light dwell, and where darkness? Evidently thou leddest them to their place, and hast often since been to visit them! How vast must be the number of thy years! Hast thou entered the store-house of the snow, and seen the arsenals of hail which I reserve for conflict with my enemies? How is the light and how is the wind distributed over the earth? Who is it that forms channels for the rain, so that it waters definite portions of the earth; and even unpeopled deserts are not forgotten? Do you know the father of the rain, or the sire of the dew-drops? Are you acquainted with the mother of ice and of hoar-frost? How is it that water becomes compressed, as it were, into stone? Canst thou string together the stars that form the cluster of the Pleiades, or unbind Orion's belt? Canst thou make the constellations appear in their season? Hast thou determined the influence which they shall exert upon the earth? Dost thou know the laws which govern them? If thou commandest, will the clouds bring rain? If thou callest for the lightnings, will they say, Here we are? Who is it that tilts the clouds, so that their contents are poured upon the earth as from bottles?

Turn now to the animal creation. Canst thou find prey for the lion? When the young ravens cry unto God in their hunger, canst thou provide them with food? Canst thou trace the life of the rock-goat from its beginning? Who was it gave the wild ass his love of freedom, and made him dwell in the wilderness in scornful contempt of men? Canst thou make a slave of the bison, and compel him to plough thy fields or to carry thy corn? Hast thou given birds their instincts? Why is the stork so careful of its young, and the ostrich so careless? The latter, on the approach of the huntsmen, leaves her eggs to be trodden under foot. She is as indifferent as though they were not her own, for God hath denied her wisdom. Dost thou give the horse his strength? Hast thou provided him with his quivering mane? Hast thou given him his caracole? His very snorting spreads terror. He rushes in his pride against the arms of the enemy. He laughs at fear, and is not dismayed though the arrows rattle upon his side. He recoils neither from sword nor from spear. He cannot contain himself at the sound of the trumpet. At every blast he neighs aloud in his eagerness for the battle. He scents it from afar, with the thunder of the captains and the shouting. Is it thy cunning that taught the hawk to fly southward in the winter-time? Doth the eagle build its eyrie on the top of lofty crags, because thou hast so commanded it; or didst thou implant in him his propensity to swoop down at the sight of blood?*

Then Jehovah said to Job, *Will the censurer of the Almighty still contend with Him? Let him who accused God now reply.* Then Job answered and said, *Lo I am weak, what can I reply? I must be silent: I have spoken, but I will say no more.* In plain English, Job hints that he is being overwhelmed rather than answered.

So Jehovah speaks again. *Prepare thyself for the contest like a man. I will question thee, and answer thou me. Wouldst thou impugn my justice, and condemn me to clear thyself? Hast thou then, an arm of power like God? or canst thou thunder with a voice of terror like His? Deck thyself now with pomp and majesty like mine, and array thyself in glory and splendour. Give free course to the floods of thy wrath. Humble the proud with a look. Trample the wicked in the dust, and cover their faces with the shadow of death. Then I will praise thee as thou hast been praising thyself.*

I will acknowledge that thy power is equal to my own. Behold now the hippopotamus, whom I made as well as thee. His bones are like tubes of brass, and his ribs like bars of iron. He is God's masterpiece. With his tusk he can mow the grass as with a scythe. He is not put about even though the river overflows its banks and bursts upon him. Yet, strong as he is, men put cords through his nostrils and catch him, even when he has his eyes wide open. The crocodile on the contrary, because I have otherwise ordained, thou canst not catch. Canst thou pass a rope through his nostrils, or pierce his jaws with a hook? Will he entreat thee with soft words for thy mercy? Will he sell himself to thee into slavery? Canst thou make a plaything of him for thy children? Are the fishermen able to trade in him? Thou canst make no impression on his hide. If thou offerest him battle, woe betide thee; thou wilt not do it a second time. He is not dismayed when he sees thee; no one would be so daring as to anger him. —And yet thou wouldst venture to stand up against me, his Maker, who am under obligation to no man, to whom all things under heaven belong. —I will not be silent about his members and the beauty of his structure. Who can lift up his coat of mail? Who will open the doors of his *face? Round about his teeth is terror. What a pride he takes in his shielding scales, fitted together so closely that not a breath can come between them! His eyes with their red glow are like the eyes of the morning. Fire and smoke seem to pour forth from his nostrils, so that his breath might kindle coals. In his neck dwells superhuman strength. Despair springs up before him. He is as destitute of fear as the hardest stone. When he rouseth himself, the bravest are filled with terror. Let any one attack him, it will be in vain. Sword and javelin and dart are all useless against him. He regards iron as straw, brass as rotten wood, and sling-stones as so much chaff. Arrows do not move him. The club affects him no more than stubble. He laughs at the shaking of the spear. He is armed underneath with spikes like those of a threshing-sledge. He causes the sea to boil like a caldron. He leaves a glistening track behind him, which gives to the water the whiteness of hoary hair. There is not his like upon earth. Created devoid of fear, he can look the loftiest boldly in the face. He is king of all the sons of pride.'*

Then Job answered and said, *I know that Thou canst do all things, and that nothing is too hard for Thee. Thou saidst, " Who is this*

*that is obscuring Providence with foolish words?"
I confess I have spoken of things I understood
not. When I said, "Listen to me while I ask
Thee questions," I had but heard of Thee with
the hearing of the ear; but now mine eye seeth
Thee: therefore I retract, and repent in dust and
ashes.*

You will observe that this confession of sin is not a renouncing of his integrity. The sin he acknowledges is not one of which a human being could have made him conscious. He had been all along, as is expressly stated in the epilogue, far more righteous than his friends. But he now began to feel

"That merit lives from man to man,
But not, O God, from man to Thee,"—

that however much better he might be than the rest of his neighbours, he was yet not faultless in the sight of God. He perceived that God was not only more powerful than man, but also holier and wiser, more to be trusted than the treacherous human heart, than erring human reason.

I need not detain you more than a moment over the epilogue. I must just remind you that, like the prologue, it is written in prose, and belongs, not to the poem itself, but merely to its setting. The most interesting verse in it is the first. The Lord said to Eliphaz, "My wrath is kindled against thee and against thy two friends; because ye have not spoken of me *aright* as my servant Job hath." At times Job had spoken foolishly; but still he had honestly, by terrible mental conflict, worked his way to the conclusion that God would do him justice sooner or later, in the next world if not in this. Whereas his friends had been telling lies to prove their piety. They had groundlessly accused him of the most grievous crimes, rather than admit a defect in their orthodox theology.

The only other noteworthy point in the epilogue is Job's restoration to prosperity. It reads in our modern eyes like an anti-climax: the attainment of faith is something so infinitely higher than the possession of "fourteen thousand sheep, and six thousand camels, and a thousand yoke of oxen, and a thousand she-asses." But at the time when the poem was written, any other *dénouement* would have been considered unsatisfactory. Every one *then* believed that good conduct must necessarily lead to good fortune. So that in no other way could Job have been thoroughly vindicated in the estimation of contemporary readers.

For the few moments that remain to me, I must return to Jehovah's speech. Is it not very disappointing? We could not help hoping that it would throw some light upon the mystery of existence; but it does not. Job complains that he is suffering wrongfully, that the ways of Providence are apparently unjust and capricious. Jehovah's only reply is to enumerate instances illustrative of His own omnipotence. The answer seems altogether irrelevant, and yet it satisfied Job. How was this?

It is curious and instructive to notice that all books of a similar nature are equally disappointing. "From the 'Confessions' of St Augustine down to Newman's 'History of my Religious Opinions,' there have been hundreds of books which have professed to give the history of an inquiring human spirit, sounding its dim and perilous way across dark seas of doubt to the clear rest and haven of faith. But read which of these books we may, we find in it two singular phenomena. First, so long as the author sets forth the doubts and perplexities by which he has been exercised, we find his words instinct with life and passion and power—they commend themselves to our understanding, and excite our sympathy; we find that he is happily expressing thoughts and emotions which have often stirred within our own souls. But,—and this is the second and more striking phenomenon,—no sooner does he begin to tell us what it was that solved and conquered his doubts, than a thick bewildering haze settles down on his words; they neither commend themselves to our sympathies nor convince our judgment. We cry in disappointment, 'Is that all?' What is there *in that* to induce faith? The man has not fairly met one of his doubts, nor solved one of his problems; he has simply evaded them, and crept by an illogical by-path to a tame and impotent conclusion."

The fact is, a complete logical solution of the problem of existence is unattainable by us. Every thoughtful man from the beginning has puzzled over it, and still it remains unsolved. Logic in this matter can go but a very little way. Last year I discussed with you the mystery of suffering from the logical point of view,[1] and you remember how little we were able to make of it. We could just discover that *sometimes* suffering was productive of good; but we could only hope, we could not prove, that in all cases it was beneficent. Hence it is that

[1] See 'Origin of Evil.'

no man has ever been driven to faith by logic.
But though scepticism cannot be destroyed by
argument, it may be conquered by emotion, and
it is for the sake of rousing emotion that the
author represents Jehovah as appealing to nature.
The poet of nature has told us:—

> "One impulse from the vernal woods
> May teach us more of man,
> Of moral evil and of good,
> Than all the sages can."

The purport of Jehovah's speech is to inspire
Job with awe and trust, by giving him a keener
sense of Nature's mysterious sublimity.

Of course the speech is ancient, not modern,
in its tone and tenor. Men in the time of Job
had but a very superficial knowledge of natural
phenomena. They had attained to no general
conceptions, such as those of law, force, consciousness, life. They had but little appreciation for the beauty of natural scenery. It was
the unusual that chiefly attracted their attention.
It is curious that the first half of Jehovah's
speech produces less effect upon Job than the
second. He is silenced by the mention of light
and dew and rain, the instinct of birds and the
gentler phases of nature; but he is not subdued.
It is the description of the hippopotamus and

the crocodile which bends his haughty spirit. A modern poet would, of course, have omitted the second half of the speech and amplified the first. He would have pointed out how the conflicting forces of the external world work together for the production of harmonious and desirable results. He would have drawn attention to some of the innumerable instances of beneficent adaptation with which Nature teems. Above all, he would have laid stress upon the fact that she is at times so passing fair, and that her beauty makes us conscious of

> "A presence that disturbs us with the joy
> Of elevated thoughts."

But the aim of the modern poet would have been identical with that of the author of the Book of Job, viz., to suggest, as vividly as possible, the wonderfulness—awesome and at the same time hope-inspiring—of the world and of life.

The Book of Job has frequently been compared to Goethe's 'Faust' and to the 'Prometheus' of Æschylus. And no doubt there are interesting analogies between them. But understood as it ought to be understood—regarded as the history of a soul—the poem which most closely resembles it is Lewis Morris's "Evensong."

There the poet, like poor Job, passes through all phases of doubt and despair, and like Job he eventually attains to faith. But in the modern poem, just as we might naturally expect, God is found by the troubled soul, not in a thunderstorm, but in the quietness and beauty of eventide.

"And through all the clear spaces above—O wonder! O glory of Light!—
Came forth myriads on myriads of worlds, the shining host of the night,—

The vast forces and fires that know the same sun and centre as we;
The faint planets which roll in vast orbits round suns we shall never see;

The rays which had sped from the first, with the awful swiftness of light,
To reach only then, it might be, the confines of mortal sight.

O wonder of Cosmical Order! O Maker and Ruler of all,
Before whose infinite greatness in silence we worship and fall!

Could I doubt that the will which keeps this great universe steadfast and sure,
Can be less than His creatures thought, full of goodness, pitful, pure?

Could I dream that the Power which keeps those great suns circling around,
Takes no thought for the humblest life which flutters and falls to the ground?

O Faith! thou art higher than all.—Then I turned from the
    glories above,
And from every casement new-lit there shone a soft radiance
    of love:

Young mothers were teaching their children to fold little
    hands in prayer;
Strong fathers were resting from toil, 'mid the hush of the
    Sabbath air;

Peasant lovers strolled through the lanes, shy and diffident,
    each with each.
Yet knit by some subtle union too fine for their halting
    speech:

Humble lives, to low thought, and low; but linked, to the
    thinker's eye,
By a bond that is stronger than death, with the lights of the
    farthest sky:

Here as there, the great drama of life rolled on, and a jubilant
    voice
Thrilled through me ineffable, vast, and bade me exult and
    rejoice:

'Exult and rejoice, O soul!' sang my being to a mystical
    hymn,
As I passed by the cool bright wolds, as I threaded the pine-
    woods dim;

'Rejoice and be sure!' as I reached my home under the
    hill,
Wrapt round with a happy content,—AND THE WORLD AND
    MY SOUL WERE STILL."

Elihu's Speech.

JOB XXXII.-XXXVII.

WHEN we were considering the Book of Job, we omitted altogether the speech of Elihu, which is manifestly an interpolation. It interferes with the unity and natural development of the poem. It attempts a logical solution of some of the difficulties Job had started, and a logical solution is altogether alien to the spirit of the poem itself.

It is curious to notice the different opinions which have prevailed among commentators as to the worth or worthlessness of Elihu's remarks. One, for example, calls him a pert and braggart boy, of weak and rambling speech; while another believes that his teaching is too wise and authoritative for merely human lips, and so supposes him to have been the second person in the Trinity. Instead of " Elihu, the son of Barachel, the Buzite, of the tribe of Ram," as we have him described in our version, the latter commentator reads: "Elihu, the blessed son of God, of the lineage of the Most High." In reality, however, Elihu speaks just as a moderately intelligent scribe might be expected to speak. And if we take his speech by itself, out of connection with the poem which it mars, it becomes interesting and suggestive. The new speaker is introduced with the remark that his wrath was kindled against Job for justifying himself, and against the friends for condemning him without being able to prove that he had done wrong. He begins apologetically.

I am young and ye are old. But, after all, it is not years which teach wisdom; that only comes from the inspiration of the Almighty. Therefore listen to me. None of you has refuted Job. I gather from your silence that you have perceived your failure. But as for me, I am full of words. I can restrain myself no longer. I must speak out. And I intend to speak plainly my honest conviction. Although I am but a man, I feel that I am inspired by the Almighty.

I could hardly believe my ears, Job, when you said, " I am pure and spotless and free from sin. God is spying out all my ways, determined to condemn and convict me." Why did you assert that He is an autocrat, giving no account of His dealings, and altogether refusing to speak to men? He does speak to them, if they would but hear. He speaks, first of all, in visions of the night. By them He admonishes us, trying to reclaim us from our evil ways, and to hold us back from destruction. Then, too, He has another way of speaking—viz., by pain, when we writhe upon our beds in agony and the angel of death comes very near. With the suffering He sends an interpreter, one of His thousand messengers, to reveal to us the meaning of our painful experience. If we listen to the interpreter and profit by his teaching, then God has pity on us. He says to the angel of death, "Deliver him from going down into the pit, for I have found a means of escape for him; he has learnt his lesson—there is no need for his being any further afflicted." And so the sorrowful soul, restored to health and joy, chants God's praises and says, "I have sinned, but I am not requited as I deserve: He hath rescued my soul from going down to the grave: I live and behold the light."

Have you anything to answer, Job? If not, listen to me, and I will teach you wisdom.

In the next chapter, Elihu proceeds to vindicate the Almighty from Job's accusation of injustice. Such an accusation, he tries to show, is irrational and unphilosophical.

God must be just, and must requite men according to their deserts, for the following reasons. First, He can have no motive for doing otherwise. He made rich and poor, high and low, alike. Why, then, should He treat them unequally? Secondly, injustice is fatal to authority. Had He been unjust, He would long ago have ceased to be worshipped. Men would have rebelled against His impious rule. Thirdly, He must take a positive interest in the welfare of His creatures, or else He would not have created them, He would not continue to sustain them. If He lived for Himself alone, He would withdraw His quickening breath, and men would return to dust. The fact that He troubles Himself to maintain the world, proves that He must have for it a kindly regard. And fourthly, His justice is demonstrated by actual facts. In the long-run it fares ill with evil-doers. For a time they may prosper, but in the end they are always overthrown—sometimes in the stillness of the night by an unseen hand, sometimes in open day and in the sight of all.

Since, then, God is just in all His dealings, it behoves every sufferer to humble himself under the divine chastisement; and to bethink himself that he may have sinned, unconsciously, if not consciously. His prayer should be, What I know not, teach Thou me, that if I have done evil, I may do so no more." Are you to dictate to God? All wise men must agree, Job, that you have spoken foolishly. Your words are like those of the wicked. You are adding wilful rebellion to your unconscious guilt. My prayer for you is, that you may be purged from your iniquities.

He now advances two more arguments in defence of the divine justice. The first is this: God cannot conceivably be unjust. He is far too exalted to be influenced, or in any degree affected, by human actions. The wickedness or righteousness of a man may affect his fellow-men; but they must be equally matters of indifference to God, who can have, therefore, no inducement to act unjustly. His second argument relates to unanswered prayers. Much of what passes under the name of prayer is but an instinctive cry of pain, like that which might be uttered by a beast or a bird. Such outcries are vain. God does not regard them. Men's prayers are unanswered because they pray amiss. They should remember that God has a purpose in afflicting them, that He gives men songs in the night of their sorrow, and eventually turns their *mourning into joy.* He has not forgotten you, Job. Your cause is before him. Wait, therefore, for Him. Great as is your *affliction, it is not so great as your blasphemous speeches have deserved.*

I still have something to say in God's behoof. He is strong, but He despiseth none. He is mighty by strength of heart. He afflicts men in order to make them conscious of their transgressions. If they listen to Him and turn from their iniquities, they will end their days in happiness. He delivereth the afflicted by their afflictions, and opens their ears by calamity. But those who wilfully stop their ears, and refuse to learn the lessons of suffering, end their days in woe.

Towards thee also, God has a merciful intention. But beware lest you frustrate this intention and provoke Him. From His anger none can deliver you. It is no good crying out against your fate. It is no good calling for death. God does not use His power to crush you, but, on the contrary, to teach and to exalt you. Instead of venturing to criticise and find fault with Him, you should rather stand in awe.

At this point Elihu proceeds to give a description of a thunderstorm, partly as being illustrative of the divine power and punishment, and partly also to connect the speech with what follows, and make it fit into the speech of Jehovah, which is said to have been uttered out of the tempest. Elihu now describes such a tempest—describes it vividly as if he actually saw it; and thus the way is skilfully prepared for the words of Jehovah, which are supposed to be heard just when the storm is at its height. It is mainly owing to this ingenious device on the part of the copyist, that the interpolation has so frequently been considered as genuine.

God is great, and we know Him not. From the depths of the sea He draweth up the clouds and forms them into a pavilion. He dischargeth lightning against His foe. The crash of the thunder announceth the fierceness of His wrath. My heart leaps out of its place for fear. Listen to the tumult of His voice, and the muttering that goeth forth out of His mouth. He doeth great things past our comprehension. He saith to the snow and to the streaming rain, "Fall ye upon the earth," and they fall,—fall in such torrents that all human labour is stopped, and men are compelled to gaze on the handiwork of the Almighty. He breathes upon the waters and they are frost-bound. Hither and thither He pilots the thunder-cloud, so that it may accomplish His behests, for good or for ill. Listen, Job. Stand still and scan the wondrous works of God.—But scan them as we may, we shall never comprehend them; we cannot tell upon what the clouds are poised, nor how it is they gleam with light. We do not know by what means the firmament has been spread forth like a molten mirror, nor why the south wind makes us warm. *Let us take heed, therefore, how we speak to God, lest we destroy ourselves by our folly.* We cannot gaze at the sun when he is shining in a cloudless sky. How awful, then, must be the majesty of God! We cannot find Him out. He is of perfect equity, but He will render account to no man. *Therefore let us fear Him, whom not even the wisest can behold.*

I should like, in conclusion, just to sum up the results of Elihu's teaching. Of his various arguments to prove the justice of God, one is worthless, and another is worse than worthless. In saying that the actual facts of experience demonstrate the divine justice, he falls into what, as we saw, was the common mistake of all the older theologians. No doubt in the long-run evil-doers generally come to grief in this world. Still there often occur glaring exceptions. We may wish it otherwise, but that does not change the facts. And God's honour cannot require from us *lies* for its preservation. It is best preserved, it is alone preserved, by honesty. The inequalities which we find in this life, the existence of which no amount of ingenuity can disprove, are, as you know, relied on in the present day as a main support for the doctrine of immortality. Then, too, Elihu's argument (which is substantially the argument of Epicurus) that God is too exalted to be influenced by human actions—in other words, that He is too indifferent to be unjust—sounds in our modern ears little short of blasphemous. Let me say, however, in Elihu's defence, that this argument is inconsistent with, and contradicted by, another which he himself uses—viz., that God, from the fact that He preserves His creatures, must be conceived of as taking an interest in their welfare.

His views in regard to suffering are partly true and partly false. He saw that affliction was disciplinary rather than retributive. But he erroneously conceived this purpose as always one and the same—viz., to make men conscious of their sins. He did not perceive that there were other lessons which suffering might teach, and other purposes which it might subserve.[1]

[1] See sermons on "Suffering" in my 'Origin of Evil.'

In regard to prayer Elihu's teaching is really fresh and valuable. Prayer is too often, as he says, but an instinctive cry for deliverance from pain, whereas it should be rather a request for enlightenment and for spiritual help.[1] If God be a loving God, there must be a wise and beneficent purpose underlying all calamity. As Elihu finely puts it, God delivers the afflicted *by* their afflictions. And so our prayer, when we are in suffering, should be, not so much that this suffering may be removed, as that we may be enabled to learn from it the lesson it was intended to teach, and to derive from it the benefit it was meant to confer. There is much need that we all lay to heart Elihu's counsel. If we examine ourselves, we shall find that our prayers are most fervent and most real, when we are merely asking for some temporal blessing. Our requests for spiritual enlightenment and help are comparatively languid and forced. We are too anxious to inform the Almighty of our wishes and bend Him to our will. But to pray in this fashion is to prostitute our noblest endowment. We should be chiefly concerned to understand the divine will more perfectly, and to obey it more implicitly. The

[1] See also a sermon on "Prayer" in my 'Origin of Evil.'

main burden of all true prayer is contained in the pregnant summary of Elihu, "That which I know not, teach Thou me; wherein I have done evil, may I do so no more." Well will it be for you, well will it be for me, if we can say, with all the fervour of which our nature is capable;—

"I do not ask, O Lord, that life may be
    A pleasant road ;
I do not ask that Thou wouldst take from me
    Aught of its load.

I do not ask that flowers should always spring
    Beneath my feet ;
I know too well the poison and the sting
    Of things too sweet.

For one thing only, Lord, dear Lord, I plead—
    Lead me aright ;
Though strength should falter and though heart should bleed,
    Lead me to Light."

Christianity and Pre-Christian Religion.

I.

PRE-CHRISTIAN RELIGION.

"He left not Himself without witness."—ACTS xiv. 17.

IN this and the following sermons I propose to contrast Christianity and pre-Christian religion, with especial reference to the doctrines of the Incarnation, the Atonement, and Redemption,—with reference, that is, to (1) the revelation of the Deity which was given in Christ; (2) the new relation towards God into which men were thereby introduced; and (3) the moral reformation effected by the Atonement.

There are persons who divide religions, as they do all other things, into two classes,—their own, and those which are not their own;

or, as they more euphemistically express it, the true and the false. Any religion, which does not number *them* among its disciples, must be of course altogether worthless. Some even go so far as to restrict the term true religion, not to the common Christianity of Christendom, but to the creed of some one particular sect or denomination. I remember hearing a man—a clergyman, I am sorry to say—find fault with her Majesty our Queen for worshipping in a Presbyterian church, on the ground that, in doing so, she was guilty of "*changing her religion.*" Such an extreme exhibition of narrowness is nowadays somewhat exceptional; but the notion that non-Christian religions, at any rate, are altogether worthless, is by no means uncommon.

That this notion is incorrect, and that all religions are true as far as they go — *i.e.,* as far as they are religions, may be seen from the following considerations. (1.) It is inconceivable that God, while revealing Himself completely to the few, should have concealed Himself as completely from the many. The Being who cared only for a small proportion of the human race, however strong He might be, however remarkable and terrible, would not be good

—*i.e.*, would not be God. (2.) If every religion which is inferior to Christianity is to be called false, Judaism cannot be called true. (3.) In many of the so-called false religions, we find, as I shall point out to you, remarkable anticipations both of Old and of New Testament teaching. And what is absolutely true in one religion cannot be absolutely false in another. (4.) The hasty characterisation of all religions but one as false religions, is countenanced neither by the Bible nor by what are called "the Fathers."[1] I might quote many confirmatory passages, but two will suffice. St Peter, who was by nature and education inclined to all the exclusiveness of a Jew, confessed on one occasion to the Gentile Cornelius, "God hath showed me that I should not call any man common or unclean." And similarly Augustine says, "There are no religions which do not contain some truth." (5.) The unwarrantable depreciation of non-Christian religions is not the best way of honouring Christianity. If they contained nothing valuable, the fact that Christianity surpassed them would be deprived of

[1] A quotation from the Fathers always impresses the persons who imagine that these primitive expositors of Christianity have said the last word upon the subject.

all significance. But if, after giving them their full due, and seeing that they did contain much that was true and good, we still find that Christianity is pre-eminently superior, we shall in the end appreciate our own religion all the more highly.

There is another equally common, but equally misleading, mode of expression—viz., the attempted distinction between natural and revealed religion. This implies that it is possible, without any revelation at all, to arrive at a certain amount of religious truth. Now there is no doubt that by a study of nature, and by self-examination, men may come to know something of God. But it is absurd to call this knowledge natural, in contradistinction to revealed; for nature and man are themselves revelations. Nature is not silent and dead. She is resonant with voices that speak to us of God:—

> "There is a tongue in every leaf,
> A voice in every rill,
> A voice that speaketh everywhere,
> In flood and fire, through earth and air,
> A voice that's never still."

"Day unto day uttereth speech, and night unto night showeth knowledge. There is no speech nor language [in one sense]; their voice is not heard; [and yet in another sense] their line is gone out through all the earth, and their words to the end of the world." By her order and regularity, by her wonderfulness, and, still more, by the mysterious power of her beauty, Nature speaks to us of her Author, and reveals to us God.—Man, too, is a divine revelation. "He who truly knows himself," said St Chrysostom, "knows God." If we are the children of God, if we have been made in His image, then He must have revealed Himself in us. If conscience be the voice of God, its teaching, however natural, must be also revelatory. In other words, apart from revelation there could be no natural religion. All religion —so far as it is religious—is revealed.

And once more, the common distinction between natural and supernatural religion is another distinction without a difference. Always and everywhere the natural and supernatural are interwoven.[1] There is nothing in the universe that is merely natural. Any one who supposes that Christianity alone is supernatural must be blind. Look but deeply enough into them, and you will discover the super-

[1] See 'Origin of Evil,' pp. 250-270.

natural in every pebble and in every blade of grass. You remember Wordsworth's words—

> "A primrose on the river's brim
> A yellow primrose was to him—
> And it was nothing more."

Nothing more? Why, the whole mystery of the universe is bound up in the heart of that tiny flower. "Natural" you may call it if you please; but it owes its existence to causes that we cannot discover or conceive. If we could trace its history up to its first beginnings myriads upon myriads of ages ago, we should have solved the riddle of life, we should have detected the method of creation, we should know the very nature of God. Since, then, the natural and the supernatural are eternally inseparable, the attempt to draw a sharp line of demarcation between them in matters of religion is misleading and erroneous.

There are two distinctions, however, which it is really important for us to recognise—the distinctions, viz., between Biblical and non-Biblical, between Christian and non-Christian, revelation. And of these the most important is the second. For while our Scriptures, taken as a whole, are superior to the Scriptures of other religions, it is possible, as we shall find, to extract sentences from other sacred writings which are almost identical with some in our own. But the revelation of God in Christ is in some respects unique. In order that we may clearly see its superiority, let us ask what had been previously achieved. And let us begin as nearly as we can at the beginning.

Long before the dawn of history, long before the time of Abraham or of Homer, our ancestors, and the ancestors of all those nations which are now classed together under the name of Aryan, were dwelling in the centre of Asia as a single and undivided people. These progenitors of Celt and Teuton, Anglo-Saxon and Indian, Scandinavian and Iranian, had in their language a word, Dyauspitar,[1] which means in English Heaven-Father. In the records of the past there is nothing more beautiful, nothing more suggestive, nothing more confirmatory of the truth of our text, than this simple fact. It teaches us that those old Aryans, thousands of years ago, had looked up to the infinite azure and been filled with awe—nay, more, that they

---

[1] The existence of this word, or one very similar to it, in the prehistoric Aryan language, is proved by the existence of the words Dyauspitar, Zeupater, and Jupiter in the derivative languages of Sanscrit, Greek, and Latin.

had looked through it and been inspired with trust. They had penetrated in thought

> "Beyond the verge of that blue sky
> Where God's sublimest secrets lie."

They had learnt to say, vaguely it may be and hesitatingly, but still with faith and hope, the words that Christ has made immortal,—" Our Father which art in heaven." [1]

But this primeval worship soon became corrupt; and we need not be surprised that it did. The unknown man who first conceived the idea and coined the expression "Heaven-Father," must have been a poet and a seer, gifted with "the vision and the faculty divine." But his was too high a platform for the most of his contemporaries to occupy. Even now we find men constantly forgetting that emblems are merely emblematic. Just as to-day the eucharistic symbol of Christ's sacrifice is often mistaken for the sacrifice itself, so those old Aryans came to consider that natural objects and phenomena not only revealed the Deity, but were themselves divine. Thus the worship of the Heaven-Father degenerated into a Phy-

---

[1] Max Müller has traced a similar primitive religion in the Semitic and Turanian branches of the human family.

siolatry, or worship of nature.[1] The great investing firmament was resolved into a number of separate entities. There was the god of dew and rain, the god of wind, the storm-god, and so on. This religion is unfolded in the Veda, which is the Scripture of the Hindus. We find there, amid much that is puerile, some truths that are of perennial sacredness and value. Though a number of inferior deities are recognised, the word Dyauspitar still survives. The consciousness of sin and the yearning for reconciliation are ever present in the Vedic hymns. We read such passages as these: "How can I get near to Varuna?[2] when shall I, with a quiet mind, see him propitiated? Absolve us from the sins of our fathers, and from those which we have committed with our own bodies. Varuna is merciful even to him who has committed sin."

As time went on, however, Hinduism became more and more corrupt, chiefly through the influence of the Brahman priests. For private

[1] There seems to have been a similar degradation of the primitive religion among the Semitic and Turanian nations. "Everywhere men begin with the idea of the sky, they rise to the idea of God, and they sink down again to the idea of gods and spirits."

[2] Varuna signifies the investing sky.

reasons of their own they introduced the system of caste, which they pretended was sanctioned by the Veda. The people were taught that "the priests alone knew what food might be eaten, what air might be breathed, what clothes might be worn, and what was the proper length of the ladles in which the sacrifices were to be offered." In a word, religion degenerated into the most absurd and degrading ceremonialism.

What is called Buddhism was a reaction against the corruptions of Brahmanism. It was founded, as you know, nearly six centuries before the Christian era, by Prince Gautama, who was afterwards called by his disciples "the Buddha"—*i.e.*, the Enlightened One. You may perhaps get the clearest glimpse of the beauty of this man's life, and the inexpressible sweetness of his character, by reading Edwin Arnold's 'Light of Asia.' His personality was, as Sir Edwin says, the highest, gentlest, holiest and most beneficent (with one exception) which has appeared since the world began. The religion which he founded has achieved greater and more lasting conquests than any other, not excepting even Christianity, and it is now the faith of 500,000,000 of the human race.

Overcome with pity for the misery and suffering which men were called upon to endure, Prince Gautama set himself to find a remedy. Leaving wife and home and all that men call good, he spent years in solitude, fasting, thinking, praying, in order that he might work out some plan of salvation. And at last he thought he had found it, in the doctrine that men were miserable on account of their desire for pleasure and their love of life. Till these are rooted out of us, he said, we shall continue to suffer, even after death. But when we have learnt that life is vanity, and when we have ceased to care for it, we enter into rest,—a rest which is finally to become Nirvana—*i.e.* to say the unconsciousness of annihilation.[1] A poor salvation this may seem to us, upon whom the light of Christianity has shone. But the means by which the Buddha taught men to achieve it were inward purifications and moral goodness. He forestalled Christ by enunciating the golden rule and preaching a doctrine of universal benevolence. But what is strangest about Buddhism is this. Though Prince Gautama constantly reminds us of a

---

[1] Sir Edwin and others would say that Nirvana is not a purely negative motion. But the distinction between ceasing to live and ceasing to exist ('Light of Asia,' p. 231), seems to me *practically* worthless. Unconscious immortality is a contradiction in terms.

still more illustrious Prince—the Prince of the house of David—yet in one respect there is an infinite difference between their religions: Buddhism makes no mention of God.[1]

There is one other religious system—viz., Confucianism—in which Christ's golden rule was anticipated, at least in its negative form. More than 500 years before the birth of Jesus the Chinese sage had written: "What you do not like when done to yourself, do not that to others." With the exception of the Buddha, Confucius has had more disciples than any other religious teacher. They now number 400,000,000. But his system, like Gautama's, is practically atheistic. It was useless to trouble, he thought, about anything superhuman,—all such knowledge being quite beyond our grasp. He was what, in these days, we should call an agnostic.

It is a remarkable fact that the two religions, which *morally* approach the nearest to Christianity, should, in this important respect, be the furthest removed from it. But they could not have survived so long, they could not have made so many converts, unless there had been some-

---

[1] Some modern scholars say that Gautama was not an atheist. But even so, since it has taken more than 2000 years to find it out, God cannot have occupied an important place in his system.

thing true in them,—unless they had been, in some degree, divine revelations. And divine revelations they were. Though God Himself seemed to be ignored, yet the goodness which God loves was insisted on. And whoever loves goodness, unconsciously, if not consciously, loves God. Some day, somewhere, without doubt this will be discovered by every sincere Buddhist and Confucian.

Before the advent of our Lord, there had been two religions—Zoroastrianism and Judaism—which aimed at leading men to worship the invisible God.

Zoroaster, who lived more than three thousand years ago, was an enthusiastic believer in the unity and purity of God. He recognised also an evil principle, a sort of Miltonic Satan, whom he supposed to have existed from the beginning. But this evil principle, he declared, was in the end to be conquered, if men would become workers together with God against it. He protested earnestly against the worship of nature and the belief in ceremonialism, to which he found his countrymen addicted. Some of you may remember Bunsen's graphic description of a scene in the life of Zoroaster, which reminds one strongly of Elijah upon Mount Carmel. Having summoned the people to a hill upon which sacrifices and auguries were being performed, he exhorted them to make their choice between good and evil; between the many gods they had been accustomed to worship, and the one true God who was Lord over all. It was not by a punctilious ceremonialism, he explained, that God was to be honoured, but by purity,—purity in the holy triad of thought, word, and deed. It was the same doctrine that was taught afterwards by Samuel: "Hath the Lord as great delight in burnt-offerings and sacrifices, as in obeying the voice of the Lord? Behold, to obey is better than sacrifice." The mistake of Zoroaster was this: Out of respect, I suppose, for the hardness of men's hearts, he made a compromise with custom, and allowed a subordinate place to the old objects of worship, such as the sun and the sacred bull. He intended that they should be at most but suggestive, symbolical emblems — like the images in the Roman Catholic Church; but they soon became more. When we remember how carefully all such symbols were excluded from the Jewish religion by the second commandment and by the reiterated injunctions of the prophets, and how notwithstanding the Jews were always relapsing into idolatry, we are not surprised to find that the religion of Zoroaster has degenerated into fire-worship and a belief in magical formulæ. And such a degeneration in religion seems inevitable. At any rate it has always taken place. The revelation of God, made at times so clear by the inspired few, becomes again obscured, owing to the blindness and foolishness of the uninspired many.

In the next sermon we shall see how much the world owes to Judaism, with its firm faith in a personal, present God, and its passionate enthusiasm for righteousness.

In the meantime I hope that what I have said already, will have served, in some small degree, to illustrate the truth of our text. The most poorly endowed of human beings, the most wretchedly circumstanced individual that is called by the name of man, has something within him that may become the germ of a higher life—has some influences brought to bear upon him that may eventually lead him into the presence of God. "An infant," says Irenæus, "cannot yet receive the food which is meant for full-grown men. So man in the beginning was unable to receive the truth in its completeness, for he was still a child." "God's purpose," says Bunsen, "to make a progressive revelation of Himself on earth, forms the inward connecting thread of history." In other words, though Christianity is the highest, it is not the only, revelation. "He has never left Himself without witness." By the beauties and the terrors of nature, by the light of imagination and reason, by the still small voice of conscience, by the teachings of human love, by that strange sense of dissatisfaction felt even in the supreme moment of success achieved or desire fulfilled, by the inextinguishable yearning for something better and more enduring than has ever been found on earth, as well as by influences too subtle for us to name or comprehend, God has been revealing Himself from the beginning until now, wherever the foot of man has trod, with a fulness and distinctness continually increasing, in proportion to the growing capacities of the race. The revelation of the almighty Father is free as the air, broad as the horizon, universal as His own divine presence;

> "And so the whole round earth is every way
> Bound by gold chains about the feet of God."

Christianity and Pre-Christian Religion.

II.

THE INCARNATION.

"God, who at sundry times, and in divers manners, spake in time past unto the fathers by the prophets, hath in these last days spoken unto us by His Son."—HEBREWS i. 1, 2.
"The Word became flesh."—JOHN i. 14.

TAKING up the subject where we left it in the last sermon, let us, before considering the Incarnation, look for a moment at the Jewish faith. Lying at the root of this religion is the idea that the human race is one, in origin and end—one, because of its dependence upon a God who loveth righteousness. Both accounts of the creation which we find in the Book of Genesis agree, in asserting emphatically that man is not merely the creature, but the child, of the Creator. In the first account, we read that man was made in the divine image. In the second, it is said that man's soul was the breath of God. And as the race was one in origin, so the Jews thought it was one in end. They believed in the gradual and universal restoration of the divine image, which had been effaced by sin. From the time of Abraham to Malachi, a period of not less than fifteen hundred years, we find among this ancient people an almost unbroken succession of spiritual seers, such as has no parallel in the world's history, who were constantly exhorting their fellow-countrymen to the practice of righteousness, and reminding them of a time when it would be completely victorious and absolutely universal.

I say this was the most radical conception of the Jewish faith. But at the same time it was an idea which the ordinary, commonplace Israelites were very slow to grasp. They fancied themselves the favourites of Heaven, because they were Jews. They imagined they could win the approval of God by the performance of rites and ceremonies. These mistakes it was the constant effort of the prophets to rectify. Among the Jews—as among all other nations—

priests and prophets had but little in common. Priests, ordained by men to observe a certain ritual, and prophets, ordained by God to disseminate new ideas, are always more or less at variance. The Jewish seers were continually pointing out the hollowness and worthlessness of mere ceremonialism. " I hate and despise your feast-days. Though ye offer me burnt-offerings and meat-offerings, I will not accept them. Take away from me the noise of your songs; I will not hear the melody of thy viols. But let justice run down as water, and righteousness as a mighty stream." "Will the Lord be pleased with thousands of rams, and ten thousands of rivers of oil? What doth the Lord require of thee, but to do justly, and to love mercy, and to walk humbly with thy God?" "The sacrifices of God are a broken spirit and a contrite heart."

Closely connected with the idea of the worthlessness of ceremonies *as such*, is another idea— viz., the worthlessness of the Jew *as Jew*. The priests were inclined to regard Israelites as the only people of God. But the prophets pointed out that the promises—the "covenant" as it was called—applied only to *faithful* Israel, to Israelites in heart, to a spiritual people and not to a privileged race. They declared that Jews, who had nothing but their ceremonialism to recommend them, would be rejected by God; while Gentiles who loved righteousness would be received. And thus they laid the basis of a spiritual and universal religion, in which nationality conferred no benefit, and in which Jehovah was the God of all kindreds and nations and tongues. This thought pervades the entire prophecy of the later Isaiah.[1]

There are two striking characteristics of Judaism, as thus represented by its highest exponents. The first is a passionate enthusiasm for righteousness. "Other nations," it has been well said, "had the idea; but to feel it enough to make the world feel it, it was necessary to be possessed with it. It is not enough to have been visited by such an idea at times — to have had it occasionally forced upon one's mind by the teaching of experience. No! 'he that hath the bride is the bridegroom.' The idea belongs to him who has most loved it. Common prudence can say, Honesty is the best policy. But Israel and the Bible are filled with religious joy." "O Lord, what love have I unto Thy law; all the day long is my study in it. Thy testi-

[1] See 'Faiths of the World,' p. 354.

monies are the joy of my heart. Thou shalt teach them to thy children, and shalt talk of them when thou sittest in thine house, when thou walkest by the way, when thou liest down, and when thou risest up. Thou shalt write them on the table of thine heart." Righteousness they regarded as the very essence of religion. To fear the Lord was to depart from evil. This was understanding, this was wisdom. This was the best possession. "She is more precious than rubies; and all the things thou canst desire are not to be compared unto her. Take fast hold of her; let her not go; keep her; for she is thy life." To this very day, whoever would be a lover of righteousness must still derive much of his inspiration from the writings of those Hebrew psalmists and seers. In the matter of religion the Jews stand out conspicuously from the rest of mankind, just as the Greeks are pre-eminent in art.

Another very striking characteristic of the Jewish faith was a vivid realisation of the presence of a personal God. Matthew Arnold is doubtless right in saying that they had no abstract metaphysical notions of the Deity—that they could not, for example, have composed the Athanasian Creed. But assuredly he is greatly mistaken when he asserts that they regarded the Almighty as an impersonal Being, that by God they merely meant *the stream of tendency by which things fulfil the law of their being*. Such a conception of God—which, by the way, is far more abstrusely metaphysical than personality—such a conception would never have called forth those outbursts of religious emotion which we find in the Old Testament. "The Lord is my shepherd, I shall not want. He maketh me to lie down in green pastures: He leadeth me beside the still waters. . . . Yea, though I walk through the valley of the shadow of death, I will fear no evil: for Thou art with me." "As the hart panteth after the waterbrooks, so panteth my soul after Thee, O God." No man could ever speak in this way of what he regarded as a mere stream of tendency.

In the next sermon we shall see what were the radical deficiencies of Judaism, and how they were corrected by Christianity. Meanwhile the fact must be noticed, that there came a decline of the God-consciousness among the Jews. Inspiration seemed at an end. The word of the Lord became precious, as the Bible has it—that is to say, scarce—in those days. The young men saw no visions, the old men dreamed no dreams.

There was no one pure enough or true enough to become a prophet of the Lord. The degeneration of the Jewish religion is significantly shown, as Ewald has pointed out, by the treatment of the name Jehovah. The Egyptians, you remember, held that the Supreme Being should be worshipped in silence; and they never bestowed upon Him any appellation. The Jews at last began to follow their example. The sacred name Jehovah, they maintained, could not be pronounced without desecration; and so it was ordained that it should never be uttered at all. This practice would gradually generate the theory, that human language was incapable of conveying any knowledge of the Almighty; that He was a God afar off, and not near at hand; and that human life was practically unaffected by His existence. Thus the God of the ancient community, who had been, as the Psalmist used to say, "a very present help," was ever retiring further and further into the mysterious distance, till at last He became a mere logical abstraction —something like the Unknowable of Herbert Spencer's philosophy.

And what of Greece and Rome? As St Paul, in his speech on Mars Hill, reminded the Athenians, more than one of their own poets had taught, in common with Judaism and Christianity, the doctrine that man was the offspring of God. The Greek dramatists had a vivid consciousness of the divine superintendence of human affairs. The main purpose of their drama, especially in the case of Æschylus, was to exhibit the moral order of the world, and to represent God's government as righteous, and always in the end triumphant. Plato had even grasped the idea of immortality, and that with a firmness and fulness never found among the Jews.[1] "The life beyond the grave was to him the only real existence: death was the enfranchisement from the prison of the body; the harbour of rest from the storms of life; the reunion of long-parted friends; the admission into the society of the wise and good of former ages; the attainment of that perfect goodness and wisdom and beauty, which had been the yearning of the embodied spirit during the years of its mortal life." Plato himself, however, saw and acknowledged that the world needed a fuller revelation than any which it had yet received. With regard to the populace, for some centuries before the time of Christ they

[1] For the opinions of the Jews on a future state, see my 'Agnosticism,' pp. 297-302.

were entirely without anything that could be called religion. The Sophists, by their shallow rationalism, had undermined every deeper sentiment connected with the old mythology; and the lofty views of the more profound philosophers the common people were incapable of appreciating.

The Romans were, at first, a very religious people, in the ceremonial sense of the word religion. Every hearth had an altar of its own, on which the sacred fire was always burning; every family was an assembly of worshippers; every father was a priest. Worship—or at least sacred ceremonies—entered into every act of the Roman's life, private, domestic, social, political. It was, however, a worship rather of the letter than of the spirit. "In all religious acts, *e.g.*, prayer had a prominent place; yet it seems rarely, if ever, to have taken the form of supplication for moral or spiritual blessing." At one time the Romans appear to have regarded the ruling of the world as a work intrusted to them by Providence; but, enervated at last by their successes, they gradually degenerated in character, until—with the exception of a few philosophers—they answered to St Paul's terrible description.

Having thus noticed one or two of the more characteristic features of pre-Christian religion, let us pass on to consider the advent of a new and higher revelation in Christ. "The Word," says St John, "became flesh, and dwelt among us, and we beheld His glory, the glory as of the only begotten of the Father." The expression "Word of God" in the New Testament, corresponds to what is called the "Name of God" in the Old. Both terms are very apt and suggestive. Among the Jews, as among all primitive people, names had a meaning; they were significant of the qualities or characteristics of the person named. The name of God, therefore, implied those divine attributes which had been already revealed and recognised. In other words, by the name of God a Jew meant *God in so far as He was known*. This you may see from such passages as the following: "They that know Thy name will put their trust in Thee." "How excellent is Thy name in all the earth!" "Do not abhor us, for Thy name's sake." And the same notion is involved in the term "Logos" (Word), a term that had been frequently used by Philo and the Alexandrine philosophers. As a name among the ancients revealed the qualities of the person named, so a word reveals the character of the thought for which it stands. And just as a word is the revelation of a thought, so Christ is the revelation of God. The Word of God, therefore, is God as uttered or manifested or expressed. When it is said the Word became flesh—or, as a Hebrew of the old school would have put it, the Name became flesh—the meaning is, that all previous revelations were supplemented, and in some degree superseded, by a manifestation of the Deity in a divinely human life.

The nature and effect of this new revelation we shall have to study somewhat in detail in the next two sermons. In the meantime, let me draw your attention to its most distinctive feature —viz., its absolute uniqueness. Account for it how you may, the life and work of Christ were so different, so superior, to those of all other men, that He must be called, in a special sense, divine. We are obliged to recognise Him as *the* Son of God. "It is common in human history," says the author of 'Ecce Homo,' "to meet with men who assert some superiority over their fellows, but they dream of nothing greater than some partial control over the actions of others for the short space of a lifetime. To a few, indeed, it is given to influence future ages. Some have appeared who have been as levers to uplift the earth and roll it in another course. Homer by creating literature, Socrates by creating science, Cæsar by carrying civilisation inland from the shores of the Mediterranean, Newton by starting science in a steady career of progress, may be said to have attained this eminence. But these men gave a single impact, like that which is considered to have first set planets in motion. Christ claims to be a perpetual attractive power, like the sun which determines their orbits. They contributed to men some discovery, and passed away: Christ's discovery is Himself. To humanity, struggling with its passions and its destiny, He says, 'Cling to me—cling' ever closer to me.' He commanded men to leave everything and attach themselves to Him; He declared Himself King, Master and Judge of men; He promised to give rest to all the weary and heavy laden; He instructed His followers to hope for eternal life from feeding on His body and blood. Further, these enormous pretensions were advanced by One whose special peculiarity, not only among His contemporaries, but among the remarkable men that have appeared before and since, was an almost feminine tenderness and humility. The 'Lamb of God,' He had been called by the Baptist. Yet so clear to Him was His own dignity and importance to the race, that in the very same breath in which He asserts it in the most unmeasured language, He alludes also to His humility. 'Take my yoke upon you, and learn of me; for I am meek and lowly in heart.' Meek and lowly He was!—naturally content with obscurity; wanting the restless desire for distinction and eminence which is common in great men; fond of what was simple and homely, of children and poor people; occupying Himself so much with the concerns of others, with the relief of sickness and want, that the temptation to exaggerate the importance of His own thoughts and plans was not likely to master Him. And yet we find that He laid claim persistently, with the calmness of entire conviction, in opposition to the whole religious world, in spite of the offence which His own followers conceived, to a dominion more transcendent, more universal, more complete, than the most delirious votary of glory ever aspired to in his dreams."

Christ was—and felt that He was—*the* incarnation. Not, mark you, as it is so often misemphasised, the *incarnation*. The Bible most distinctly teaches that all men are incarnations. "God breathed into man's nostrils the breath of life, and man became a living soul." St Paul, who in the second epistle to the Corinthians speaks of Christ as the image of God, applies the same term to men generally in the first epistle.[1] And in his speech on Mars-hill, he *deduces* the glory of God from that of man. "Forasmuch as we are the offspring of God, we ought not to think that the Godhead is like unto gold or silver or stone:" that is to say, the Deity must be conceived of as an immaterial, spiritual Being, since His nature is akin to our own. Moreover it is distinctly the teaching of the Bible that we, in whom the divine image has been effaced, may and should become eventually as perfect as Jesus Himself. The same apostle who tells the Colossians that in Christ dwelleth all the fulness of the Godhead, prays for the Ephesians,[2] that they too may be filled with the self-same fulness. The Saviour is described in the New Testament, not merely as the only-begotten—*the* Son of God in the fullest sense—but He is also described as the first

[1] xi. 7. [2] iii. 19.

begotten,[1] the first-born of many brethren.[2] And His brethren, the other sons of God,[3] are to grow up into Him in all things till they come to a perfect man, to the measure of the stature of the fulness of Christ.[4] But that is in the far-off future. In the meantime Christ stands alone, a unique figure in the history of the world, pre-eminently God manifest in flesh, the *express* image of the Father.

[1] Heb. i. 6.   [2] Rom. viii. 29.
[3] John i. 12; Rom. viii. 14, 19; Phil. ii. 15; 1 John iii. 1, 2.
[4] Eph. iv. 13.

Christianity and Pre-Christian Religion.

III.

THE ATONEMENT.

"God was in Christ, reconciling the world unto Himself."
—2 Cor. v. 19.

THE word atonement is synonymous with reconciliation. It means etymologically, as you see, at-one-ment—the bringing to an understanding those who have misunderstood one another, the reconciling those who had previously been at enmity. Hence it is manifest that all relevation is, in a greater or less degree, atoning. It will attract men towards God, in so far as they can learn from it what He really is. But the pre-Christian relevations were vague and difficult to interpret. Nature, for example, is sometimes beautiful and beneficent and lovely;

but sometimes also, with her earthquakes and whirlwinds, her pains and diseases, she seems to suggest to us a Power which does not care whether we live or die, whether we have all that heart can wish, or suffer lifelong, unmitigated anguish. Conscience, again, has told every man ever born into the world that there is a distinction between right and wrong, that he should do the one and avoid the other, that right-doing is praiseworthy and wrong-doing abominable. This much conscience tells him; but *what* he must do in order to act rightly, he has to discover for himself. And the discovery is not always easy. The Feejee Islander kills his parents when they begin to grow old, and he thinks he is thereby doing them a service; for he is afraid that otherwise they would be too feeble to make their way into another life. Jael the wife of Heber the Kenite, invited the vanquished warrior Sisera into her tent, offering him, as it seemed with feminine kindliness, refreshment and repose. He trusted her; he fell asleep; and she killed him on the spot. She thought she had acted nobly. Deborah and Barak chanted a pæan in her honour, and declared that, in doing what she did, she came to the help of the Lord. As if the God of righteousness required to be supported by treachery and meanness worthy only of a fiend! History, moreover, "which, to him who reads it rightly, is but the God of truth working out truth," is by no means easy to decipher. In the long-run, right has always prevailed, and evil has always proved itself to be foolish and injurious:—in the long-run, but not necessarily in the life of the individual. The tower of Siloam, may fall upon the righteous. The wicked may be in great power, and may "spread himself like a green bay-tree,"—even till he dies. And so we may be often misled into mistaking good for evil, and evil for good. These primeval revelations, then, of nature and conscience and history, are very difficult to interpret.

Hence men have often formed the most erroneous and unworthy conceptions of the Deity. Some have regarded Him as indifferent to human welfare, others as positively vindictive. Epicurus, for example, taught that it was a waste of time to worship the gods; for they were too agreeably employed to do men harm or good.

> "They haunt (he said)
> The lucid interspace of world and world,
> Where never creeps a cloud or moves a wind,
> Nor ever falls the least white star of snow,
> Nor ever lowest roll of thunder moans,
> Nor sound of human sorrow mounts, to mar
> Their sacred everlasting calm."

The belief that God is indifferent is bad, but the belief that He is vindictive is worse, and the latter conception has been the more common of the two. It lies, of course, at the root of all the sacrifices of heathendom. Savages almost always look upon their gods as powerful and capricious beings, naturally inclined to do them harm, but liable to be turned from their purpose by a grateful savour, or a costly gift, or the pleasing sight of blood.

To a superficial observer it might appear that the sacrifices of Judaism implied the same sort of belief. We know that this was the view commonly held in degenerate times by the masses of the people. But the original intention of these sacrifices was something very different. They are to be distinguished from the sacrifices of heathendom, by the fact that there existed among the Jews a mercy-seat. This was a constant witness to them that they did not need to *extort* mercy from a grudging Deity, but that, on the contrary, He wished to do them good. A Jewish sacrifice was intended to typify self-surrender; it was symbolical of a determination to serve the God of righteousness. The mere giving up of a thing was not sufficient, as the Jews were taught by the story of Cain. The spirit of the worshipper must be right with God. The sentiment of his heart must correspond with the meaning of the symbol. Under the Levitical dispensation, you remember, the Jews were obliged to offer up the first-born of animals as dead sacrifices, and the first-born of men (through the rite of circumcision) as living sacrifices. The first-born represented their strength, their vitality, their endurance. Hence the meaning of the sacrifice was, that all which was best in the nation should be devoted to the service of God. The same remark applies to the Passover. That yearly festival was a symbol of the people's consecration. Their being sprinkled with the life-blood of the paschal lamb typified the dedication of their own lives to Jehovah. So, too, with the ceremonial purifications and the sacrifice of the day of atonement. In conforming to these requirements, they acknowledged the fact that they belonged to the peculiar people, and that they desired to participate in its duties and its privileges. If a man refused to comply with these conditions, he cut himself off from the congregation of faithful Israelites. "Without the shedding of blood there could be no remission." Not, of course, that the blood of bulls and goats compensated for sin or annulled it. It merely represented the worshipper's state of heart; it symbolised the fact that he was conscious of his sin, and anxious to give it up—that he desired to become a worthy member of the nation which felt itself chosen as the representative of righteousness.

Such was the original intention of the Jewish sacrifices. But the misinterpretation of symbols is one of the commonest of human weaknesses, and the Jews were constantly supposing that their own institutions meant the same as those of heathendom. They were constantly acting as if the God of righteousness were a Moloch or a Baal. Instead of regarding the sacrifices they offered as emblems of a desire to depart from iniquity and to conform to God's will, they looked on them as a means of purchasing immunity, so long as they might please to continue in sin. Against such notions as these we find the prophets continually protesting. They were so strongly impressed with the magnitude of the mischief arising from this misinterpretation of the ceremonial law, that they often spoke of sacrifice as useless, and even worse than useless. In Jeremiah, for example, we read, " Thus saith the Lord of hosts, I spake not unto your fathers concerning burnt-offerings and sacrifices; but this I commanded

them, Obey my voice, and walk ye in my ways."
Similarly, in Isaiah, we read, " To what purpose
is the multitude of your sacrifices unto me ? saith
the Lord. Bring no more vain oblations; in-
cense is an abomination unto me." But in spite
of all their protests, the prophets were rarely
successful in eradicating from the Jewish minds
their heathenish notions of sacrifice.

One reason, perhaps, why the Jews were so
inclined to look upon God as tyrannical and
capricious was this: they had little or no faith
in a future life.[1] There are one or two well-
known passages in the Old Testament where
immortality is referred to; but generally we find
it ignored. Under the Levitical dispensation the
rewards promised to right-doing were temporal,
and temporal only. For example, look at the
26th chapter of Leviticus: " If ye walk in my
statutes, and keep my commandments; then I
will give you rain in due season, and the land
shall yield her increase, and I will rid evil beasts
out of the land ; " and so on for ten verses. " But
if ye will not hearken unto me, and will not do
all these commandments ; I will appoint over you
terror and consumption and burning ague ; and
ye shall sow your seed in vain, for your enemies

---

[1] See note p. 205, and 'Agnosticism,' pp. 297-302.

shall eat it. I will send wild beasts among you, which shall rob you of your children, and destroy your cattle;" and so on for twenty-five verses. There is no reference whatever to any possible effect which their conduct might have upon them in a future state. The author of the 89th Psalm says: "O Lord, where are Thy former loving-kindnesses, which Thou swarest unto David? Remember how short my time is: wherefore hast Thou made all men in vain?" The writer of Ecclesiastes speaks after the same fashion: "Whatsoever thy hand findeth to do, do it with thy might; for there is no work, nor device, nor knowledge, nor wisdom, in the grave." And even the prophets, who were never tired of alluding to a future universal reign of righteousness, rarely suggest to their hearers the possibility of their own personal immortality. Isaiah himself said, "The grave cannot praise Thee, death cannot celebrate Thee." The few passages in the Old Testament that refer to a future life, evidently had but little influence in moulding the belief of the masses of the people. And amid the chances and troubles of this life, those who are not supported by a firm faith in another, inevitably come to think that "the ways of the Lord are not equal"—that He is neither just nor good.

Evidently then, notwithstanding the teaching of nature and conscience and history, and notwithstanding the more definite teaching of specially inspired individuals, there was still need of something more.

> " And so the Word had flesh, and wrought
> With human hands the creed of creeds,
> In loveliness of perfect deeds,
> More strong than all poetic thought."

In Christ the lessons of all previous revelations were gathered up, explained, and consummated; and the falsity of the views which had kept humanity from God was fully and for ever proved. A consciousness of guilt had led men to believe that they were beneath the notice of the Almighty; or that if He considered them at all, it would only be to condemn and to punish. But Christ was "a propitiation." The word so translated in our Bible means literally the mercy-seat. We noticed just now that under the Old Testament dispensation, the mercy-seat was a constant witness to the Jews of the long-suffering and favour of God. While the barbarians around were pouring out their blood, and their children's blood, to appease the anger of their gods, the Jews were reminded by the mercy-seat that Jehovah was more willing to give than they were to receive. So Christ is a propitiation—a mercy-seat, as it were, from which God reveals Himself to us as a God of love. "He is our peace," says St Paul—that is, the revelation to us that we may, if we will, be at peace with God. "God was in Christ, reconciling," not Himself unto the world, but "the world unto Himself"—teaching men they had greatly erred, in supposing that He was indifferent in regard to human welfare, or vindictive in regard to human sin. "Christ died" as He lived, "the just for the unjust," not to bring God to us, but "to bring us to God"—to prove to us that He was already near. "By Him we have received the atonement," for now our old misunderstandings have been removed. "With His stripes we have been healed;" for had He not suffered, we could not have known God as we do. It is inconceivable that the inner nature of the Deity could ever have been manifested to us, except by the self-denial of a divinely human life. Christ's suffering was not a sacrifice which God *exacted*, in order that He might be APPEASED. No; it was a sacrifice which He *provided*, in order that He might be REVEALED.

"God is love." That is the Christian revelation. All other lessons which Christ taught,—

about the righteousness and justice of God, or about the duty and destiny of man,—all other lessons are summed up in that one primary truth, just as every possible colour is contained in pure white light. Christ voluntarily surrendered Himself, in life and in death, to the one task of revealing the Father. It is impossible to discover a single selfish action in the whole career of the Redeemer. He never gave a thought to His own physical comfort, and yet was always mindful of the wants of those who were about Him. He would not use His extraordinary powers for His own advancement, but was never tired of employing them for the good of others. The great Teacher of the ages was not self-absorbed, but could spare time to be kind and genial even to little children. He who found it His meat and drink to do His Father's will, was no gloomy egotist, but was fond of showing His sympathy for men by joining them at the social board or the marriage-feast. He who was so strong as never to yield to the fiercest temptation, was yet so gentle as to make allowance for sinners whom society would have hounded to destruction. He who had been all His life homeless, knowing not where to lay His head, was careful to provide a home for His mother, even when He was in the very agony of death. His anger itself was a proof of His kindness to men. He was indignant with the Pharisees and Scribes, not because they were sinners, but because they, and such as they in all time, persist in creating obstacles for those who would enter into the kingdom of heaven. He who was, in an altogether unique sense, the Son of God, delighted to call Himself the Son of man; went about continually doing good; sought not to be ministered unto, but to minister; and declared that He was ready, like a good shepherd, to lay down His life for the sheep. Thus Christ's work from the first was one of reconciliation. His whole career was sacrificial and atoning. From the very beginning of His ministry He gave Himself unreservedly to the world. His death was but the last and steepest step of the altar of self-sacrifice He had been so long ascending. But on Calvary His divine patience and forbearance were brought out in greater relief. Here was "love deeply wronged, daring to love on even unto death, in the face of the enormity that had wronged it." Here was the most absolute sinlessness united to the most perfect sympathy for men. Here was divine goodness, and that goodness was self-sacrificing. Here was the old

Aryan belief in the Heaven-Father[1] worked out in very deed. The theory had become a fact. The lesson of His death was the lesson of His life, repeated with greater fulness, and taught with greater power—the lesson that God is love. And so the cross has come to mean all that Christ did and taught and was. Once a symbol of disgrace, it is now an emblem of triumph. It is the noblest word in human speech. It represents all that is divinest in the universe of God.

[1] See p. 188.

Christianity and Pre-Christian Religion.

IV.

REDEMPTION.

He "gave Himself for us, that He might redeem us from all iniquity, and purify unto Himself a peculiar people, zealous of good works."—TITUS ii. 14.

WE have in the previous sermons been engaged in comparing Christianity with pre-Christian religions. We saw that God had never left Himself without witness, but that everywhere and to all men He had revealed Himself with more or less distinctness, in proportion as they were able to bear it. We then passed on to consider the Incarnation, or the new and higher revelation which was given in Christ. We saw how this last revelation, by reason of its clearness and fulness, naturally and necessarily involved *the* Atonement. God was in Christ, reconciling the world unto Himself, removing men's misunderstandings, and teaching them that He was a God of love. In the present sermon, I have to ask you to consider Redemption, or the reformation of character which is inevitably effected in the genuine disciples of Christ. "He gave Himself for us, that He might redeem us from all iniquity, and purify unto Himself a peculiar people, zealous of good works."

We have already noticed the heathenish idea of sacrifice, which represents it as something required in order to appease the anger of the Deity; and we have contrasted this with the Scriptural view that God is *waiting* to be gracious. There is also a heathenish idea of redemption, which has sometimes been adopted by so-called Christian sects. Among the many perversions of Christianity, this is the most horrible and the most blasphemous. It has been held that, for the believer in Christ, sin is a matter of no moment whatsoever. He has borne, it is said, the punishment of *all* our sins, and so we need not be afraid of having to bear the punishment of any. He died, in fact, that we might sin with impunity. He, so to speak, *compounded* for all the enormities which it might ever please us to commit. In a word, the God of righteousness became incarnate for the sake of encouraging iniquity!

In a less extreme form this theory has unhappily been exceedingly common. I allude to the notion that belief—as it is called—if not everything, is at any rate far more important than conduct. This idea is most mischievous in its results; and if you come to look at it, is in itself absurd. The belief which does not show itself in conduct is but a spurious belief. If a man says he believes in Christ, and acts continually as if Christ had never lived, what are we to infer? Why this; that he persuades himself he believes, merely because he does not disbelieve. But not to disbelieve and to believe are two totally different things. It is impossible really to believe in the value of the Redeemer's work, without endeavouring to be redeemed; and to be redeemed is to be saved, not from punishment, at least not in the first instance, but from sin; to be saved, not in spite of our sins, but from the sins themselves; to be saved, not from the wrath of God, but from the thraldom of our baser self. "With the heart man believeth unto righteousness." In other words, he who really believes in Christ must become, as a matter of necessity, Christ-like. "He died," we are told, "to put away" [not punishment, but] "sin, by the sacrifice of Himself." "He has washed us," we read, "from our sins in His own blood"—blood meaning, of course, the life which He sacrificed in His atoning and reconciling work. We are to be "redeemed from our vain conversation." We are to be "renewed in the spirit of our minds." We are to be "created again unto righteousness." Our conscience is to be "purged from dead works, to serve the living God." "God is just," we are told, "and the justifier of him that believeth"—that is, the righteous God enables us, through Christ, to become ourselves righteous. Christ is to be "made unto us righteousness, and sanctification, and [in a word] redemption." "He gave Himself for us, that He might redeem us from all iniquity, and purify unto Himself a peculiar people, zealous of good works."

The redemption, then, at which Christ aimed, was a redemption from sin. Now let us inquire how He proposed to effect this, and why it was He succeeded, when others before Him had failed. Centuries prior to His advent, the Jews, as we have seen, had a passionate enthusiasm for rightcousness, which distinguished them from all other nations upon earth. But we know how they had deteriorated by the time Christ came. And we cannot be surprised that their ardour cooled. They had no criterion of wrong but specific prohibitions, and no criterion of right but temporal prosperity. The latter was false, and was distinctly declared to be so by Christ: the good man, He taught, was not always prosperous, nor was the bad man always in adversity. And as to the Jewish criterion of wrong, there is something very damping to enthusiasm in the constant reiteration of "thou shalt not." But the Jews kept on multiplying their negative commandments indefinitely. For example, they discovered that there were thirty-nine different ways in which the Sabbath could be broken. The tying and loosing of knots on that day was long felt to be a delicate problem; but finally, it was decided that knots which could be managed with one hand might be considered Sabbatic knots, but that those which required both hands must on no account be touched. In the time of our Lord, the Pharisees and Scribes were learned in all this traditional lore, and punctilious in observing it; yet at the same time the great majority of them were altogether indifferent, if not hostile, to real goodness. And no wonder. They were so afraid of doing wrong, that they had neither time nor inclination to do right. A certain amount of *abandon*, an enthusiasm that will carry us beyond the strict requirements of the law, is necessary for the attainment of anything like eminence in virtue. And it is just this enthusiasm which Christ supplied. He aimed at redeeming men by the "attractive power of His own personality."

The first thing that must strike any one who reads carefully the history of Christ, is the immense importance He attached, not merely to His mission, but to Himself. Every great teacher, with this single exception, in exact proportion to his greatness, has been willing to be cast into the shade by the glory of the truth which he wished to teach. But not so Christ. He was frequently placing Himself before His disciples as an object for veneration and worship. They must be willing, He taught, to leave everything for Him. They must not count their lives dear unto them, if His service should demand their death. Their spiritual nature was to be nurtured by communion with His spirit, in such a way that they might be said to "eat the flesh and drink the blood of the Son of man." Their devotedness to Him was to be so passionate and intense, that in comparison with it, all other loves would seem but as hatred.

It is by this demand that Christ is distinguished from the rest of the world's teachers. It is because He made it, and had a right to make it, that His success has been so marvellously great. Much of what He taught had been already anticipated. Gautama, Confucius, and Hillel[1] had pronounced the golden rule. The Stoics had urged on their disciples the duty of treating all men, if not as brethren, at least as fellow-citizens. But this teaching had had comparatively little effect. The philosophers might exhort to unselfishness, but instinct and habit were too strong, and were frequently reasserting themselves. The influence of mere teaching is always very small. Juvenal, to use a familiar illustration, was a Stoic, trained up in the doctrine that the wise and good of all nations were alike citizens in the city of God; and yet the mixture of races in Rome excited in him the bitterest contempt. Nay, it was this partial realisation of the ideal of his own philosophy, which made him the cynic and the satirist that

[1] The last two, however, had only given it in its negative form.

he was. So far is it possible for theory to be divorced from practice.

But Christ not only taught, He inspired. He appealed not so much to the intellect as to the hearts of men. "The passions which other teachers had sought to put under the control of Reason, He aimed at controlling by the creation of a yet more powerful passion— an all-absorbing attachment to Himself." He knew that if selfishness can be eradicated, sin will be destroyed. All sin is in the last resort but the undue appreciation of self. "The difficulty of discovering what is right commonly arises from the prevalence of self-interest in our minds; and as we generally behave rightly to any one for whom we feel affection or sympathy, Christ considered that he who could feel sympathy for all would behave rightly to all." He endeavoured to create in men this universal sympathy for their fellows, by first creating in them an enthusiastic sympathy for Himself. He knew that we must inevitably grow like what we supremely love. "If ye love me," He said, "ye will keep my commandments." He was the very impersonation of unselfishness. His whole career was one prolonged self-sacrifice. "He loved us, and gave Himself for us." To love Christ, therefore, is to love Love. It is to be filled with a divine enthusiasm for goodness which converts self-denial into the highest joy.

This it was, then, at which Christ aimed, and this He actually succeeded in accomplishing. "He convinced men," says the author of 'Ecce Homo,' "that He was a person of altogether transcendent greatness, and that yet He had devoted Himself, of mere benevolence, to their good. He showed them that for their sakes He lived a hard and laborious life, and exposed Himself to the utmost malice of powerful men. They saw Him hungry, though they believed Him able to turn stones into bread; they saw His royal pretensions spurned, though they believed that He could in a moment take into His hand all the kingdoms of the world and the glory of them; they saw Him at last expire in agonies, though they believed that, had He so willed it, no danger could harm Him, and that, had He thrown Himself from the topmost pinnacle of the Temple, He would have been received softly into the arms of ministering angels. Witnessing His sufferings, and convinced that they were voluntarily endured, men's hearts were touched, and an agitation of gratitude, sympathy and astonishment, such as nothing else could ever excite, sprang up in them. And when, turning from His deeds to His words, they found this very self-denial which had guided His own life, prescribed as a principle which should guide theirs, gratitude broke forth in cheerful obedience, and the Law and the Lawgiver were enshrined in their hearts for inseparable veneration."

It was in this way that Christ succeeded in giving men a universal test of right, infinitely better than the most elaborate system of rules— better, just because it was a test which was at the same time an inspiration. It was not by the mere statement of the golden rule that He revolutionised the world; it was because He implanted it in men's inmost hearts. "There have been not a few who have found it possible to conceive for Christ an attachment, the closeness of which no words can express—an attachment so absorbing that they have said, 'I live no more, but Christ liveth in me.' Now such a feeling carries with it of necessity the feeling of love for all human beings. They have been made sacred by a reflected glory. It matters no longer what quality men may exhibit, amiable or unamiable; as the brothers of Christ, as the objects of His love in life and death, they must be dear to all to whom He is dear. The true disciple of Christ must think of the whole race, and of every member of it, with awful reverence and hope. If some human beings are abject and contemptible, if it be incredible to us that they have any high dignity or destiny, do we regard them from so great a height as Christ? Are we likely to be more pained by their faults and deficiencies than He was? Is our standard higher than His? And yet He associated with these meanest of the race. No contempt for them did He ever express; no suspicion that they might be less dear to the common Father; no doubt that they were capable of becoming perfect even as He was perfect. There is nothing of which a man may be prouder than of this; it is the most hopeful fact in human history. An eternal glory has been shed over the human race by the love Christ bore it. And so, along with the law of love, the power of love was given." The chief apostle of Him who was made a curse for sin, had grown so like his Master as to be able to say—"I could wish that myself were accursed from Christ for my brethren, my kinsmen according to the flesh."

To be a Christian, then, it is not enough to be a member of a Christian Church. "Many walk," says St Paul, " of whom I have told you that they are the enemies of the cross of Christ." To be a Christian, it is not enough to profess a belief in certain propositions about Christ and His work. " Not every one that saith unto me, Lord, Lord, shall enter into the kingdom of heaven." To be a Christian, it is not enough to be free from what are commonly called sins. It was to the man who had kept all the commandments from his youth that the Saviour said, " One thing thou lackest"—that one thing without which he could not enter into the kingdom of God. We sometimes think it is comparatively easy now to be a Christian—easier far than in the old times of martyrdom. But it is not. The *spirit* which was in the martyrs must be in us, or we are unworthy to bear the name of Christ. The spirit which impelled them to sacrifice themselves for Him in death, should inspire us to sacrifice ourselves for Him in life. He should be to us as He was to them—more dear than anything else the world contains. We should think it our highest joy to take up the cross of self-denial and follow Him " *whithersoever* He goeth."

This is a lofty standard. We may feel as if we could never attain it. But unless we have a sincere desire to do so, calling ourselves after the name of Christ is nothing short of blasphemy. The accusation is constantly brought against Christianity, that those who profess it are not better than their neighbours, but, on the contrary, rather worse, narrower in their sympathies, harsher in their judgments, more petty in their aims, more grossly selfish in their actions—a peculiar people indeed, but only in the sense of being peculiarly disagreeable. Woe betide us if we do anything to justify this accusation! Sir, if Christ is nothing more to you than any ordinary historical personage; if your heart has never been touched by the old, old story of the Cross; if you see no beauty in a life of self-denial; if you have no intention of making any sacrifices in behalf of your fellow-men for whom Christ died,—then, for God's sake, I adjure you, do not call yourself a Christian. Why must you bring the name of Christ into contempt? Is it not enough to treat Him with indifference? Can you not be satisfied with ignoring Him? What harm has He done you, that you must positively insult Him? Will nothing content you but to crucify the Son of God afresh, and put Him to an open shame?

Christmas-Day

"On earth peace, goodwill toward men."—LUKE ii. 14.

THERE is considerable difference of opinion as to what is the best reading and the best rendering of this passage. According to Dean Alford and the Revised Version, we should understand it to mean, peace among the men towards whom God has a goodwill—that is, among those in whom He is well pleased. According to the Vulgate the meaning should be, peace to men who exhibit a goodwill. This is the sense adopted by Keble in his Christmas Hymn. The reading of the Authorised Version is not, perhaps, the best; but as being more familiar, and at the same time so thoroughly in harmony with the spirit of the day, I shall take it as a motto.

It must be confessed that the conduct of

professing Christians has often been such, as to make the angel's song sound like an ironical sarcasm on Christianity, rather than a eulogy. Church History, for example, to a passionate lover of peace and goodwill, must be very melancholy reading. Almost every page of it tends to obscure the beauty of Christ's character, and to hide the meaning and purpose of His life. It is concerned almost entirely with dogmas, formulas, definitions,—for which Christ cared nothing. Jesus most assuredly never would have said "Whosoever will be saved, it is above all things necessary that he thus think of a doctrine." The Christianity of Christ consisted in living a certain life. The Christianity of Christendom resolved itself into "thinking of" certain dogmas.

For a long time the fiercest controversy raged as to whether Christ were *homoousios* or *homoiousios*,—*i.e.*, whether He were in substance the same as the Father, or only similar. These two words differ by one letter—the smallest in the Greek alphabet; and this difference pretty well represents the importance of the discussion. If Christ was decided to be *homoousios*, the world would be none the better; if *homoiousios*, none the worse. For just think. The controversy was almost meaningless,—to the non-philosophical public, quite meaningless. This word "substance," you must know, means in metaphysics not what it means in common language, but just the opposite. It stands, not for what is tangible and palpable, but for what is intangible and impalpable. It represents, not what appears to the senses, but what does not so appear. The substance of anything is, roughly speaking, that which it is conceived to be in itself, in contradistinction to our perception of it. By Christ's substance would be intended not His body, nor even His mind, but rather the secret and hidden essence of both. You will observe the difficulty of the idea. And not only is it difficult, but it is one about which there has always been the greatest possible disagreement. The word "substance" has been the most serious battle-ground of metaphysicians from the beginning until now. It may still be considered an open question as to what its exact positive meaning should be. Men are at one as to what they do *not* mean by the word; but when they attempt to define precisely what they *do* mean by it, there is endless diversity and confusion. And yet, as if Christianity were nothing more than a logomachy, it was round this word "substance" that the fourth century expended the greater part of its enthusiasm. Can you conceive of a sadder spectacle? There was the whole world lying in wickedness, waiting to be converted to Christ, waiting to be taught the new commandment and to be inspired with the zeal necessary to obey it; and His ministers, the bishops and pastors of the Church, were jangling as to whether His substance, whatever that might be, were *homoousios* or *homoiousios!*

And there were many other controversies, equally fierce and equally futile. As, *e.g.*, whether Christ had two natures or one. The Monophysites said that the divine and human nature were blended at His conception; the Nestorians, on the contrary, declared that they always remained distinct. There were scores of sects quarrelling over hundreds of doctrines,— all more or less vague and mystical, not to say incomprehensible. And the bishops century after century kept on persistently excommunicating one another, or being excommunicated, according as their power waxed or waned. For centuries excommunication seemed to be the chief work of the Christian Church. Poor Athanasius, Bishop of Alexandria, was expelled ten times from his see, and sometimes nearly lost his life in the tumult that attended his expulsion; and the only accusation against him was, that he did not "think of" the Trinity in the same way as his opponents, who happened for the moment to be in the ascendant.

And in the present day, though there is less bloodshed, there is, I am afraid, almost as much hatred. I remember that in the preface to the second edition of his Belfast Address, Professor Tyndall said he was not surprised at the bitter things which had been uttered against him by Christians, when he remembered how bitterly they were in the habit of recriminating one another. " 'Tis true, 'tis pity; pity 'tis, 'tis true." They have been so busy shouting their party shibboleths, and wrangling over their little points of doctrine or of ritual, that they have altogether forgotten their chief business in the world. But this is not Christ's fault. Any one who reads His New Testament intelligently, must see that it was a very different result at which Christ aimed. We noticed in a previous sermon that His endeavour was to redeem men from selfishness, and to create in them a universal sympathy for their fellows. Of this sympathy, peace and goodwill are the invariable characteristics: peace, or the absence of quarrelsomeness; goodwill, or the actual performance of deeds of kindness. These are essential characteristics of genuine discipleship. Without them, any profession of religion is but hypocrisy and cant. St John does not mince matters, but declares plainly—"If a man say, I love God, and hateth his brother, *he is a liar.*"

Let us to-day apply this test of discipleship to ourselves. Of all the provisions for our spiritual welfare in this human life, there is perhaps nothing more helpful than the periodical recurrence of days like the present. They break the spell of routine. It would be the greatest conceivable calamity, if all days were exactly alike. We are creatures of custom; and custom means, generally speaking, thoughtlessness and indifference. For you and for me these days are no less needful than they are for the hard-worked masses. Our work may be light and even enjoyable, but we are apt to become too absorbed in it. We are apt to look upon our professional duties, or upon our personal culture, as the exclusive business of our lives. You remember in Dickens's 'Christmas Carol,' when the ghost of Scrooge's former partner is lamenting his misspent life, Scrooge tries to console him by saying, "But you were always a good man of business, Jacob." "Business!" cried the ghost, wringing its hands; "mankind was my business; the common welfare was my business; charity, mercy, forbearance, benevolence, were all my business. The dealings of my trade were but a drop of water in the comprehensive ocean of my business." This comprehensive nature of our work in life we are all of us too apt to forget in the pressure of our daily occupations. The constant recurrence of these occupations gives them an undue importance in our eyes. And we have so little opportunity of *considering* our ways. Apart from days like the present, there is no such thing as leisure for us. That is precluded by the multiplication of books, if by nothing else. Do you not sometimes wish that a good angel would stifle for a little that passion for writing them, which is so characteristic of our age? Would it not be an enormous relief, if for a single year no fresh books were issued from the press? As it is, books take up too much of our time—time which would be better spent in thought.

A day such as this then, which we cannot, if we would, spend as a common day, is an inestimable blessing. We are compelled to turn aside out of our ordinary life-path, and submit ourselves to the peaceful influences of this quiet resting-place. Our Christmas cards, our Christmas carols, our Church services and decorations, our social gatherings, all remind us of the peace and goodwill foretold eighteen centuries ago. We are drawn, in spite of ourselves, nearer to our fellows. The very greeting of "A Merry Christmas to you!" which custom has taught us to give to one another, suggests to us that, if we are not hypocrites, we are really taking a very wide interest in the welfare of our fellow-men. The good feeling of this festive season is irresistibly contagious. We have probably all of us done something, at the sacrifice of time and money, to make this a merry Christmas for some of the children of our common Father. The air is resonant at this moment with the echoes of the angel's song. It is a marvellous triumph for Christianity, that on one day of the year at any rate kindness and amiability reign supreme, and all antagonistic emotions have to hide themselves for very shame.

But it was Christ's aim that every day should be in this respect a Christmas-day. Is that the case with us? There was a curious institution in the middle ages, half beautiful, half grotesque. When private feuds had become very numerous and very fierce, an attempt was made to oppose them, by what was called the ecclesiastical truce or peace of God. It is not known exactly how this arose; but it was proclaimed in several cities, and was religiously observed. According to this truce, feuds were legally stopped for four days in the week. The bell tolled on Wednesday, to intimate that, on pain of judicial punishment, all hostilities were to cease till the following Monday. And until the Monday accordingly, they were suspended; but *then they were always faithfully resumed.* On the same principle, we are too apt to return again after a day like the present to our old routine, which with the most of us is more or less a routine of selfishness. Shall it be so this year? Is it really so hard to be a Christian, that we can only accomplish it on one day out of 365? After manifesting peace and goodwill on the 25th of December, must we relapse again into practical paganism on the 26th? We cannot be always making presents, but we may be always doing good. We may show others by our manner that we are interested in their welfare. I have known men with whom it was a privilege to shake hands; to talk to them for five minutes was as refreshing as a week's holiday. We may not be able to do any great thing for Christ, but the simplest act of kindness is a service with which He will be well pleased. Shall we not, then, set ourselves diligently to cultivate the Christian temperament, and to manifest the Christian spirit? Peace and goodwill are their own exceeding great reward. There is a happiness within the reach of every man, far sweeter than any merely selfish gratification—the happiness of making others glad. There is a beauty that might belong to the plainest of us—the beauty of a benevolent expression. Wordsworth, you know, speaks of

> "Benignant looks,
> That, for a face not beautiful, do more
> Than beauty for the fairest face can do."

There is a nobility, the glory of which cannot be outvied by the descendant of a hundred earls—the nobility of thoughtful consideration for others. When peace and goodwill are universal, human society will be, as Christ wished to make it, a heaven upon earth. He never expected this result to be a speedy one. "I came not to send peace, but a sword." This, he foresaw, would be the first effect. But so gentle a nature could not calmly have uttered such a terrible prophecy, unless he had looked forward to something very different in the future. And He did. He foresaw that there would come a time when all men would be drawn to Him, and love one another for His sake, even as He had loved them. And so they will in the sweet by-and-by.

> "It came upon the midnight clear,—
>   That glorious song of old,
> From angels bending near the earth
>   To touch their harps of gold :
> 'Peace to the earth, goodwill to men,
>   From heaven's all-gracious King.'
> The world in solemn stillness lay
>   To hear the angels sing.
>
> Still through the cloven skies they come,
>   With peaceful wings unfurled;
> And still their heavenly music floats
>   O'er all the weary world.
> Above its sad and lowly plains
>   They bend on heavenly wing
> And ever o'er its Babel sounds
>   The blessed angels sing.
>
> Yet with the woes of sin and strife
>   The world has suffered long;
> Beneath the angel-strain have rolled
>   Two thousand years of wrong.
> And men at war with men, hear not
>   The love-song which they bring.
> Oh hush the noise, ye men of strife,
>   And hear the angels sing !
>
> And ye beneath life's crushing load,
>   Whose forms are bending low,

Who toil along the climbing way
  With painful steps and slow,
Look now! for glad and golden hours
  Come swiftly on the wing.
Oh rest beside the weary road,
  And hear the angels sing!

For lo! the days are hastening on
  By prophet bards foretold,
When with the ever-circling years
  Comes back the age of gold,
When peace shall over all the earth
  Its blessed banner fling,
And the whole world SEND BACK the song
  Which now the angels sing."

The Rest of Faith.

"Rest in the Lord, and wait patiently for Him."
—Psalm xxxvii. 7.

REST! Wait patiently! Who ever did? Who ever can? Restlessness and impatience seem to be inseparably connected with humanity. They are manifested by all classes at every stage of their existence, from the child who grows weary of its newest toy, to the philosopher who is dissatisfied with the result of his patient, lifelong thought. Rest! Some men know not what it means; they have never in their lives experienced it. And for others, it has no sooner come than gone, vanished like some transient dream of bliss.

You have often, I daresay, felt strangely saddened by the restfulness of nature. How beautiful she appears on a summer's evening, when the setting sun bestows on the landscape a parting gift of glory, when the voice of the zephyr murmurs the tired earth's lullaby, and when all things seem sinking into rest! Beautiful? Yes, but suggestive of a mournful and startling contrast :—

> " For, in the deepest hour of nature's peace,
> The human heart's disquiet will not cease."

On the serenest evening which the world has ever seen, there was one exception to the common restfulness. "Man's heart taketh not rest even in the night." And therefore nature's serenity, though beautiful, is very, very saddening. We are shocked at her want of sympathy. How can she be so placid when we are so perturbed?

Yet rest cannot be quite impossible for man, for it has been occasionally achieved. The Psalmist, for example, had practised what we find him preaching in our text. "The Lord is my shepherd," he says, "I shall not want. He maketh me to lie down in green pastures: He leadeth me beside the still waters. . . . Yea, though I walk through the valley of the shadow of death, I will fear no evil; for Thou art with me." "My soul waiteth upon God. My expectation is from Him. He is my rock and my defence. I shall not be moved." Faber, too, had

The Rest of Faith.

attained to a restfulness not less perfect than the Psalmist's. You remember his words:—

> "I love to trace each print where Thou
>   Hast set Thine unseen feet.
> I cannot fear Thee, Blessed Will,
>   Thine empire is so sweet.
>
> I love to lose my will in Thine,
>   And by that loss be free.
> I find my strength in helplessness,
>   And meekly wait on Thee.
>
> Ill that God blesses is our good,
>   And unblest good is ill,
> And all is right that seems most wrong
>   If it be Thy sweet will."

You will observe that the rest to which the Psalmist and Faber and a few such men have attained, is an intelligent and intelligible rest. There can be no rest for us in circumstances; they are ever changing. There can be no rest in self; for self is too much at the mercy of circumstances. There can be no complete rest for us in other men; for they may play us false, or be taken away by death:—

> "There is no union here of hearts
>   That finds not here an end."

The only perfect rest conceivable for man is a rest in the Lord—a confidence in the love and wisdom of Him who is the same yesterday, to-day, and for ever.

You will observe, further, that all forms of restlessness and impatience resolve themselves into a want of faith. They amount to practical atheism. We all, I suppose, profess to believe, and think that we believe, in God. And yet we are constantly acting and feeling as if we did not. We fancy that we could have arranged the circumstances of our life much better than they have been arranged for us by Providence. When we look forward to the future, we are afraid things will not turn out well unless we have a hand in ordering them. We are restless under bad fortune, as if we were quite sure it was an unmitigated evil. We are impatient for good fortune, as if we were at the mercy of a niggardly tyrant, who would keep it from us if he could.

Let us take an illustration or two. We young men perhaps afford the most striking example. We probably, more than any other class, are characterised by a feverish restlessness and a tremendous impatience. We want to build our Rome in a day. We should like to reap the fruit of our labours almost before we have sown the seed. We desire to put the top-stone on to our building without having laid a good foundation. When we first sketched out for ourselves our life's plan, and saw the goal in the far-distant future, we determined that its attainment was worth any amount of effort and of perseverance. But we soon grew weary. We thought we were not having so good a time of it as we deserved. And we turned aside from the path we had marked out, in pursuit of ignoble pleasure or still more ignoble sloth. My brother! it is our restlessness and impatience, our eager craving after ease and pleasure, our indisposition to endure hardness and conflict, our longing to enjoy the present moment however meanly, rather than work out patiently some future good however glorious—it is these things that mar us, that keep us from ever becoming what we might have been. Burns's lament is so true of us:

> " O man, while in thy early years,
> How prodigal of time,
> Misspending all thy precious hours,
> Thy glorious youthful prime."

There is no cure for this restlessness but faith. Faith in the future, and in the God of the future, will alone help us worthily to discharge our present duty. Of necessity a good deal of drudgery precedes any kind of success. An aspirant for musical fame once asked a celebrated violinist, how long it had taken him to become a proficient in his art. The reply was, "Sixteen hours a-day for twenty-five years." And it is the same in all vocations and in every sphere. No success worth having was ever achieved without tremendous toil. Now there is nothing that would enable us to endure this necessary "hardness" like a steadfast faith in God—an unwavering confidence that He will give us what is best. Such a faith would teach us to hold pleasure at its true worth. We should make it our *first* aim to do our life's work bravely, accepting pleasure gratefully when it came in the path of duty, but refusing to turn aside in its pursuit. And so every day, as it passed over us, would find us nearer to our goal. We should be living an ideal life, in which progress was united to repose.

There is another very common form of restlessness, arising not from the mere absence of enjoyment, but from the actual presence of pain. Here is a man who has failed to obtain something on which he had set his heart—or having obtained it, it does not please him as he thought it would; or, it may be, some source of happiness has been taken from him which he had long been privileged to possess. How he chafes and frets! How he resents this interference with his plans! How sure he feels that Providence has made a mistake! To any one in such a predicament I should like to offer two suggestions. The first is this: Your present adversity, my friend, may be the best means—perhaps the only means—to a great prosperity which is in store for you at no distant date. Many a man has said, like Jacob, "All these things are against me," when they were in reality paving the way to a happiness greater than any for which he had ever hoped. "Quarrel not with God's unfinished providence." Your life is not yet over. *Wait.*

> "Out of evil cometh good,
>   Joy is born of sorrow;
> Sighs that rend the heart to-day
>   Die in bliss to-morrow."

So it often has been. So it may be with you.

But secondly, I would remark, it is a great mistake to imagine, as all those who are chafing under difficulty or disappointment seem to imagine, that happiness is the chief end of life and that we have a right to as much of it as we like to demand. The end of life is not happiness but duty. God has a purpose to fulfil in our existence—at least so we profess to believe; and surely it must be evident that *with this purpose* an indefinite amount of happiness might be quite incompatible. We forget that, both as individuals and as members of a race, we require discipline, training, development. It may be absolutely necessary that we suffer—necessary for the strengthening and perfecting of our own character, or necessary for the teaching and enlightenment of the race. "Sorrow," says J. P. Richter, "seems sent for our instruction, just as we darken the cages of birds when we would teach them to sing." I have pointed out to you before,[1] that some of the noblest characteristics of humanity could never have been conceivably developed without the instrumentality of grief. My sorrowing friend, benefits may accrue to you from your suffering which could not have been otherwise conferred. It will give you strength and stability of character; it will make you sympathetic, pitiful, and kind; it will bring you nearer to Him who is "a very present help in trouble."

But besides the benefit that you will *gain* from suffering, think of those which it may be thereby in your power to *confer*. There are not

[1] See 'Origin of Evil.'

only lessons which sorrow enables men to learn;
there are also lessons which it enables them to
teach. You are suffering perhaps, in the providence of God, not so much for your own sake as
for the sake of others. And can you conceive
of any higher glory than thus to be a sacrifice
for the world? If poor Job can now see the
priceless value of his woe, if he can see how
thousands and tens of thousands have been
helped by the story of his conflict, you may be
very sure that he is thankful for having been
permitted to achieve so much. "He remembers
no more the anguish." He will now be ready
to exclaim, "My light affliction, which was but
for a moment, has worked out for me a far more
exceeding, and an eternal, weight of glory." And
Job has many companions in his educative work.
Every one who bears suffering as it should be
borne, belongs, in virtue thereof, to the noble
army of martyrs, by whose pain the world is
made better. Many a weak woman, unknown
beyond her family circle, has taught lessons of
patience and resignation and faith and unselfishness, with a clearness and a force which could
not be surpassed. Not a few of us, probably,
will look back throughout eternity to some such
sufferer as to our highest spiritual teacher

Thoughts like these should help us to bear affliction bravely, to rest in the Lord and wait patiently, until He reveals to us the meaning and the blessedness of our grief. We may have to wait, perhaps till the great hereafter, but then assuredly we shall see that we have not suffered in vain.

> " With aching hands and bleeding feet
>   We dig and heap, lay stone on stone ;
> We bear the burden and the heat
>   Of the long day, and wish 'twere done.
> Not till the hours of light return,
>   All we have built shall we discern."

Our restlessness and impatience, once more, involve a practical disbelief in immortality. Though we constantly *say* we " believe in the resurrection of the dead and the life of the world to come," we chafe and fret when our wishes are thwarted, as if there were no life but the present, as if the grave were the end of all things for us. Here is a man somewhat advanced in years, who begins to feel that life is not going to be to him what he had once believed it would. Age is coming upon him, and not one of the expectations of his youth has been fulfilled. He was not, perhaps, highly gifted by nature, or he had but few early advantages, or he was more scrupulously conscientious than his neighbours; but be the cause what it may, he has to confess to himself that he has not been successful. It is too late now; he is too old to hope for better things. As to waiting patiently, there seems nothing to wait for but the falling of the curtain upon a very unsatisfactory play. He feels disgusted, chagrined, annoyed, enraged. If that be your case, sir, I ask, do you, or do you not, believe in another life? If you do not, I have no consolation to offer you. If there is no future, your fate is a very hard one, and unless you have done anything to deserve it, a very cruel and unjust one. But if there is a future life and you believe in it, why should you despond? Your threescore years and ten, compared to the eternity that is before you, are really less than a second in a lifetime. There are some exquisite lines of Mr Greg's which are full of consolation for you:—

> "Yes, I have failed; that golden prize
>   Of life—success—ambition's boast,
> Which dazzled once my boyish eyes,
>   I strove for, prayed for, and have lost.
>
> Yet I may *not have lost* the prize—
>   It only may not yet be won;
> I see with dim and tearful eyes—
>   The goal may be still farther on.

> That star again, like morning sun,
>   May rise upon some happier shore,
> And where a nobler race is run,
>   My Master bid me try once more."

The lesson of our text is a lesson we all need to learn. Circumstances are continually arising, in your life and mine, which tend to make us restless and impatient. Sometimes our plans are frustrated, our hopes disappointed, our labours nullified; sometimes we have to bear pain and disease, bodily and mental prostration; sometimes those whom we have benefited are ungrateful, and render us evil for good—or those whom we trusted and loved deceive and wound us; sometimes our staunchest, truest friends are taken from us by death. To one and all of us then the advice of the Psalmist is applicable, or will sooner or later become applicable. When trouble comes upon us, we become restless and impatient, as if we had never heard of God. We are always ready to preach patience; why cannot we practise what we preach? We can exercise faith for other men; shall we never exercise it for ourselves? Is it likely that in a well-ordered universe—and we profess to believe that the universe is well ordered—

is it likely that *our* welfare alone has been overlooked? If it were our destiny to fight impotently against surrounding forces which were bound in the end to destroy us, then there would be an excuse for our anxiety and foreboding. But if there be a God, a loving God, a God who is making all things to work together for good, then our fretful impatience is puerile and contemptible. Have we not the glorious hope of everlasting life?

Yes. But this very hope often makes us restless and impatient. We should like—instead of a hope—to have possessed a demonstration. We should like to know exactly the kind of existence that awaits us in the future. We should like, in this life, to be allowed some communion with those whom we have loved and lost. And yet, in the present state of our mental development, it may be quite impossible for us to understand any fuller or clearer revelation than that which has been given to us. Even if it were possible, it might be supremely inexpedient. There is probably no other discipline so useful for us as that of the comparative ignorance in which we are compelled to remain. At any rate, I think, we might bring ourselves to the "*sure and certain* hope" that the Author of a world so beautiful, that He to whom we owe all the joy and happiness of life, is caring also for our future, and doing in regard to it that which alone is best. Can we not wait —wait like men—" for the far-off interest of tears?"

Against Censoriousness.

"Judge not."—MATTHEW vii. 1.

THE wisest maxims are always susceptible of a ridiculous interpretation. This is the kind of interpretation which thinkers of a certain school are wont to put upon the sayings of Christ. Having made up their minds that the Christian religion is impracticable and altogether unsuited to the exigencies of human life, they proceed to explain Christ's injunctions in a way which will support this gratuitous hypothesis. They tell us that social order—nay, the very existence of society—would be at an end if we were to act upon the precepts of the Nazarene. They maintain that the meekness of spirit which Christ inculcated, would involve the abrogation of criminal prosecutions and civil punishments; and such an abrogation, they assert, would be absolutely fatal. Of course it would. Christ

Himself said, however, that His mission was not to destroy the law, but to fulfil; and He certainly did not narrow, but on the contrary enlarged, its borders. But this of course is, consciously or unconsciously, ignored. Just notice, if you please, the unphilosophical injustice of which these thinkers are guilty. In studying Aristotle or Herbert Spencer, they try to discover the *best* meaning which the author's words are capable of bearing; but in regard to Christ's teaching, they always select the *worst*. It is really too bad. No amount of absurdity or inconsistency is too great to be attributed to Jesus. In fact, the more ridiculous they have made His teaching appear, the more confident do they seem that they have expressed His real meaning. "Judge not!" they exclaim, for example. "Why, it is impossible to fulfil that command; and if it were possible, it would be detrimental!" Very true in one sense. Everybody knows that if we are certain a man has committed a crime, we cannot help judging him to be guilty. And everybody knows that if we did not award punishment, where punishment was due, society would be destroyed. Christian charity itself demands that we be very strict and inexorable in these kinds of judgments. What Christ is here warning us against is not social or legal judgment, but moral. By a moral judgment I mean the attempt to sum up the worth or worthlessness of a human character, considered not in regard to such and such actions, but as a whole. We may see very clearly that association with certain persons would be injurious to ourselves or to our families, and it is our bounden duty to form such judgments, and to act upon them. But this does not warrant our attempting to estimate a man's moral standing in the sight of God. The reason why Christ forbids our passing such judgments is that they would be invariably wrong. Let me try and make this plain.

In the first place, we have not sufficient data. "We see a few of the actions which a man performs, we hear a few of the words he utters; and that is all we know of him. Yet some of us imagine that, on the strength of this knowledge, we can form a complete and infallible judgment in regard to his moral worth." We could not make a greater or more foolish mistake. The question whether a man is good or bad, very good or very bad, how good or how bad, is a highly complex question, depending on an almost infinite variety of circumstances. In order to arrive at a correct decision, we must know the history of the man's ancestors for hundreds of years past, and the different tendencies towards right and towards wrong which they have transmitted to him. We must know the exact quantity and quality of his brain, together with the value of his whole *physique*, considered as an instrument of the will. We must discover with how much ability he was endowed by nature, and how far his faculties have been improved by voluntary effort or injured by voluntary neglect. We must be familiar with the advantages and disadvantages, the trials, temptations and privileges of his trade or profession. We must ascertain the climate and other characteristics of the place in which he lived, and investigate their adaptation or want of adaptation to his particular temperament and constitution. We must glean information regarding the schoolmasters and clergymen from whom he received, or failed to receive, instruction. We must know what books he had it in his power to read, what he actually did read, and what were beyond his reach. And so I might go on multiplying *ad infinitum* data which are essential to a correct solution of the problem—data which must be fully known and accurately estimated, before a moral verdict can be legitimately pronounced. " Many of us are born," says the author of 'John Inglesant,' " with seeds within us which make moral victory hopeless from the first, the seeds of disease, of ignorance, of stupidity." A few of us, on the other hand, the descendants of a long line of cultured ancestors, have had refinement and goodness in our blood to start with, so that we involuntarily shrink from vice, almost as we shrink from pain. Circumstances over which a man has had absolutely no control, may have conspired to render his conflict between duty and inclination either easy or terrific, may have made it almost impossible for him to do right, or almost impossible for him to do wrong. And the circumstances which have had this effect are infinitely subtle, complex, and involved. They can be fully understood only by omniscience. So that it is impossible to say of any human being how far he has made himself what he is, or how far his character may have been determined by extraneous forces; in other words, how far he is, or is not, responsible for himself.

Again, we can never see what goes on in another's heart. We may detect his sins; but whether he has struggled against them, and to what extent, we can never tell. The moral conflicts in which each of us is engaged are known only to ourselves and God. "We may be able to say," observes Mr Greg, "this man has lied, has pilfered, has forged! and that man has apparently gone through life with clean hands. But can we say that the first has not struggled long, though unsuccessfully, against temptations under which the second would have succumbed without an effort? We know that one is generous and open-handed, and another close, niggardly and mean; but the generosity of the one, as well as the niggardliness of the other, may be a mere yielding to native temperament. In the eye of heaven, a long life of beneficence in the one may have cost less exertion, and may indicate less virtue, than a few rare, hidden acts of kindness, wrung by duty out of the reluctant and unsympathetic nature of the other." Burns's words are as true as they are beautiful:—

> "Who made the heart, 'tis He alone
>   Decidedly can try us:
> He knows each chord, its various tone;
>   Each spring, its various bias.
> Then at the balance let's be mute;
>   We never can adjust it:
> What's done we partly may compute,
>   But know not what's resisted."

And it is but a very partial computation we can give even of what is done. We are ignorant of the larger portion of men's deeds. "We do not know half the acts of wickedness or of virtue of our most immediate friends. How little, comparatively speaking, does the world know of ourselves! Of how many of our best, and of our worst, actions and qualities are our most intimate associates utterly unconscious! How many virtues does the world give us credit for that we do not possess! How small a portion of our evil deeds ever come to light! Even of our few redeeming goodnesses, how large a portion is known only to God!" We are, then, in all cases ignorant of the majority of the facts, upon which an accurate moral judgment must depend.

But further, even if we were acquainted with the facts, we should be incapable of estimating correctly their moral significance. This is owing, partly, to the misleading influence of self-esteem. There is in each of us an ineradicable bias in favour of ourselves, and of everything belonging to ourselves. According to an old Indian legend, there once appeared among a nation of hunchbacks a young and beautiful god. The people gathered round him; and when they saw that his back was destitute of a hump, they began to hoot and jeer and taunt him. One of them however, more philosophical than the rest, said:

"My friends, what are we doing? Let us not insult this miserable creature. If heaven has made us beautiful, if it has adorned our backs with a mount of flesh, let us with pious gratitude repair to the temple and render our acknowledgments to the immortal gods." This quaint legend illustrates very forcibly some of the curious delusions resulting from self-esteem. We are apt to plume ourselves even on our defects. We are apt to condemn those who differ from us, merely because they differ. And as for those bad points in our own character which *even we* must acknowledge, we think them much less serious than they really are; we put them down to evil tendencies inherited from our forefathers, or to the force of unpropitious circumstances, while we make no such amiable allowances for the faults of other people. In a word, there is a large number of our shortcomings which we do not recognise at all, and with the rest we deal far too leniently. So that it will evidently go very hard with men, when we subject them to our moral criticism. We naturally compare them with ourselves: but the self which we use as a standard is not our real self; it is far too flattering to be correct. Our self-esteem for ever keeps us from thoroughly knowing ourselves.

But we are misled even more seriously by the difficulty of understanding others. It is simply impossible for us duly to appreciate the thoughts and feelings of those who are very differently constituted from ourselves. Try as we may, we shall never see things as they appear from an opposite point of view. We shall never be completely successful in ascertaining the condition of another's mind and heart. If men would only remember this, they would be saved from a good deal of religious intolerance. They fancy they are passing judgment on the facts of a case, when in reality they are but criticising their own distorted view of the facts. Beliefs and practices *mean more* to those who adopt them, than they can ever mean to those who are opposed to them. But this is so difficult to grasp. Broad Churchmen look upon Low Churchmen as fanatics, if not fools; and the latter return the compliment by regarding Broad Churchmen as infidels, if not atheists. And even when they do not go so far as this, each is apt to regard the other as a sort of mental or spiritual monstrosity, which it is surprising Providence should have permitted to exist. The impossibility of understanding or sympathising with those who greatly differ from ourselves, is strikingly illustrated in a poem called

"Hilda," by Dr Walter Smith, from which I extract the following verses:—

"'Twain are they sundered each from each,
　　Though oft together they are brought;
Discoursing in a common speech,
　　Yet having scarce a common thought.
The same sun warmed them all their days;
　　They breathe one air of life serene;
Yet moving in their several ways,
　　They walk with a whole world between.

I think they never meet without
　　Some sharp encounter of their wits;
And neither hints a faith or doubt
　　The other does not take to bits.
For what the one regards with awe,
　　The other holds a creed outworn;
And what this boasts as perfect law,
　　That turns to laughter with his scorn.

Thus on their several ways they go,
　　And neither other comprehends;
Yet it was God who made them so,
　　And they do serve His several ends.
That seeks for light to walk in it,
　　And this for God to live in Him;
One questions with a searching wit,
　　The other trusts where all is dim.'

Now if these two persons judge one another, their verdicts will most certainly be incorrect. The first will say that the second is impiously sceptical. The second will assert that the first is blasphemously credulous. And yet perhaps, in the sight of God, each may be doing the best he can to seek and to hold the truth.

We see then, do we not? that Christ's injunction is pre-eminently reasonable. The facts upon which a moral judgment should be based, are for the most part unknown to us, or known only in a distorted and untruthful form. And even if we were perfectly acquainted with the facts, we should be prevented, by the very constitution of our nature, from estimating them with the slightest approach to accuracy. In these days of spectroscopic analysis, you can obtain more certain knowledge about the composition of a distant star, than you can ever hope to obtain in regard to the moral worth of an intimate friend. What would you say of any one who asserted that he knew the exact value of all the land upon the earth's surface, when he did not know the extent of that surface, and was thoroughly acquainted only with a few square miles of it? The attempt to pass a moral judgment upon a fellow-creature is not a whit less impertinent, not a whit less absurd. A man's moral worth can be correctly and completely estimated by God alone. Therefore, judge not.

The Greatness of Man.

"When I consider Thy heavens, the work of Thy fingers, the moon and the stars, which Thou hast ordained; what is man, that Thou art mindful of him? and the son of man, that Thou visitest him? For" (or rather *but*) "Thou hast made him a little lower than the angels, and hast crowned him with glory and honour. Thou madest him to have dominion over the works of Thy hands; Thou hast put all things under his feet."
PSALM viii. 3-6.

OVER the professor's chair in the metaphysics class-room in the University of Edinburgh, where it was once my happiness to study, is inscribed the maxim, first uttered by Phavorinus:—

"On earth there is nothing great but man;
In man there is nothing great but mind."

That maxim is the lesson of our text. True greatness consists, not in weight and extension, but in intellectual power and moral worth. When the Psalmist looked up to the heavens, he was at first overwhelmed with a sense of his own littleness. The sun, moon and stars appeared to him so majestic, that he said, " Lord, what is man, that Thou art mindful of him ? and the son of man, that Thou visitest him ? " Man seemed, in comparison, insignificant and unworthy of the divine regard. But, on second thoughts, David perceived that this was an entire misconception of the matter, and that man could not be inferior to the heavens; for God had, in point of fact, made him only a little lower than the angels—than the Elohim, is the word in the Hebrew. This term, in the Elohistic portion of the Pentateuch, is applied to the Almighty instead of the term Jehovah. God had made man, we may therefore read, a little lower than Himself; had crowned him with glory and honour; had given him dominion over the works of His hands: and had put all things under his feet. So far from being insignificant in comparison with the heavens, man is of infinitely more value than they.

This is a lesson which constantly needs to be repeated. Many fall into the Psalmist's mistake, but comparatively few escape from it as satisfactorily as he did. You remember Bildad argues[1] as if human beings were altogether contemptible

[1] Job xxv. 5, 6.

when compared with the heavenly host. Even the stars, he says, are not pure in God's sight; how then can that worm man be pure? You will often hear Bildad's remark quoted, by well-meaning persons, as if it were a beautiful expression of humble piety. And this depreciation of mind in favour of matter is, likewise, a common failing with scientific investigators. Never, it seems to me, was there so much need to enforce the lesson of our text as there is to-day.

The progress of science has had a tendency to make us underrate our manhood. For our relations to time and space seem so paltry, when we compare them with those of the material world. If the Psalmist was overawed by the heavens, much more must they overawe thoughtful and imaginative minds in our own day! There are but 5932 stars visible to the naked eye, and David did not even suspect the existence of any others. His view of their origin was, that they were suddenly called into existence on a certain Thursday, two thousand years before the time of Noah. They were intended, he thought—the whole 5932 of them—to adorn his firmament or to light up his roads. Could he have heard the Lady in "Comus," he would have imagined that she was describing a scientific fact, when she speaks of the stars

> "That nature hung in heaven, and filled their lamps
> With everlasting oil, to give due light
> To the misled and lonely traveller."

How different are our heavens from his! The telescope has brought 75,000,000 of worlds within the range of human vision. We know that many of these are hundreds of times greater than our own sun; and there is every reason to believe that most of them (like him) have planets revolving around them. We know that the volume of the sun is $1\frac{1}{2}$ million times as large as that of the earth. We know it is so far distant, that if we could travel towards it day and night at the rate of 60 miles an hour, it could not be reached in less than 180 years. We know that Neptune is 30 times as far away from the sun as we are, and that therefore it would take any one at the same rate 5400 years to traverse the intervening space. Some of the *nearest* fixed stars are billions of miles away from us; so that if we travelled as before 60 miles an hour, it would require 90,000,000 of years to perform the journey. And we know that these so-called fixed stars are not really at rest, but that they are moving in orbits hundreds of millions of miles in diameter, which orbits, owing to the distance, appear to us like mere mathematical points.

The light from Sirius, though travelling, as all light travels, at the rate of 192 miles per second, takes 16 years to reach us. There is light about us to-day, which started on its course from some far-off world before we were born. And light is ever winging its way from yet more distant spheres, which, if it ever reaches us at all, will reveal the condition in which it left them ages and ages ago. Facts such as these, when we succeed in partially realising them for a moment in our imagination, give us an overwhelming sense of the vast tracts of space over which the physical universe extends.

Again its duration in time is no less stupendous than its extension in space. Myriads of ages ago our earth was a mass of molten liquid. Myriads of ages before that, it consisted entirely of glowing gas.[1] Myriads of ages hence, the fire that still remains in the interior will have burnt out; and when that internal source of heat has been exhausted, our globe will be no longer capable of maintaining animal or even vegetable life. "Then," says Mr R. A. Proctor, "her desert

[1] See 'Agnosticism,' pp. 105-112.

continents and frost-bound oceans will in some degree resemble the arid wastes which the astronomer recognises in the moon. Long as has been, and doubtless will be, the duration of life upon the earth, (and it has certainly existed for myriads and myriads of years), it seems less than a second when compared with those two awful time-intervals,—one past, when as yet life was not, and one future, when all life shall have passed away. Long after the earth has ceased to be the abode of life, other planets will become fitted for this purpose. Even these time-intervals will pass, however, until every planet in turn has been the source of busy life, and afterwards become inert and dead. Then, after the lapse perchance of a lifeless interval, compared with which all the past eras of the solar system were utterly insignificant, the time will arrive when the sun will be a fit abode for living creatures, and will continue so during ages infinite to our conceptions. We may even look forward to still more distant changes, seeing that the solar system is itself moving round an orbit, though the centre around which it travels is so distant that at present it remains unknown. The end, seemingly so remote, to which our earth is tending —the end, infinitely more remote, towards which the solar system is tending—the end of our galaxy—the end of systems of such galaxies as ours,—are but the beginnings of fresh eras comparable with themselves. The wave of life which is now passing over our earth is but a ripple on the sea of life within the solar system; and that sea of life is but a wavelet on the great ocean of life that is coextensive with the universe."

And if, as is believed by some, our earth is being slowly forced nearer to the sun, into which it will ultimately fall,—a similar fate being in store for the whole solar system, for the system of which that forms a part, and so on *ad infinitum;* if this be so, then Shelley's magnificent verse will be literally true;

> "Worlds on worlds are rolling ever
> From creation to decay,
> Like the bubbles on a river,
> Sparkling, bursting, borne away."

In the presence of such thoughts as these one is tempted, like the Psalmist, to say in despair, "What is man?" We, who are considered tall if we are seventy-two inches high, who cannot walk faster than three or four miles an hour, who die almost as soon as we are born, must feel very, very insignificant, if we look only at our relations with space or time, and then compare ourselves in these respects with galaxies of worlds. We shall be inclined to adopt the poet's words,—

> " See how beneath the moonbeam's smile
>   Yon little billow heaves its breast,
> And foams and sparkles for a while,
>   And murmuring then subsides to rest.
> Thus man, the sport of bliss and care,
>   Rises on time's eventful sea,
> And having swelled a moment there,
>   Then melts into eternity."

This kind of sentiment is just now in the air. *E.g.*, one of the characters in Buchanan's 'New Abelard,' speaks as if we were too insignificant and contemptible for immortality. "Shall we survive," she asks, "while suns go out like sparks, and the void is sown with the wrecks of worn-out worlds?" And I daresay most of you remember the following passage in 'Natural Religion': "The more," says the gifted author of that remarkable book, "the more our thoughts widen and deepen, as the universe grows upon us and we become accustomed to boundless space and time, the more petrifying is the contrast of our own insignificance, the more contemptible become the pettiness, shortness and fragility of the individual life. A moral paralysis creeps upon us. For a while we comfort ourself with the notion of self-sacrifice; we say, What matter if I pass, let me think of others! But the *other* has become contemptible no less than the self; all human griefs alike seem little worth assuaging, human happiness too paltry at the best to be worth increasing. The whole moral world is reduced to a point; the spiritual city, 'the goal of all the saints,' dwindles to the 'least of little stars'; good and evil, right and wrong, become infinitesimal, ephemeral matters; while eternity and infinity remain attributes of that only which is outside the realm of morality. Life becomes more intolerable the more we know and discover, so long as everything widens and deepens except our own duration, and that remains as pitiful as ever. The affections die away in a world where everything great and enduring is cold; they die of their own conscious feebleness and bootlessness." And I might give you many more illustrations. One of the most striking characteristics of the modern mind is the tendency to think less of man, in proportion as larger views have to be taken of the universe in which man dwells. Human beings are often nowadays regarded as mere ripples upon the infinite ocean of matter.

But this way of looking at things seems to me thoroughly erroneous—I may say absurdly erroneous. It assumes that we have nothing on which to pride ourselves except our physical extension and our physical weight. It assumes that we are merely small masses of matter. But our real glory lies in that which is not material, in that which is absolutely destitute of extension and weight—viz., in our mental powers. The proper comparison to make, is not between the small bulk of a human being and the vast bulk of the material world, but between a human being who has a mind and the material world which has not. Why should we be depressed by the knowledge we have acquired of the physical greatness of the universe? That very knowledge is a proof of our own more amazing glory. The material universe does not know itself. We know both ourselves and it. And since, further, we are endowed with sensibility, imagination, memory, hope, affection, reason, conscience, will —and the material world is not so endowed— *we* are in reality great, *it* is comparatively insignificant. A single human soul infinitely transcends in importance the entire universe of matter. If we would but remember this, the more progress that we made in science, the more we should be elevated and cheered—the more we should be stimulated to walk worthy of the vocation wherewith we have been called.

That there is not the slightest incompatibility between true science and true religion, was long ago seen and acknowledged by our illustrious fellow-countryman, whose remains were last week received into Westminster Abbey.[1] No one was ever more worthy of that honour—the last and greatest honour which the world can pay. The writings of Charles Darwin are supposed, by those who have never read them, to be subversive of faith in a Creator. This is precisely the opposite of the truth. There are no books so full of illustrations of the design and purpose and adaptation to be found everywhere in nature,— no books, therefore, which give one such an exalted view of the wisdom and beneficence of God. I cannot but regard it as a most happy omen that the author of the 'Origin of Species' should have been buried where he was, and that men like Canon Farrar and Professor Huxley should have stood side by side at his tomb. I cannot but see in it a prophecy that science and religion, after so many centuries of conflict, will before long learn to understand and love one another,

[1] This sermon was preached the Sunday after Darwin's funeral.

and that, even in your time and mine, they may be joined in a happy and indissoluble union.

But though there is no necessary incompatibility between science and religion, though a growing knowledge of the physical universe need not make us despise ourselves, but should rather give us a deeper sense of our God-given dignity and glory,—yet it must be confessed that many modern scientists have been too much engrossed with the marvels of the macrocosm. The still greater wonders of the microcosm have been ignored or forgotten. The language of very many thinkers nowadays is the first hasty utterance of the Psalmist—" What is man ?" And the answer they give to the question is this: Man is but a mote in the sunbeam, a grain of sand in the desert, a ripple upon an infinite ocean, an atom in immensity. They forget that he is an atom which feels and knows and thinks, which imagines and reasons and hopes and loves, an atom that can transcend its normal limits in space and " dwell far in the unapparent " in communion with the Unseen, an atom that believes itself endowed with " the power of an endless life." The Psalmist, on second thoughts, perceived that his feeling of despondency had been illegitimate. " Thou madest man," he continues, "a little lower than Thyself; Thou gavest him a nature like Thine own, differing in degree rather than in kind; Thou crownedst him with glory and honour; Thou madest him to have dominion over the works of Thy hands; Thou hast put all things under his feet."

This will be the ultimate conclusion of the deepest and clearest thinkers. The profoundest philosopher America has produced, who has recently been taken to his rest in a ripe old age, combined in a remarkable degree the intensest appreciation of nature with the intensest appreciation of man. No one ever thought more of nature than did Emerson; but he believed, truly enough, that she derived much of her glory from her relation to us. "O rich and various man," he exclaims, "thou palace of sight and sound, carrying in thy senses the morning and the night and the unfathomable galaxy, in thy brain the geometry of the city of God, in thy heart the power of love and the realms of right and wrong!"

The doctrine of man's paltriness is no less pernicious than erroneous. So morbid a belief must react injuriously upon character. There is nothing more enervating than depression; and the worst form of depression is self-contempt. In one of his most interesting letters of advice to a young convert, Pelagius says he will begin by laying down what human nature can do, lest from an insufficient conception of its powers, too low a standard of duty and exertion should be taken. Men are careless, he says, in proportion as they think meanly of themselves; and for this reason the sacred writers often endeavour to animate us by styling us "sons of God." Pelagius was right. We should resist every attempt, whether proceeding from scientists or religionists, to make us take a paltry view of our place in the universe. Such attempts can only proceed from science or religion falsely so called. They are based, as I have shown, upon an untrue assumption. They are condemned alike by fact and by Scripture. And if we allow ourselves to be influenced by them, the result will be disastrous in the extreme. If we believe that we are more insignificant than the dead and mindless world around us, we shall never give ourselves much trouble about character. A certain amount of prudence, of course, is necessary for self-preservation, and for procuring the esteem of our fellow-men, without which life would be unendurable. So far, we may be prudent—or, as it would be euphemistically called, virtuous. But beyond this we shall not care to go. On the other hand, if we remember that our spiritual nature is akin to God's, made only a little lower than His, made perhaps as nearly like His own as it was possible for God Himself to make it, then we are stimulated to cultivate the manhood with which we have been endowed—to *agonise*, if need be, till we become perfect, even as He is perfect.

Punishment.

"God is a consuming fire."—HEBREWS xii. 29.
"God is love."—1 JOHN iv. 16.

ARE these two statements reconcilable with one another, and with the facts of experience? They *seem* to be contradictory; but they are not, on that account, to be rejected—for an apparent paradox is often the most accurate expression of the truth. We get into the way of dwelling upon one side or aspect of a truth, either because that aspect has been most frequently brought under our notice, or because it is most congenial to our habits of thought and modes of feeling; and at last we forget—if we ever knew—that the truth has other, equally important, aspects. The complete truth is of course very different from our one-sided and distorted view of it. One half of a truth, if mistaken for the whole, is equivalent to falsehood. This is illustrated by the celebrated quarrel regarding the nature of a certain shield. One person said it was made of gold, and another that it was made of silver. They were both right, and both wrong. They had been looking at it from different points of view; and one had seen only the inside which was silver, the other only the outside which was gold. The attainment of perfect truth always involves a combination of partial views, and often requires the reconciliation of apparently irreconcilable facts. Till we have reconciled the contradiction however, till we have removed the difficulty, we cannot accept them both. And it is just as impossible to hold a *theological* contradiction as to think that twice two make five. If a man professes to believe statements which appear to him to be contradictory, he is not manifesting faith, he is, in plain English, telling a lie. Before he can actually believe seemingly contradictory statements, before he can do anything more than dishonestly profess to believe them, he must be shown that the apparent contradiction is not real, that the statements, though seemingly irreconcilable, are in fact only different aspects of one and the self-same truth. And since truth is many-sided, we are never more likely to attain it than when we are examining seeming paradoxes.

Now our text sounds paradoxical. Let us inquire if these two apparently irreconcilable statements can be brought into harmony.

That "God is a consuming fire" cannot be doubted. The *nature* of the unseen Power that punishes the wrong-doer will always be a matter for controversy; but the fact that retribution, in some form or other, follows sin, has never been and can never be disputed. Professor Huxley, in one of his lay sermons, has the following striking passage: "The happiness of every one of us, and more or less of those connected with us, depends upon our knowing something of the rules of a game, infinitely more complex than chess. It is a game which has been played for untold ages, every man and woman of us being one of the two players in a game of his or her own. The chess-board is the world, the pieces are the phenomena of the universe, the rules of the game are what we call the laws of nature. The player on the other side is hidden from us. We know that his play is always fair, just and patient. But also we know, to our cost, that he never overlooks a mistake or makes the smallest allowance for ignorance. To the man who plays well, the highest stakes are paid, with that sort of overflowing generosity with which the strong shows delight in strength. And one who plays ill is checkmated, without haste but without remorse."

The fact of punishment, then, is indisputable. The only question admitting of controversy is this, Can punishment be traced to any reasonable and intelligible cause?

The most common view perhaps has been, that the invisible Power, who works against the sinner, is a spiteful and revengeful Being, dispensing pain and anguish in haughty anger that His commands have been disobeyed. For example, Tacitus, in speaking of some great disasters which had befallen the Roman arms, says: "It is evidently not our welfare that the gods have at heart, but the due retribution of our crimes." And unfortunately a similar doctrine has not unfrequently been taught by professedly Christian theologians. "There are people," says Diderot, " of whom we must not say that they fear God, but that they are frightened of Him. Considering the picture that is sometimes drawn for us of the Supreme Being, of His readiness to anger, of the fury of His vengeance, of the great numbers of those whom He allows to perish, as compared with the few to whom He is pleased to stretch forth a saving hand,—the most righteous soul must be tempted to wish that He did not exist."

I am sorry to say it, but say it I must, that the blackest devil ever described or imagined would be adorable, in comparison with the horrible caricature of Deity which some have professed and endeavoured to worship, under the mistaken opinion that He was the God revealed by Christ. I know of nothing sadder, nothing more shocking, in the history of religion, than the general prevalence of degrading and blasphemous conceptions of the Almighty. They are often instilled into children, consciously or unconsciously, almost as soon as they can speak. A little Scotch girl, five or six years of age, was reproved by her mother for doing something wrong, and was told that God would not be pleased with her if she did it. "Pooh!" she said, "God will be too busy *burning up the bad people* to attend to me." Now that child—I can vouch for the truth of the story—was the granddaughter of a Scotch minister, had received what would be called religious instruction, and yet she thought of God as a being whose main business, whose supreme delight, consisted in "burning up the bad people." And this is no solitary instance. Would to God that it were! A great many grown-up persons hold similar views, and they find much to countenance them in the pages of certain theologians. The laws of the being whom these writers call God, are represented as the mere arbitrary exactions of His caprice. He does not command or forbid things because they are essentially right or wrong; but, on the contrary, the terms right and wrong mean only that certain things have been commanded or forbidden by Him out of pure self-will. He punishes every dereliction from His statutes, simply and solely from motives of wrathful vindictiveness. His very "love" is the crowning proof of the meanness of His nature; for the few rare individuals upon whom He chooses to bestow it are selected at random, without the slightest show of reason; not because they deserve to be loved; not in order that, by being loved, they may be purified and ennobled: no, He selects them simply and solely for the gratification of what is called "His glory." Such a blasphemous representation of the Deity, Milton justly puts into the mouth of the hideous sorceress (the personification of sin) whom he represents as guarding the gates of hell. She speaks to Satan of

> "Him who sits above and laughs the while
> At thee, ordained His drudge, to execute
> Whate'er His wrath (which He calls justice) bids."

If justice were synonymous with wrath, it could not be divine. Ages ago Protagoras said, "None but a beast would punish merely because evil had been done." If the unseen Being who punished our wrong-doing consumed in order to destroy, if He were *satisfied* by wringing out agony from erring hearts, He would be not Love but Hate, not a God but a Fiend. And if such a Being *were* the strongest Power in the universe, it would be the bounden duty of every true man, not to worship but to execrate Him, not to obey Him but to resist Him—if need be, even unto death. In that case, it is to be hoped there would always be

> "Souls who dared look the omnipotent tyrant in
> His everlasting face, and tell him that
> His evil was not good.

There is a very striking passage on this subject in John Stuart Mill's 'Examination of Sir William Hamilton's Philosophy.' "If, instead of the glad tidings that there is a Being in whom all the excellences which the human mind can conceive exist in a degree inconceivable to us, I am informed that the world is ruled by a Being whose attributes are infinite, but what they are we cannot learn, nor what are the principles of His government, except that the highest human morality which we are capable of conceiving does not sanction them,—convince me of it, and I will bear my fate as I may. But when I am told that I must believe this, and at the same time call this Being by the names which express and affirm the highest human morality, I say in plain terms that I will not. Whatever power such a Being may have over me, there is one thing which He shall not do,—He shall not compel me to worship Him. I will call no Being good who is not what I mean when I apply that epithet to my fellow-creatures; and if such a Being can sentence me to hell for not so calling Him, to hell I will go." A noble sentiment, though one curiously inconsistent with utilitarianism, which asserts pleasure to be the sole end of life. This is one of many passages in Mill's writings which go to prove that he was wiser and nobler than he knew. It is precisely the sentiment of the prophet Isaiah : "Woe unto them that call evil good, and good evil; that put darkness for light and light for darkness, bitter for sweet and sweet for bitter."

But neither the facts of experience nor the

statements of the Bible, rightly understood, give any countenance to the theory that the world is governed by a tyrant. In the 'Lay Sermons,' from which I just now quoted, Professor Huxley continues: "My metaphor [about the invisible player] will remind some of you of the celebrated picture, in which Retzsch depicted Satan playing at chess with a man for his soul. Substitute for the mocking fiend in that picture a calm strong angel, who is playing for love (as we say) and who would rather lose than win, and I should accept it as an image of human life." Or rather, I would suggest, substitute a being stronger and calmer than an angel, who not only would rather lose than win, but who aims solely at enabling us to be victorious, and whose condign punishment of false moves has no other purpose than to teach us our folly and make us wiser for the future.

There is nothing more needful than punishment for the wellbeing of the human race. The necessity for it could not have been avoided by any conceivable possibility. Our moral freedom, without which we should have been merely animals or machines, carries with it inevitably the liability to sin. Sin is injurious to us, because the pleasure that follows from it is at best of a low type, and has to be paid for by a too prodigal expenditure of pain. Theft, murder, adultery, evil-speaking, lying, and so on, must from their very nature be prejudicial to the welfare of society, with which the welfare of every individual member is inextricably involved. Imagine, *e.g.*, a lawless tribe of savages. Particular members of this tribe might, for a time, find pleasure in robbing their friends and murdering their enemies, but it could not be long before the tribe was annihilated. Any supernatural interference to ward off the punishments of crime would soon lead to the destruction of society. And just as punishment is necessary for the welfare of society in general, so is it necessary for the self-development of every individual in particular. It lies in the very nature of things that duty and inclination must sometimes be incompatible; and a noble character is only to be achieved by the sacrifice of inclination, when it would interfere with duty. Now, nothing can afford us a stronger inducement to resist temptation, nothing can be a greater help to us in our moral conflicts, than the *certain knowledge* that suffering, sooner or later and in various forms, will inevitably follow sin. From the greatest punishment of wrong-doing—namely, the deterioration of our character—God Himself could not save us; no, not even by a miracle. It is conceivable that He might interfere so as to save us from *some* of the consequences of our evil deeds. It is conceivable, for example, that He might refrain from visiting us with those pangs of conscience, which may be supposed to come more directly and immediately from Himself. But were He to do so, He would be inflicting on us the greatest possible injury: He would be doing his best to destroy us. The withdrawal of punishments would prevent us from achieving that character which is the one thing worth living for, and without which we may well be described, in the emphatic language of the Bible, as being lost, as having perished.

It is very often stated, by persons who profess to be expounding the doctrines of Christ, that God is Justice as well as Love. The Bible does not say so. It merely says that God is just. The meaning of this distinction we may take to be, that justice is not something opposed to love, but is rather its necessary outcome. It is just that the sinner should be punished in proportion to his sin, because only in this way can he be saved from that sin, which is the consummation that love desires. In other words, just punishments may be regarded as expressions of love. I forget who it is who says, "A God all mercy is a God unjust." If by mercy he meant withholding punishment, we may say with equal truth, "A God all mercy is a God unkind." "Nothing emboldens sin," says one of Shakespeare's characters, "so much as mercy." But to do anything that emboldens sin is in reality to act most unmercifully. Eli, in the treatment of his children, is a type, not of affection, but of indifference. It is only a sickly sentimentalism that withholds punishment, when punishment would be useful. God is too merciful for this. "Whom the Lord *loveth* He chasteneth."

Plato, in his 'Gorgias,' argues, in reference to the punishments inflicted by society, that the man who manages to avoid them is to be pitied; for, as vice is a disease of the soul and punishment is its cure, he who gets off scot-free is left, so far as society is concerned, to die of his disease. And we may argue in a similar manner regarding punishments in general. Just as the caustic applied by a physician is meant to destroy the disease which might otherwise destroy the body, so the fire of retribution is intended to consume the sin which might else consume the sinner—which might eat away his manhood, and leave him wasted, marred, ruined, lost. God is not "satisfied" with the suffering that follows sin. The suffering is merely a means to an end, and that end is joy. God's glory can be no selfish pride. It must consist in the welfare of His creatures. "The Lord's portion is His people." Hence, as Faber has finely said—

> "God's justice is the *gladdest* thing
>   Creation can behold.
>
> .   .   .   .   .   .
>
> There is a wideness in His mercy
>   Like the wideness of the sea;
> There is a *kindness* in His justice
>   Which is more than liberty."

So the two apparently contradictory statements of our text are really quite consistent. The first is a corollary easily deducible from the second. If God be love, He *must* punish. Hence the fact of punishment is not an argument *against* the divine benevolence, but an additional argument for it. On the one hand, a retributive fire, consuming only to destroy, would be diabolical. On the other hand, a love which withheld the punishment essential to our wellbeing would be contemptible, and equally destructive. It would harm us while meaning to be kind. Out of pity it would ruin us. The love which consumes *in order to save* is alone worthy of being called divine.

As long as the universe contains a single sinner, the fire of love must be a consuming fire.

The Gifts of the Spirit.

"There are diversities of gifts, but the same Spirit. There are differences of administrations [or rather services], but the same Lord. There are diversities of operations [or workings], but it is the same God which worketh all in all. . . . The manifestation of the Spirit is given to every man to profit withal."
—1 Con. xii. 4-7.

INTELLECTUAL progress consists in discovering the unity which underlies all diversity. In early ages the world seemed a chaos. Everything appeared to be totally different from everything else. Thousands and tens of thousands of conflicting agents were supposed to be at work in the production of natural phenomena. The woods appertained to one set of deities— the dryades; the mountains to another set— the oreades. Every star and every planet had a moving principle peculiar to itself. Storms and earthquakes, pestilences and eclipses, were thought to be the work of a variety of beings, who were guided by all sorts of different motives, and whose future action it was absolutely impossible to predict. There were gods many and lords many, who found in the material universe a convenient playground for their manifold caprices. The history of science records the gradual discovery in this primeval chaos of the unifying principle of Law. Over and over again, phenomena that seemed altogether dissimilar, have turned out to be merely different operations of one and the self-same force. The apple, which falls to the ground, once seemed to have nothing in common with the moon, which does not so fall. But now we know that both are equally under the control of gravity; that the moon is attracted no less than the apple; and that the tendency to fall earthwards, produced in it by this attraction, is one of the factors determining its course. Whenever we compare phenomena—no matter how distant they may be from each other in time or space, no matter how diverse they may at first sight appear—we now always expect to find in them an underlying unity of thought and purpose and mode of working; and sooner or later these expectations are fulfilled. In a word, throughout the entire physical universe, there are diversities of operations but the same reign of law.

This unity in the midst of diversity is to be

found also in the spiritual sphere. There are diversities of gifts, says the apostle, but the same Spirit. The enumeration of these gifts, a few verses later on, is not of course intended to be exhaustive, but merely illustrative. Those which St Paul mentions may be roughly divided into two classes. The first, or secular class, includes the gifts of teaching, of healing and of government. The second, or religious class, includes those of prophecy and of tongues. What this last precisely was, I do not know. But there would seem to have been a very great and unholy emulation among the Corinthian Christians to possess it. They looked upon it as a peculiarly spiritual endowment. St Paul was anxious to show them that this state of mind was foolish and wrong. The gift of tongues, he says, is only one of many spiritual gifts, and by no means the best. He declares that in comparison with charity, or the enthusiasm of man for man, this highly coveted gift of tongues is nothing worth. He mentions a crucial test by which spiritual gifts may be known, and their relative value determined. "The manifestation of the Spirit is given to every man to profit withal;"—that is, as we see from the context, for the purpose of doing good therewith. Even a secular endowment, such as the power of healing, becomes a gift of the Spirit to him who is desirous of using it worthily—of using it for the welfare of his fellow-men. Such a desire is an inspiration that can only come from above, and this inspiration transforms what would otherwise be a mere natural endowment into a sacred spiritual gift. The mistake of the Corinthians was similar to one that is not uncommon in the present day. It is sometimes imagined that a man in holy orders is, *in virtue of those orders*, a better Christian than a layman, that a clergyman as such is, in an especial degree, under the guidance of the Spirit of God. So foolish and unscriptural a supposition is not at all necessary, in order to vindicate the usefulness of the clergy as a class of teachers. If in the choice of his profession a clergyman has followed the guidance of his natural inclinations and sympathies and gifts, and if he has made a good use of his education and of his leisure, he will often be able, in cases of mental or spiritual difficulty, to render the greatest assistance to men, who have had to devote the most of their time and the best of their energies to purely secular pursuits. But after all, even in spiritual matters, there is no exclusively clerical prerogative. I pity the clergyman who has not sometimes been ministered unto, when he went to minister. If he has never been taught by a layman some spiritual lesson, more valuable than any he was able at the time to impart, the chances are that he is not a specially inspired priest, but rather a peculiarly obtuse man. *Profitableness*, according to the apostle, is the sole test and criterion of spiritual gifts. He is the most highly gifted man who does the most good. Human endowments are very diverse, but in so far as the world is made better by them, they are all to be regarded as divinely bestowed. There are diversities of gifts, but it is the same Spirit from whom they have all been derived.

And further, not only do different gifts proceed from the same Spirit, but there are different developments of the self-same gift. Let us take, for example, the instinct of worship. If anything deserves to be called pre-eminently a gift of the Spirit, it is surely the tendency in the human heart to recognise and reverence God. Yet the developments of this instinct are various in the extreme. The instinct is God's work, the development of the instinct is man's. The office of the Spirit, you will observe, is not to provide us with an infallible set of doctrines or an immaculate set of actions. His work is to give us powers, instincts, emotions, and sentiments, which will be differently developed in different individuals.

> "God fulfils Himself in many ways,
> Lest one good custom should corrupt the world."

There would be no use in our receiving a certain set of opinions, however correct; there would be no advantage in our having a certain set of actions extorted from us, however excellent. Barren uniformity is death. Our spiritual life consists essentially in our *co-operation* with God. And the co-operation of different individuals, under different circumstances, leads of necessity to a diversity of opinions and of practices. For instance, the attempt to form a conception of God is, in every case, due to the divinely given instinct of worship, but the conceptions actually formed will vary according to circumstances. Some men will be so anxious to represent God to themselves, that they will give too much licence to their imaginations, and thus tend to anthropomorphism; others will be so fearful of irreverence, that they will scarcely venture to assign Him any determinate attributes, and thus tend to pantheism You remember Lord Houghton's words—

> 'It must be that the light divine,
> That on your soul is pleased to shine,
> Is other than what falls on mine.
>
> For you can fix and formalise
> The Power to which you raise your eyes,
> And trace Him in His palace skies.
>
> You can perceive, and almost touch,
> His attributes as such and such,
> Almost familiar over-much.
>
> You can His thoughts and acts display,
> In fair historical array,
> From Adam to the judgment-day.
>
> I cannot think Him here or there;
> I think Him ever everywhere,
> Unfading light, unstifled air."

We probably think both these conceptions erroneous, and have another of our own. And yet it is not the light divine that varies; the difference lies in the medium through which it comes to us—the medium, viz., of our previous training. Thus very different conceptions of God may be the outcome of the same yearning after Him, the same delight in communion with Him; in other words, there may be different developments of the same spiritual gift.

So it is, too, in regard to the outward forms and ceremonies of worship. All emotions, both natural and spiritual, may be very variously expressed. Some, for example, mourn for the departed in black raiment, others in white; some, when they would pay respect, uncover their heads, others uncover their feet; some, if they are strongly moved, try and make the greatest possible show of their feelings, and pour forth their sentiments in a torrent of words, while others endeavour to assume a preternatural calmness—nothing short of silence can express the intensity of their emotion. Similarly, the self-same desire to honour God, may manifest itself in the most diverse ways. Some will think it necessary to go through the most elaborate ritual, while to others a bald simplicity will seem more in harmony with the solemnity of worship. Some will feel that music draws them heavenwards, others that it ties them down to earth. Some will find that they can hardly pray without a set form of words, others that they can hardly pray *with* it. And so it may come about that two men, equally anxious to honour God, may adopt quite opposite modes of doing so. There are diversities of workings, and yet it is the same God who worketh.

What we have to look for in the spiritual, as in the physical, sphere, is not uniformity but unity—unity manifested through diversity.

Just as in nature, the action of any single law is exhibited in a countless variety of forms, some of which may seem at first sight to violate it; so in religion, the self-same gift, the work of the same Spirit, leads to the most diverse opinions and the most dissimilar modes of worship. Just as in nature, under the influence of forces identically the same, there is a constantly progressive evolution of higher forms of life; so in religion, under the influence of the one Spirit, there is a continual development of more accurate opinions and more excellent practices. Creeds and rituals may differ, and do differ of course, in moral value; and yet, so far as they are honestly held and honestly performed, they may all be regarded as developments of the same divinely implanted instincts, of the same divinely inspired emotions.

This is a lesson which many find it very hard to learn. They imagine uniformity to be a necessary test of the divine operations. They suppose that the Spirit of God can only be manifested through certain opinions and practices, more or less similar to their own. Some time ago, the author of a book upon religious denominations was told that, in a particular village in the north of Scotland, he would find a small sect which was rapidly becoming extinct, but the members of which felt quite sure that they alone were in the way of salvation. He went to the village in question, and was there directed to a cottage, in which lived the chief representative of the expiring sect. The great man happened to be out, so the visitor entered into conversation with his wife. He said he had been given to understand that the sect to which she belonged was small in numbers. To this she assented, explaining that there had been defection after defection from unsoundness of views, till at last, as she pathetically put it, "There is only just myself and Jock left, and I'm na sae very sure o' Jock." Now we may smile at the ridiculous narrow-mindedness of this foolish old woman, who supposed that she was the only person in the universe whom God had vouchsafed to instruct; but after all, she is merely an extreme illustration of a state of mind that is by no means uncommon. There are, unhappily, very many who delight in reducing the operations of the Spirit to a minimum. They seem to find supreme comfort in the assurance that He is working only in the select few, who agree in doctrine and in practice with themselves.

It is sometimes urged against the Church of England as a great disgrace, that it embraces those who hold the most diverse opinions and adopt the most diverse practices. But this is in reality our Church's greatest glory. "A wise man," said Bacon, " will sometimes hear ignorant persons disputing, and know well within himself that their meaning is the same, though in words they cannot agree about it. We may well suppose, then, that God above seeth in some men's contradictions that they intend the same thing, and accepteth of both." If there be anything in which we may take a holy pride, it is in the fact that our Church has succeeded in partially mastering this lesson — the hardest lesson in the school of Christ. But broad as our communion is undoubtedly becoming, the Spirit's influences are infinitely broader still. God's "tender mercies are over all His works." In heaven, if not on earth, men will discover that their differences were much less, and their agreement much greater, than at the time appeared. All honest, earnest seekers after God are in heart united, whether they know it or not. Though distinct as the billows, they are one as the sea; though distinct as the colours of the rainbow, they are one as the pure white light which those colours compose. The mount of Truth has many paths. Those who are ascending by different ways look too often upon each other with suspicion and contempt. But they will all be led onwards and upwards by the Holy Ghost, till eventually they find themselves standing side by side before the throne of the Eternal.

"The saints of many a warring creed
    At last in heaven have learned,
That all paths to the Father lead
    Where Self the feet have spurned.

Moravian hymn and Roman chant
    In one devotion blend,
To speak the soul's eternal want
    Of Him, the inmost Friend.
One prayer soars cleansed with martyr fire,
    One choked with sinner's tears;
In heaven both meet in one desire,
    And God one music hears.

Whilst thus I dream, the bells clash out
    Upon the Sabbath air,—
Each seems a hostile faith to shout,
    A selfish form of prayer.
My dream is shattered; yet who knows,
    But in that heaven so near,
These discords find harmonious close
    In God's atoning ear?"

The Triune God.

"The Father, the Son, and Holy Ghost."—MATT. xxviii. 19.

CHRIST commanded the disciples to baptise their converts in the name of the Father, the Son, and the Holy Ghost. He did so, because these three sacred names sum up all that is most fundamental in the Christian faith. They represent to us the whole of the divine operations, so far as we are concerned. God in Nature, God in Christ, God in our own hearts; God the Creator, God the Atoner, God the Sanctifier; this is the God in whom we, as Christians, profess to believe. Let us examine our belief in detail.

First of all, God is in Nature.[1] Men may know that He exists, and may know something about Him, from a study of the external world alone. The order, regularity, and above all the

---

[1] For the complete proof of this assertion, see my 'Agnosticism,' part i.; 'Belief in God,' chaps. iv. and v.; and 'Personality,' section 4.

progressive development which modern science has brought to light, demand some explanation. He who can find it in blind atoms must have a mind that is easily satisfied. No profound thinker was ever an atheist. Nature does not, it is true, tell us what is the kind of connection between God and the world. Whether the forces of the material universe are parts of His own essential power, or something quite different from Himself; whether they were *made* by Him, or merely *used*, Nature does not say. But according to the teaching both of common-sense and of the highest criticism, she does declare that these forces are in some way controlled and governed by a Mind and Will. The results produced by their interaction are such as intelligence might be supposed to aim at; and contrariwise, it would be flying in the face of all experience to imagine that these results have been brought about by the fortuitous play of unintelligent atoms. Plain, unsophisticated men have always seen God in Nature, and so have the deepest and most original thinkers. But a little thought, just like a little learning, is a dangerous thing. Atheism is the product of careless and superficial thinking. In defence of the assertion that profound thinkers have always been theists, I might quote the opinions of the ablest men in antiquity; but, lest any one should detract from the value of these quotations, by saying that their authors would have been wiser if they had lived in the nineteenth century, let me rather refer to two of the leaders of modern science—viz., to Herbert Spencer and Charles Darwin, whom no one will accuse either of being behind the age or being prejudiced in favour of theology. "The belief," says Herbert Spencer "common to all religions, in the omnipresence of something which passes comprehension, is a belief which the most unsparing criticism leaves unquestioned, or rather makes even clearer. It has nothing to fear from the most inexorable logic; but, on the contrary, it is a belief which the most inexorable logic shows to be more profoundly true than any religion supposes." "No man," said Darwin, "can stand in the tropic forests without feeling that they are temples filled with the varied productions of the God of nature, and that there is more in man than the breath of his body."

Further, Nature suggests the fatherliness of this omnipresent Power. I mentioned to you before [1] that the old Aryans, before the dawn of

[1] See p. 188.

history, had a word in their language, *Dyaus-pitar*, which meant Heaven-Father. There was a survival of this idea among the Greeks and Romans, in the words "Zeupater" and "Jupiter." The same conception is found among the Semitic races, or at any rate in one of them. It is, as I said just now, an idea suggested by Nature. He who is perceived to be controlling and guiding things, is also perceived to be controlling and guiding them with a view to the wellbeing of sentient and intelligent creatures. The happiness of these creatures may be seen to be *at least one* of the ends for which Nature exists and works. This has been admitted by many who are popularly regarded as altogether hostile to religion. It was acknowledged even by John Stuart Mill, in spite of his constitutional tendency to pessimism. "Endeavouring," he says, "to look at the question without partiality or prejudice, and without allowing wishes to have any influence over judgment, . . . there does appear to be a preponderance of evidence that the Creator desires the pleasure of His creatures. This is indicated by the fact that pleasure, of one description or another, is afforded by almost everything. The mere play of the faculties, physical and mental, is a never-ending source of pleasure. Even painful things may give pleasure, by the satisfaction of curiosity and the agreeable sense of acquiring knowledge. And moreover pleasure, when experienced, seems to result from the normal working of the machinery; while pain usually arises from some external interference with it—from the collision of the organism with some outward force, to which it was not intended that it should be exposed." And, lastly—a point which Mill does not notice—pain is necessary as a stimulus to self-preservation; it is required as a warning, to make us avoid conduct which would be injurious or fatal. All this leads to the conclusion that the great omnipresent Power has exercised a kindly thoughtfulness for our welfare,—that we may, in a word, venture to call Him by the name of Father. And let me ask you to notice that, *apart from this fatherliness*, the Power underlying Nature would not be entitled to the name of God. There is nothing divine in mere strength; that may be possessed by a mass of dirt. There is nothing divine in wisdom and skill, as such; since they may be used for purposes of torture. Power and wisdom will suffice to make a devil, but not a God. Nature however does more than exhibit to us power and skill; she suggests a kindly intention toward us, a thoughtful consideration for us on the part of her Author: and in doing so, she makes us conscious of a God.

But the teaching of Nature is not altogether unmistakable. The forces of the material world sometimes work against us, as well as for us. Their beneficent results are visible only upon the whole, and not in all the details of their operation. Some have suggested that matter was intractable—unwilling, as Plato put it, to receive the divine ideas. Theologians have often maintained that Nature was corrupted by the Fall. But, be the cause what it may, the world around us has sometimes suggested a capricious injustice, instead of a fatherly beneficence. And even if this apparent contradiction in the teaching of Nature had never arisen, even if she had always declared unwaveringly in favour of the divine Fatherhood,—she could never have afforded a *complete* revelation of the Deity. The character of a person cannot be fully unfolded in any impersonal work. Hence God, though suggested by Nature, was only fully revealed by Humanity; the Father is completely known only through the Son.

In almost every age and country there have

been men like Isaiah, or Zoroaster, or the psalmists—men possessed by a passionate enthusiasm for righteousness, and who declared that there was a righteous Being at the heart of things, with whom they themselves were in personal communion. The Jewish nation, in particular, was remarkable for a long succession of these spiritual seers, which culminated eventually in Christ. "God, who at sundry times and in divers manners spake in time past unto the fathers by the prophets, hath in these last days spoken unto us by His Son."

Account for it how you may, the character and life and work of Christ are unique, unique to such an extent that He deserves to be called *the* Son of God. In a far higher sense than any earlier or later prophet could attach to the words, He was able to say—" I and my Father are one; he that hath seen me hath seen the Father." Hence it is through Christ that we may pre-eminently be said to have "received the atonement";[1] for it is pre-eminently through Him that we have come to know the real nature of God. Though the Fatherhood of God had been revealed in Nature, it had been revealed so dimly that it required a poet or a seer to

[1] See pp. 213-225.

discover it.[1] In Christ it became so plain that "the wayfaring man, though a fool," need not mistake it. The conception of the divine Fatherhood belongs nominally to the Jewish dispensation; yet while the word "Father" is applied to God two hundred times in the New Testament, it is applied only three times in the Old. Instead of the "untractableness" suggested by Nature, the life of Christ verified His own assertion—"my meat is to do the will of Him that sent me." And so with His last breath He was able to say "It is finished!" God had been completely revealed.

But even the divine revelation in Christ, full and complete though in one sense it was, even this was not enough, for it was still *external* to man. Christ's revelation needed itself to be revealed. Just as the Father is fully known only through the Son, so the Son is fully known only through the Holy Ghost. In other words, it required a revelation of God in the individual heart, to supplement and explain the teaching of Nature and of Christ. This was fully effected only when the Saviour had passed away. "If

[1] P. 189.

I go not away," He said, "the Comforter [or, rather, it should be rendered the Helper] will not come to you." The ultimate purpose of Jesus was to quicken men's inner, spiritual nature. While He was with them, they never grasped this purpose; they supposed it was a carnal life, of power and authority and dominion, to which He was calling them. But when He was gone from them in the flesh, and was with them only in the spirit, then they began to see that, unless His life had been a failure and His death a mistake, it must have been something inward and spiritual at which He had aimed. They saw that the vocation to which they had been really called was neither more nor less than to become sons of God. And thus "after the Saviour had disappeared as an outward authority, He reappeared as an inward principle of life." Men perceived that there was something higher than living *with* Christ, something higher even than living *for* Christ,—that it was at once their duty and their glory to live *Christ*. They discovered, as He foretold they would, that God was not only in Nature and in Jesus, but in themselves; and that if they yielded to His influences, they too would become, in a sense, divine.

The Deity had been latent, so to speak,

within men from the first. For what were their moral aspirations but the Spirit of the universe in communion with their spirits, inspiring them, impelling them, all but forcing them, to become co-workers with Itself? And to some extent this truth had from time to time been recognised and acknowledged. But the essential unity of God and man, the fact that the finite life might be possessed and suffused by the Infinite life, the possibility of a human apotheosis[1]—all this became clearer after Christ had passed away. We now regard it as our destiny to be "filled with all the fulness of God." We believe that we ought, even now, to be able to say—"It is not I who live, but God who liveth in me." And it is just because we are thus conscious of an indwelling Deity, whose presence within us makes our lives divine, that we may be said, in the language of theologians, to live under the dispensation of the Spirit.

It must not be supposed, however, that we can draw a strict line of demarcation between the dispensations of the Father, Son and Spirit, or that one was over before the next began.[2] In a

---

[1] See 'Agnosticism,' pp. 376-378.
[2] The system of Sabellius, the reader will remember, involved this false distinction.

sense, they have always been coexistent. We have still the dispensation of the Father, for Nature is yet around us to suggest God's beneficent care. We have still the dispensation of the Son, for we can, in imagination at any rate, converse with the historic Christ; and there are men and women about us to-day in whom the crucified Nazarene re-lives. Further, under the old Jewish dispensation—the dispensation of the Father, as it would be called in theological language—there had been men who prefigured and typified Christ; who by the lives they lived shadowed forth, partially and vaguely but still really, the great truths which Christ made so plain. And long before the day of Pentecost God's Spirit had been influencing men, both in their common yearnings and aspirations, and in the deep religious communion which psalmists and prophets enjoyed. We however may be said to live peculiarly under the dispensation of the Spirit, in the sense that we have attained to a clearer consciousness than the ancients of an indwelling God.

And, once more, not only should we remember that it is impossible strictly to distinguish between the dispensations, but we should also remember that the God of each dispensation is the same.[1] In the words of the old creed, "the Father is God, the Son is God, and the Holy Ghost is God; yet are they not three Gods, but one God." It is the same kind and holy Being, who appeals to us in the physical beauty of nature, in the moral beauty of Christ, and in those yearnings after a beautiful character of our own which, do what we will, we can never completely extinguish. And, strictly speaking, God is only known *as God* when He is recognised as Father, Son, and Spirit. No one knows the full meaning of the first expression who has not, in his heart of hearts, experienced the full meaning of the last. Just as it is good when a child believes in his father's love, and better when he learns to admire and reverence his father's character, but best of all when the father becomes part of his inmost life,—a guiding principle, a restraining power, the source of his highest satisfaction and of his noblest development: so, though it is good to realise the existence of God the Father, and better to realise the existence of God the Son, it is best of all to realise the existence of God the Holy Ghost. Not only is the

---

[1] The first Christian writer who distinctly taught a doctrine liable to the charge of Tritheism was Philoponus, in the middle of the sixth century.

teaching of God in the heart fuller, deeper, and clearer than His teaching either in Nature or in Christ, but His inspiration will gradually enable us to become perfect, even as our Father in heaven is perfect. Theoretically, God may be much to a man who believes in the Father, and more to a man who believes also in the Son; but *practically*, God is nothing to any one who is not yielding to the influence of the Holy Ghost. *God without us* is but a subject of curious speculation. It is *God within us* that is the sum and substance of all true religion and of all real life.

> "We hear His voice when thunders roll
>   Through the wide fields of air;
> The waves obey His dread control,
>   Yet still He is not there.
> Where shall I find Him, O my soul,
>   Who yet is everywhere!
>
> Oh, not in circling depth or height,
>   But in the conscious breast;
> Present to faith, though veiled from sight,
>   There doth His Spirit rest.
> Oh, come, thou Presence Infinite,
>   And make Thy creature blest!"

The Connection between Reason and Faith.

I.

THE RELIGIOUS USE OF REASON.

"Be ready to give a reason to every man for the hope that is in you."—1 Pet. iii. 15.

"Believe not every spirit, but try the spirits whether they be of God."—1 John iv. 1.

"Prove all things."—1 Thess. v. 21 [or rather it should be, "test all things;" δοκιμάζετε πάντα is the Greek expression. The word δοκιμάζειν is applied first and specially to the testing of metals for the purpose of seeing if they are pure].

TRUE religion involves the harmonious and complete development of all parts of man's nature. False religion consists in the attempt to get rid of, or to suppress, certain parts in favour of the rest,—the senses, for example, in favour of the intellect, or reason in favour of faith. I want to show you in this and the following sermons that there is nothing incompatible between the last-mentioned faculties, but that, on the contrary, they imply and involve one another.

It is, I am afraid, a very common opinion that the exercise of faith necessitates a violent suppression of reason. Some persons are so afraid of their intellects, so certain their own judgment would lead them astray, that they would seem to regard the human mind, not as the breath of God, but as a corrupting influence infused into man by the devil. Others, again, though not so distrustful of the powers of reason, appear to imagine there is *no virtue* in believing anything in which there can be perceived the slightest glimmering of meaning. Religion, they think, consists in professing to believe that which cannot be understood. In proportion as they comprehend what they profess, their profession, they fancy, loses its value. Even so wise a man as Bacon was once foolish enough to say, "The more incredible anything is, the more honour I do God in believing it." Now the term incredible is equivalent in plain Saxon, as you know, to unbelievable; and unbelievable means incapable of being believed. Bacon's assertion therefore amounts to this, that the more incapable of being believed anything is, the more we honour God in believing it. So that to believe what cannot be believed at all would be the acme of religious achievement! Alas! at that rate the perfection of piety is quite beyond our reach.

The absurdity of this determination to set reason at defiance, and to eliminate her altogether from the sphere of religion, may be shown in various ways. In the first place, the irreligiousness of reason has never been proved. Those who object to the use of reason, generally endeavour to justify their objection by some show of argument. They reason against reason. But this attempt to *prove* the worthlessness of reason is self-contradictory. If she be so unreliable, her testimony cannot be relied on against herself. The arguments she provides and accepts may, in this case as in others, be but paralogisms, and therefore she may after all be valid, in spite of her pretended proof of invalidity. Reason then can never reason down herself.

In the second place, *faith* is not, as it is sometimes misrepresented, the belief of what is contrary to reason. "The human spirit is not a thing divided against itself, in which faith and reason subsist side by side, each asserting as absolute, principles contradicted by the other." Though religion contains much that the reason cannot fully comprehend, yet, in so far as it is true, it can contain nothing that is positively contradicted by the reason. For we are so constituted that we cannot believe a contradiction. No power in the universe, for example, could make us think that we both existed and did not exist in the same indivisible moment of time.[1] We might be persuaded that it was desirable for certain purposes to *profess* a belief in both these contradictory statements, but omnipotence itself could not compel us really to believe them. Now faith cannot require us to say that we are doing what, by the very constitution of our nature, we are for ever precluded from accomplishing. If it did, then in order to be religious we must be dishonest, in order to have faith we must first become liars.

In the third place, *revelation* is not inconsistent with the use of reason, but on the contrary implies it. Revelation of course is divine and supernatural: it is an act, or series of acts, on

---

[1] It is scarcely necessary to say that, for this statement to be true, the term "exist" must be used in precisely the same sense in both instances. We must not, *e.g.*, understand "potentially" in one case, and "actually" in the other.

the part of Him who is above Nature. But the very purpose of this supernatural intervention is, as the word itself implies, *to reveal*,—to make plain what was before unknown or obscure. To treat revelation as if it could never be understood, is practically to deny that it is revelation —is practically to assert that God's purpose is not to reveal, but to conceal, Himself. Further, all religions profess to be revealed. In what way then are we to decide between their rival claims, in what way are we to estimate their relative merits, but by the use of reason? We may select for adoption in the end that which appears the most credible, or, following Bacon's curious axiom, that which appears the most incredible; but in both instances we have used reason as a means of distinguishing the wheat from the chaff. The only difference is, that in the one case we conclude our investigation by selecting the wheat, in the other by selecting the chaff.

In the fourth place, *worship* is not inconsistent with the use of reason, but on the contrary implies it. The value of worship depends on the nature and character of that which is worshipped. The mere feeling of reverence is not everything; for this feeling is possessed by all who have any semblance of a religion. As Shakespeare puts it—

> "An idiot holds his bauble for a god."

That which is of the first moment is not the feeling, but the object upon which the feeling is bestowed. And what but reason—using reason in the wide sense which makes it include conscience—what but reason can decide upon the rival claims to worship, put forward on behalf of the diverse deities of different religions? "If there were no criterion," says Professor Caird, "outside the sphere of feeling to which we could appeal, any one man would have as good a right to his religion as any other. Religion must indeed be a thing of the heart; but in order to elevate it from the region of subjective caprice and waywardness, and to distinguish between that which is true and false in religion, between the lowest and most corrupt and the highest and purest forms of religion, we must appeal to an objective standard. That which enters the heart must be discerned by intelligence to be true. It must be seen as having in its own nature a right to dominate feeling,"—as deserving and demanding reverence and awe. "Religion by its very nature contains, and must ever contain, an element of mystery, but a religion all mystery is an absurd and impossible notion. In order to awaken humility and awe, or indeed any emotion whatever, an object must be something more than the blank negation of thought. In the presence even of finite excellence, of human genius and learning, we may be conscious of feelings of deep humility, of silent, respectful admiration; and this, too, may be reverence for the unknown. But that which makes this reverence a possible and a wholesome feeling is, that it is reverence, not for a mere blank inscrutability, but for what I can think of as essentially the same with my own, though far excelling mine in range and power. In like manner the grandeur which surrounds the thought of the Absolute—the infinite reality beyond the finite—can only arise from this, not that it is something utterly inconceivable and unthinkable, but that it is for thought the realisation of its highest ideal of excellence." A God altogether unknown is as impossible a conception as a God altogether known. A Being who deserves to be called God must not only be infinite, and therefore incapable of being entirely comprehended; but He must also be infinitely good, and therefore capable of being partially comprehended. If the object of our worship were altogether unknown, we should not be able to say whether He were good or bad, whether He were God or devil. "Ye worship," said Christ with holy contempt to the woman of Samaria, "ye worship ye know not what; we know what we worship." This knowledge or understanding of the object worshipped was, Christ added, the special sign of a healthy spiritual state. "Salvation is of the Jews." Those were in the soundest spiritual condition to whom God had been most plainly revealed, and by whom therefore He was best understood.

In the fifth place, let me ask you to notice a fallacy involved in the common notion that the use of reason in religious matters implies doubt, and that this doubt is antagonistic to faith. There are, I must point out, two kinds of doubt. There is one which aims at, and leads to, belief; and there is another which is self-contained and self-contented. This latter kind of doubt is scepticism. The first kind is called by philosophers Cartesian doubt, after Descartes. In that most interesting little book of his, 'The Tract on Method,' which gives an autobiographical sketch of his mental development, Descartes describes how, in the course of his studies, he made the discovery that there was no opinion so absurd as not to have been held, and held tenaciously, by some one. This discovery led him to the conclusion, that it was necessary to investigate the grounds of all his beliefs. "I made it my business," he says, "to reflect in each matter upon what might fairly be doubted and prove a source of error; and so I gradually rooted out from my mind all the errors which had hitherto crept into it. Not that in this I imitated the sceptics, who doubt only that they may doubt, and seek nothing beyond uncertainty itself; for, on the contrary, my design was simply to find ground of assurance, and to cast aside the loose earth and sand, that I might reach the rock and clay beneath."

Now, analogous to this Cartesian doubt in matters of philosophy, there is, in matters of religion, what we may call (after our texts) Petrine, Johannine, or Pauline doubt. The doubt which is implied in thoughtful investigation is not antagonistic to faith, but is on the contrary its essential prerequisite. Faith always involves, as O. W. Holmes remarks, the disbelief of a lesser fact in favour of a greater. While we are estimating the relative value of facts, our minds may be said to be in a state of doubt; but unless we have estimated their value, we can never be sure that the fact we have accepted is the greater. You have heard the criticism upon a certain law-book called 'Dirleton's Doubts,' offered by Lord Chancellor Hardwicke: "Dirleton's doubts," he said, "were better than other people's certainties." They were better, because the investigation of them led to knowledge; whereas supposed certainties, not based upon investigation, are nothing more than ignorance. The same truth is expressed by Tennyson in the often-quoted, and often-misunderstood, lines—

> "There dwells more faith in honest doubt,
> Believe me, than in half the creeds."

Tennyson's meaning is just this,—If you or I profess a creed without quite knowing what it means, without stopping to consider what grounds there may be for accepting it, without asking ourselves whether the words commend themselves to our judgment as they did to the judgment of those who first used them, our profession is not faith, but falsehood. Not until we have investigated its meaning, not until it is seen to be the expression of what we have good reasons for believing, can we honestly call the creed our own. Such investigation is always very solemn, and often very painful work; but it is absolutely necessary that we make it, according to our opportunities and abilities, if our faith is ever to be worthy of the name. Do not be deterred then from honest inquiry, by the foolish talk you will sometimes hear about the irreligiousness of doubt. The doubt which aims at reaching truth is not irreligious, but is expressly commanded in our texts. It will cost you much mental labour, it may cost you much spiritual anguish, but your reward will be great. In the end you will be able to say—

> "Doubt in misty caverns
> 'Mid dark horrors sought,
> Till my peerless jewel,
> Faith, to me she brought."

Sixthly and lastly, I may just point out that our Church does not claim for its formularies either infallibility or finality. In the twenty-first Article we read: "General councils, forasmuch as they are an assembly of men whereof all be not governed by the Spirit and Word of God, may err, and sometimes have erred, even in things pertaining to God." The Church of England thus claims for itself the right to examine its creeds afresh from time to time, to compare them anew with divine revelation, to inquire whether they are the best possible expression of the truth, and if not, to modify them in accordance with the progressive teaching of the Holy Ghost.

Nothing, then, prevents us, but on the contrary everything invites us, to the use of reason. Stupidity is not faith. Superstition is not religion. Asserting that we believe what we have never taken the trouble to inquire whether we believe or no, is not piety, but cant. Persuading ourselves we believe what we dare not investigate, for fear of discovering that we disbelieve, is not orthodoxy, but hypocrisy. Professing that we believe what we see to be contrary to reason, and therefore essentially unbelievable, proves not our regard for religion, but only our indifference to truth.

What keeps men from reflecting on matters which they *say* are of the highest moment is, for the most part, either indolence or pride. They do not care to begin a task of which they cannot see the end; or they fancy they know so much already, that reflection can teach them no more. Some may be deterred from religious thought and inquiry by a mistaken idea of reverence,—by supposing that the objects with which religion is concerned are altogether unintelligible by finite faculties. That this is a mistaken idea of reverence, I have endeavoured to prove. But, for those who profess to believe in the inspiration of the Bible, the matter should require no proof. The mere statement of my texts should be sufficient: "Be ready to give a reason to every man for the hope that is in you;" "Believe not every spirit, but try the spirits whether they be of God;" "Test all things."

The Connection between Reason and Faith.

II.

THE LIMITATIONS OF KNOWLEDGE.

" Canst thou by searching find out God? canst thou find out the Almighty unto perfection?"—JOB xi. 7.

IN the last sermon, I was endeavouring to show that we might, and that we ought, to use our reason in religious matters. I have now to remind you of the fact that, use our reason as we will, there is much which must remain unknown.

Some persons seem to imagine, if they were to think at all there would be nothing left for faith—if they tried to understand matters, mystery would be at once annihilated. And indeed the achievements of modern science might seem, at first sight, to lend some countenance to this most foolish opinion. To a careless student it may appear as if there were nothing which we had not found out, or were not on the point of finding out. We have analysed the material universe into about five dozen elements and half-a-dozen forces. We have studied the laws of these elements and of these forces, till we seem almost as well acquainted with Nature's habits as with our own. We have measured, weighed, and even discovered the composition of sun and moon and stars. We have examined the human brain, until we seem fairly in the way of localising the mental faculties. In a word, we have been making such progress in knowledge, that there is almost an excuse for our imagining that we are going to master everything. But a little reflection will show that our knowledge after all is but superficial, and that our ignorance is profound. We do not know the ultimate nature either of matter or of force. We have no means of telling whether the component atoms of the physical world are solid substances—according to the general conception of them, or merely centres of energy—according to the theory of Boscovitch. We cannot say whether or no the hardness of matter be more than the result of "a rapid motion in something that is infinitely yielding." In a word, we do not know whether matter and force are two things or one. We know even less of the nature of life. We are acquainted with some of its conditions, but we have not been able to form a theory as to what it is itself. And less still, if that were possible, do we know of the mystery of our own personality. The materialist, of course, is ready with an explanation. We are, he tells us, a mixture of carbon, hydrogen, nitrogen, and oxygen, with a dash of phosphorus and iron. But if that explanation fails to satisfy us, if we incline to the supposition that we are something more, we shall find ourselves face to face with an absolutely insoluble problem. Did you ever ask yourself, "What am I? What is this mysterious being who thinks and feels and remembers and wills, of whose existence I am so sure, but whom I have never seen, and can never see?" Did you ever ask that question, and wait for a reply? If so, you are waiting yet.

Thus, you see, the slightest reflection will suffice to convince us of the limitation of human knowledge.

But there is an erroneous theory as to the nature and causes of this limitation which is unfortunately popular at present,—the theory of those very negative philosophers who have chosen to style themselves Positivists. According to them, we can only know our feelings.[1] On this ground they tell us a man can never know that he has a soul or mind; for the soul cannot be felt, and what cannot be felt is for us practically non-existent. It is easy to show the fallacy involved in this doctrine. What do you mean when you speak of a sensation or feeling? Manifestly the term is a single abstract word for a concrete double fact. It means something felt by some one. The *some one* is as important a part of the conception as the *something;* for without the some one to feel, the something would not be felt. In other words, a soul or mind is the necessary condition of feeling. Since then feelings could not exist without the mind to feel them, it is absurd to argue that the mind does not exist, because it is not itself a feeling.[2] And though we do not, as I have intimated, know what this mind is, it is to be remembered, on the other hand, that we do not know what a feeling is. Pleasure is pleasant, pain is painful;

[1] I use here, for the sake of simplicity, the common word feeling. The technical term would be "phenomenal states of consciousness."

[2] See my 'Personality,' sections 1 and 2.

that is all we can say; but what pleasure and pain are in themselves, what it is that makes things pleasant or painful, we cannot in the faintest degree conceive. And mystery is not restricted to that which is mental. The most commonplace material object is full of it. You remember those profound lines of Tennyson's:—

> "Flower in the crannied wall,
> I pluck you out of the crannies,—
> Hold you here, root and all, in my hand,
> Little flower; but if I could understand
> What you are, root and all, and all in all,
> I should know what God and man is."

If, then, the fact of an underlying mystery does not prevent us from saying that we know such things as pebbles and primroses, it need not prevent us from saying that we know the human soul.

The Positive philosophers tell us, again, that, just as we are unable to recognise the existence of the mind, so we are unable to recognise the existence of God. "I have swept the heavens with my telescope," says Lalande, "and have not found a God." "I do not believe in the existence of God," said Clifford, "for I have not seen His brain." It is the same kind of foolish argument by which they would make us disbelieve in our own souls. Anything that could be felt would not be a soul. Anything that could come within the sweep of a telescope would not be a God. If a man persists in looking for an object where he might have been quite sure that it could not be, the fact of his failing to find it proves nothing but his own perversity. And not only is it impossible to see God by any combination of lenses, but it must be admitted also that the ordinary attempts to prove His existence all fall short of certainty. There is one way however in which it may be proved to demonstration, and that is by examining, after the manner of Hegel, the nature of thought. Thought, or mind, is the presupposition of everything. All that we know, even of that which we call matter, is certain states of consciousness which it produces in us. So that, without thought, there could be nothing. But the thought which is the presupposition of all reality is not yours or mine or any other individual thinker's, for the world existed before we perceived it. Our limited consciousness, therefore, implies the existence of a consciousness that is unlimited; our finite thoughts necessitate the existence of an Infinite Thinker.[1]

[1] This is more fully explained in my 'Belief in God,' pp. 69-76.

Our knowledge, then, is not restricted to that which the senses can teach. Reason may lead us to the supersensuous; reason may bring us to God. But,—and here we come upon the real limitation of our religious knowledge, the most fundamental limitation,—though reason will teach us to *know* God, it will never enable us to *fathom* Him. My text, you will observe, was uttered by Zophar: "Canst thou by searching find out God? canst thou find out the Almighty unto perfection?" Foolish persons sometimes make wise remarks by accident; but they generally spoil the effect of these rare flashes of wisdom by adding, in the same breath, something that is very unwise. Zophar does so in the present instance. The first part of his sentence is false, for we *can* find out God. "If thou shalt seek the Lord thy God, thou shalt find Him, if thou seek Him with all thy heart and with all thy soul." But the second half of Zophar's sentence is profoundly true; we *cannot* find out the Almighty *unto perfection*.

We are, and shall ever be, precluded from a perfect knowledge of God, by the fact that He is infinite and that we are only finite. If we could completely understand Him, we should perceive the meaning of all His actions. But this we can never hope to do. "The monarchy of the universe," says Bishop Butler, in his sermon upon Ignorance, "is a dominion unlimited in extent and everlasting in duration: the general system of it must therefore be quite beyond our comprehension. And since there appears such a subordination, and reference of the several parts to each other, as to constitute it properly one administration or government, we cannot have a thorough knowledge of the parts without a complete knowledge of the whole." Now, we are only acquainted with an infinitesimal part of the universe, and so we cannot entirely comprehend even that small fraction. We see, for example, not only in heathen lands, but even about us here in London,—we see men and women living in the midst of such terrible surroundings, that nothing but a miracle—which is never worked — could save them from the lowest abyss of wretchedness and degradation. If what we saw were all that there was to be seen, then we should be justified in saying that the Being who created them for such a fate was cruel and unjust. But how if, somewhere in the future, there be compensation in store for these hapless souls! It may be that, if we could see this compensation, and if we remembered, on the ther hand, that much will be required from him to whom much has been given, we should be almost inclined to envy some for whom our hearts now bleed, and to weep for others whom now we look upon as pre-eminently fortunate. Still, we can never *prove* that the ways of the Lord are equal. And though we sometimes discover, even in this lfe, that His dealings are less unequal than at first appears, though we may hope to make many more such discoveries in a future state, yet the limitation of knowledge which is due to our being finite can never be altogether removed.

But at present we have not reached a full use of the powers that are really latent within us. The law of the universe we know to be development. This is the favourite word with modern scientists. It is also the teaching of the highest philosophy. We know that this law has been exemplified in our own individual history. What a marvellous change did we undergo between our babyhood and our youth! Still more wonderful was the change from youth into manhood, in those years when we acquired the habit of thinking for ourselves. And if we are living our best, we are still conscious of making progress. Who then shall limit the development of which we are capable, if there be an eternity before us in which it may be achieved? Our powers, though they can never equal, may be constantly approximating, to the very powers of God Himself.

The limitation of knowledge, then, affords no valid argument against the use of reason. The fact that reason will not teach us everything, does not justify us in refusing to derive from it such instruction as it is able to impart. "If a man were to walk by twilight, must he not follow his eyes as much as if it were broad day and clear sunshine? Or, if he were obliged to travel by night, would he not give heed to any light shining in the darkness? It would not be altogether unnatural for him to reflect how much better it were to have daylight; he might perhaps have great curiosity to see the country round about him; he might lament that the darkness concealed many extended prospects from his eyes, and wish for the sun to draw away the veil: but how ridiculous would it be to reject with scorn and disdain the guidance and direction which that lesser light might afford him, because it was not the sun itself!" Not less foolish is the man who refuses to use his finite reason because it is not infinite.

And, further, the limitation of knowledge affords no valid argument against the exercise of faith. We saw in the previous sermon that our faith, to be worth anything, must be a reasonable faith. But the limitation of knowledge does not prevent it from being reasonable. Not only will reason teach us much, but it will also supply us with suggestions as to why we do not know more. Our powers must, in the nature of things, be limited: for we could not have been created infinite; and finitude means limitation. Further, we need not take offence at knowledge being for us a gradual acquisition. To do so would be as absurd as if a child were to grumble because it was not born grown up. The process of growth is the very purpose of our existence. Nor need we be angry at "the sore lets and hindrances" by which we are at present trammelled, such as the distractions of business, the petty worries of life, or the easily exhausted powers of our physical organism. For the value of knowledge, like that of everything else, is enhanced by the difficulties amid which it has been achieved. And even if, as is quite possible, certain things have been purposely concealed from us which we have already the natural capacity for understanding, this concealment may be eminently wise and kind. "There is no manner of absurdity," says Bishop Butler, "in supposing a veil on purpose drawn over some scenes of infinite power and wisdom and goodness, the sight of which might some way or other strike us too strongly; or that better ends are designed and served by their being concealed, than could be attained by their being exposed to view." In a word then reason teaches us much, even putting us in the way of understanding why it does not teach us more; and thus we are led up to a reasoning and reasonable faith.

The Connection between Reason and Faith.

III.

THE FUNCTION OF FAITH.

"*HAVING boldness, . . . by the blood of Christ, . . . let us draw near . . . in full assurance of faith. Let us hold fast the confession of our hope without wavering. . . . Call ever to remembrance the former days, in which, when first enlightened, ye endured a great conflict of suffering, . . . and took joyfully the spoiling of your goods, knowing that ye had for your own a better and an abiding possession. Cast not away your confidence. . . . Now, faith is the substance of things hoped for, the proof of things not seen. . . . By faith we understand that the worlds were framed by the word of God, so that what is seen was not made of things which appear. . . . He that cometh to God by faith must believe that He is, and that He is the rewarder of them that diligently seek Him.*" The writer then proceeds to mention instances of patriarchal faith,—the most illustrative example, perhaps, being that of Moses: "*By faith, Moses, when he was come to years, refused to be called the son of Pharaoh's daughter, choosing rather to suffer affliction with the people of God than to enjoy the pleasures of sin for a season, esteeming the reproach of Christ greater riches than the treasure in Egypt,—for he had respect unto the recompense of the reward. By faith he forsook Egypt, not fearing the wrath of the king,—for he endured as seeing Him who is unseeable. . . . The time would fail me to tell of Gideon and of Barak and of Samson and of Jephthah, of David also and Samuel and of the prophets, who through faith subdued kingdoms, . . . escaped the edge of the sword, . . . turned to flight the armies of the aliens, or (contrariwise) were tortured, stoned, or sawn asunder, being destitute, afflicted, tormented, not accepting deliverance, that they might obtain a better resurrection. . . . These all having had witness borne to them on account of their faith, received not the promises, God having provided some better thing for us, that they without us should not be made perfect. Wherefore let us also, seeing we are compassed about by so great a cloud of witnesses, lay aside every weight, and sin which doth naturally enwrap us, and let us run with patience the race that is set before us, looking unto Jesus, the Author and Perfecter of our faith, who for the joy set before Him endured the cross and despised the shame. . . . Consider Him who endured such gainsayings at the hands of sinners, that ye be not wearied and faint in your souls. Ye have not yet resisted unto blood in your striving against sin."*—Hebrews x. 22 to xii. 6.

We have seen that religion implies and necessitates the use of reason. We have seen, further, that there are many fundamental religious problems of which reason is unable to give us a complete solution. We have now to consider the function of faith, which comes in to help us at the point where reason fails.

That faith begins where reason leaves off is curiously illustrated by the fact that, according to our text, it is faith which teaches us "the worlds were framed by the word of God." Now, as I intimated in the previous sermon, it is possible to demonstrate the existence of a divine

Creator, by a reflective examination of our conscious experience. But since this demonstration was first given to the world by Hegel, and from its excessive abstruseness is somewhat difficult to understand; and since further, as I mentioned before, the ordinary logical arguments for the existence of God are not perfect demonstrations, it follows that, as far as the majority of men are concerned, the divine existence must be, as our text asserts, a matter of faith.

Now, let us try and discover what faith is. And let us begin by inquiring what is implied in the ordinary man's faith in the existence of God. Though it has not been proved to him by absolutely perfect demonstration, it has nevertheless more or less of a rational basis. The most ordinary man can hardly have failed to perceive some sort of *adaptation* in the world around him and in himself. *There* is a beautiful landscape, and *here* is an eye which sees it, a mind which appreciates it, and a heart which is moved by it. Very dense indeed must be the human being to whom the idea has never occurred, that the landscape and the eye and the mind and the heart were made with some sort of view to one another. But this suggestion does not amount to certainty. Sometimes what appears to be design turns out to be accident. Still, as the appearances of design are multiplied, the possibility of their being all due to accident becomes smaller; and when it is remembered that there are semblances of design extending over a universe which is for us practically infinite in space and time, the possibility of their being all due to accident becomes infinitesimal. The atheist then adopts an irrational belief, for he assumes that this smallest conceivable possibility outweighs the largest conceivable probability. The ordinary man on the contrary, who believes in God because of the adaptation which he seems to see around him, adopts a rational belief. His reason has not proved the divine existence to demonstration, and yet it has afforded him arguments that are all but irresistible. Faith then implies a reasonable belief in the existence of God.

But faith, says the author of our text, implies a belief that God is, *and* that He is the rewarder of them that diligently seek Him—that is to say, it implies a belief in God, not only as the Creator, but as the moral Governor of the universe. The Hebrews had taken joyfully the spoiling of their earthly goods, because they knew there was in store for them a better and an abiding possession. Moses had chosen to suffer affliction with the people of God, because he felt that the pleasures of sin were only for a season, and because he had respect unto the recompense of the reward which was attached to the reproach of Christ. The noble army of martyrs refused to accept deliverance, in order that they might obtain a better resurrection ; and though they had not themselves received the promises, they died in peace, feeling that they, and those who should come after them, were members of a kingdom which would be perfected in God's good time. Even Jesus, the writer says, endured the cross and despised the shame *for the sake of* the joy that was set before Him.

Now the moral government of the universe, in which all these believed, can never be demonstrated ; at least, no one has ever yet succeeded in demonstrating it. Even those who are able to prove conclusively by reason that God is, are not able to prove in the same manner that He is *uniformly* the rewarder of them that diligently seek Him. It cannot be shown that it will always go well with the good, for sometimes it seems to go very ill with them. Faith implies the conviction that these apparent exceptions to moral government are not real. And far more reasons can be discovered in support of this conviction than can ever be arrayed against it. As a rule, good men are honoured for their goodness; or, if they suffer wrongfully, they, generally speaking, have an inward peace which is sweeter than any outward applause. These and similar arguments, moreover, acquire additional force if read in the light of the Gospel. It is the blood of Christ, our author tells us—that is, the sacrificial life of Christ—which pre-eminently gives us boldness. It is in the light of the Cross that we best discern the infinite value of character, and he who has learnt this lesson can "endure all things." On the whole then, though we have not arrived at demonstration, we have strong rational grounds for believing that the Ruler of the universe is not indifferent to our actions, that the wages of virtue is not to be dust, that sooner or later it will be well with the righteous; and if later, that there will be compensation for the delay. Hence faith is not a belief in anything unintelligible or irrational. The proof of what is believed, though not by any means complete, is good so far as it goes. The Hebrew Christians, you will observe, endured their great conflict of sufferings *after they were enlightened*—that is, after *reasons for faith* had been presented to them.

But though there is an intellectual element implied in all true faith as its ground, the term "belief," if used as a synonym for faith, is terribly misleading. Faith involves far more than any mere mental assent. An intellectual belief by itself no more constitutes faith than the foundation alone constitutes a building. The belief of the head must be supplemented by the confidence of the heart; and confidence is an active emotion or sentiment, which inevitably shows itself in corresponding conduct. It is true that the term "belief" is occasionally used in this sense, as when we speak of a man's "believing in himself." The man who believes—who knows—that he is, or is to be, a great man, will act accordingly. But this is not its commonest signification, and is not generally suggested to us by the word. It commonly signifies merely a passive, tacit assent, which is certainly not Christian faith. "Thou believest that there is a God," says St James [or rather, that "God is one," as the best MSS. read]. "So far well; but if that is religion, the very devils themselves are conspicuous examples of piety." Confidence, rather than belief, is the proper synonym for faith. St Paul not only says, in the Epistle to the Romans, that we are saved by faith, but in the same Epistle he also asserts that we are saved by hope. So, too, the author of our text speaks of faith as implying a "full assurance"; he describes it as "the confession of hope"; and in urging his readers to cherish it, he says, "Cast not away your confidence."

Now confidence, as I have said, is an emotion or sentiment which necessarily shows itself in conduct. There can be no mistake, therefore, as to whether a man is possessed of faith. "By their fruits ye shall know them." It is not easy —it is, in fact, often impossible—to tell what a man believes, in the ordinary sense of the word; for he may say he believes one thing, when all the time he knows he believes another; he may even think he believes something, when in reality he does not. But, just as it would be absurd for us to make asseverations of bravery, when we were visibly trembling at the very smell of powder, so is it ridiculous to profess a confidence that God will render to every man according to his works, when we are acting as if this were, to say the least, unlikely. He who is confident cannot act as if he were in doubt. Faith made Moses refuse to be called the son of Pharaoh's daughter; it led him to despise the treasure in Egypt, and to set at nought the wrath of the king. It inspired men with such courage and strength, that they subdued kingdoms, escaped the edge of the sword, turned to flight the armies of the aliens; or, if it were otherwise ordained — if they were tortured, stoned, sawn asunder—it helped them to bear their agony without a murmur. It enabled the Hebrew Christians originally to endure their great conflict of sufferings, and to take joyfully the spoiling of their goods; it would help them in the future, says the writer, to run with patience the race set before them, and in their striving against sin to resist unto blood—that is, to the extent even of laying down their lives.

The test of faith therefore according to our text is conduct, or, in theological language, works. This might seem at first sight inconsistent with the teaching of the Epistle to the Romans. But the difference is only on the surface, and is explained by the different objects which the two writers had in view. As Professor Blackie has well pointed out, the author of the Hebrews aimed at giving a full and complete exposition of the nature of faith; while St Paul, in the Romans, was endeavouring to expose the vanity of a certain kind of works, and of works generally *if put forward as a substitute for faith*. The works which are depreciated in the Epistle to the Romans are the ceremonial and legal works, mainly of an external character, on which the Jews plumed themselves, in virtue of which they fancied that they were better than their neighbours and had special claims upon the favour of the Almighty. All such pretensions St Paul sweeps away. He shows, in the first place, that they imply a total misapprehension of the nature of morality, which is something essentially different from external ceremonialism. He is not a Jew who is one outwardly, and the circumcision which is outward in the flesh is not the real circumcision. But he is a Jew who is one inwardly, and the important circumcision is that of the heart and spirit. The apostle points out also, in the second place, that when confronted with the moral law—with an ideal of perfection to which finite creatures can never completely attain—all men, even the best, must confess themselves sinners. You see, then, that it was not against works *as such* that St Paul is arguing, but against works put forth as a meritorious claim, or against the vain conceit of self-righteousness, which implies a contemptible moral standard and a degraded condition of the heart. Faith, on the contrary, involves a steadfast belief in an ideal morality, which as yet we are far from having realised, but towards which it should be our constant endeavour to approximate. Hence faith is the spring of all noble acts.

"And here," continues Professor Blackie, "we have a true key, not only to St Paul's glorification of faith in the Romans, but also to the emphasis given to that doctrine by Luther and Calvin, and other prominent fathers of the Protestant Church. As the Jews in St Paul's time believed in the saving power of the ceremonial law, so Christians in the age of the Reformers had been seduced, by the teaching of the priesthood, to adopt the opinion that certain works, principally of an external and irrational kind, performed in obedience to Church authority, might be substituted for the application of the moral law to all the relations and details of life." Thus individual acts of real or imaginary virtue were divorced from that spirit of confidence in God which ought to inspire them, and religion was made to consist in observances which had no vital connection with a noble life or a manly character. It is the function of faith to stimulate us, not to isolated acts of spasmodic and intermittent virtue, but to a steady and consistent course of lifelong welldoing. In this very epistle to the Romans, the apostle shows that, so far from excluding works, Christian faith, if it be genuine, leads to a much higher type of righteousness, to a far better class of works, than any which Judaism had been capable of producing. What the law could not do, in that it was weak through the flesh, is to be accomplished in us, who have been taught by Christ to walk, not after the flesh, but after the spirit. The teaching of our text, then, we may take to be the teaching of the entire New Testament, that faith is confidence manifested by conduct.

At first this confidence may be but feeble. After grappling in vain with some of the insoluble problems of existence, we are burdened with a sense of failure. Till we began to use our reason, we thought we knew everything, and that the intellectual difficulties which troubled others were capable of being easily dissipated. But, after reflection, we discovered that we knew scarcely anything, and that many of the difficulties we had treated so slightingly were nevertheless insuperable. We can only say, in the words of Tennyson—

> "I falter where I firmly trod,
> And falling with my weight of cares
> Upon the world's great altar-stairs,
> That slope through darkness up to God,
> I stretch lame hands of faith, and grope,
> And gather dust and chaff, and call
> To what I *feel* is Lord of all,
> And faintly trust the larger hope."

But our confidence will grow in proportion as we act upon it, until at last it will become *the very substance of things hoped for.* We shall feel as certain that God will reward us according to our works, as if we already had the reward in our possession. In acting according to the promptings of faith, we are animated by the divine spirit, we are moved by the divine will, we are living the divine life—it is, in fact, no more we who live, but God who liveth in us. Faith thus becomes in the end a *proof* of things not seen, more certain even than the demonstrations of reason. There may be a flaw in arguments that appear quite cogent; but there is no possibility of our mistaking our experience, for that is what we feel it to be. Thus in time we may rise from the lower levels of faith to the higher, until we are able to say, in the later words of the Laureate—

"Closer is He than breathing, and nearer than hands and feet."

God grant that you and I, before we meet again, may have made some progress in this higher faith! We must remember that the use of reason, important though it be, is only a means to an end. The purpose of reason is to lead us to faith; the purpose of faith is to prompt us to conduct:[1] and it is this conduct alone that will enable us to say, in the emphatic language of St Paul, " I *know* whom I have believed."

> " For meek obedience, that is light—
> And following that is finding Him."

---

[1] On the connection between creed and conduct, see my 'Church and Creed,' pp. 92-104.

THE END.

PRINTED BY WILLIAM BLACKWOOD AND SONS.

WORKS BY PROFESSOR MOMERIE.

I.

PERSONALITY;

THE BEGINNING AND END OF METAPHYSICS,

AND A NECESSARY ASSUMPTION IN ALL POSITIVE PHILOSOPHY.

Fourth Edition, revised. Crown 8vo, 3s.

"This is a little book, but it contains more sound philosophy than many pretentious treatises....... In an admirably lucid way the author scatters to the winds the baseless assumptions of the sense philosophy."—*British Quarterly Review.*

"It is not often that we have to complain of the brevity of a sermon or of a treatise on philosophy; but in the case of a little book of the latter kind, recently published anonymously, we have found the arguments so cogent, the style so clear, and the matter at issue so important, that we heartily wish that the writer had allowed himself room for the fuller treatment of his subject....... We confidently refer our readers to this well-reasoned volume."—*Modern Review.*

"Professor Momerie's remarks on the doctrines of the defenders of empiricism present a close, and thoroughly scientific, examination of the views these thinkers put forth as to the nature of sensation, perception, and cognition....... The arguments are throughout conducted with marked logical power, and the conclusions are very important in relation to the present aspect of philosophical thought in England."—*Scotsman.*

"The work under our notice will well repay the careful reading of those who wish to have at their command plain answers to modern positivism."—*Ecclesiastical Gazette.*

"His discussion of these questions stamps Dr Momerie as an acute metaphysician, a philosophical scholar, and a powerful dialectician."—*Glasgow Herald.*

"When published anonymously received a very hearty welcome by all who were interested in the advent of a new writer of great power, of happy diction, and of independent thinking."—*Montrose Standard.*

WILLIAM BLACKWOOD & SONS, EDINBURGH AND LONDON.

And all Booksellers.

II.

THE ORIGIN OF EVIL;

AND OTHER SERMONS.

Sixth Edition. Crown 8vo, 5s.

"Professor Momerie has done well to publish his sermons; they are good reading.......A real contribution to the side of common-sense religion."—*Saturday Review.*

"We decidedly recommend them to persons perplexed by the speculations of modern science."—*Spectator.*

"This is a remarkable volume of sermons. Though it consists of only about 300 pages, it contains an amount of thought and learning which might have been expanded into a bulky folio."—*Glasgow Mail.*

"These sermons are some of the very best produced in this country within the last hundred years."—*Inquirer.*

"The author is an original thinker, whose sympathies are very wide."—*Guardian.*

"Those who preach may learn much from their perusal."—*Christian World.*

"Out of the common run, they give one a refreshing sense of novelty and power."—*Glasgow Herald.*

"Die Vorträge zeigen allenthalben eine schöne Harmonie zwischen Schriftwahrheit und Lebenswahrheit."—*Deutsches Litteraturblatt.*

"Der Verfasser behandelt in diesen Vorträgen wichtige Fragen aus dem Gebiet des christlichen Lebens. Wir heben besonders die über das Leiden hervor, in denen der Verfasser tiefe beherzigenswerthe Gedanken ausspricht. Wir nehmen keinen Anstand, diese Vorträge zum Besten zu rechnen, was über diesen Gegenstand gesagt worden."—*Christliches Bücherschatz.*

"The author of the 'Origin of Evil' will go sadly astray if he does not make his mark on the age."—*London Figaro.*

"We should almost like to have heard these sermons preached. We are willing to read them carefully, and recommend them to others for like reading, even though, in almost every instance, we dissent from the author's pleading."—*National Reformer.*

"These sermons are everything that sermons ought *not* to be."—*English Independent.*

III.

DEFECTS OF MODERN CHRISTIANITY;

AND OTHER SERMONS.

Third Edition. Crown 8vo, 5s.

"Throughout Mr Momerie's attractive little volume the morning air of the new world breathes through the dry leaves of the old theology."—*Westminster Review.*

"There is an intellectuality, spirituality, and a simplicity in Mr Momerie's sermons, that should make them models for young preachers."—*Christian Union.*

"Professor Momerie, by his former books, has already laid the foundation of a reputation as a philosophical thinker and an able expositor of religious subjects. The present volume is marked by equal ability, intellectual force, independent and original thinking, and will confirm the favourable opinion which he has already produced.......Whatever views readers may detect as different from their own, they will not fail to admire the author's powerful enforcement of the practical side of Christianity.......There follows, as the second part of the volume, nine lectures on the Book of Job; and we have not read before, within the same compass, a more masterly and interesting exposition of that great poem.......There are also three admirable sermons on 'The Connection between Reason and Faith,' which will repay repeated reading.......The volume deserves to be widely read; and whether readers agree or not in all respects with the author, they will not rise from the perusal without feeling that Christianity is something grander than they have ordinarily realised it to be, and that the Christian life is the bravest and most beautiful life possible."—*Aberdeen Journal.*

"Very fresh and striking."—*Globe.*

"Although he is a polished and accomplished scholar, he simply defies the conventionalities of churches and schools."—*Literary World.*

IV.

THE BASIS OF RELIGION;

BEING AN EXAMINATION OF 'NATURAL RELIGION.'

Second Edition. Crown 8vo, 2s. 6d.

"As a controversialist, Professor Momerie is no less candid than he is remorselessly severe."—*Scotsman.*

"As a revelation of the pretentiousness of that philosophy [Positivism], Dr Momerie's powerful essay is very valuable."—*Fifeshire Journal.*

"The result of profound study and earnest thought.......This attempt to sketch out a basis for rational theology is fitted to the needs of the times. ......Professor Momerie has won for himself a name as one of the most powerful and original thinkers of the day."—*Globe.*

"Professor Momerie has wide views of men and things, resembling in this quality the author of 'Ecce Homo' himself, and he has attacked from the Cambridge University pulpit the book 'Natural Religion,' accusing it of considerable vagueness of conception and of considerable misconception of critical points of its own argument. The present book presents the substance of these sermons in the form of a brief essay.......We would recommend our readers to see for themselves how those confusions of thought, by which the school of writers—of whom the author of 'Natural Religion' is an eminent representative—seek to save religion when supernaturalism has disappeared, are exposed. We are certain they will be charmed with the accurate philosophical thinking of Professor Momerie, with his unpretentious display of keen logical reasoning, conveyed in lucid and forcible language, which arrays and adorns it like a well-fitting garment."—*Eskdale Advertiser.*

"Greater force is given to this essay, since the author is himself an advanced thinker."—*Christian Union.*

V.

AGNOSTICISM.

Third Edition. Crown 8vo, 5s.

"To readers who do not demand that 'the scheme of salvation in its fulness' should be enunciated in every sermon, this volume, which is happily free from rhetoric, and for the most part from any ostentation of the reading which it indicates, will be interesting from its acuteness, learning, and insight."—*Saturday Review.*

"This is a really good book. It is profound in thought, large and comprehensive in view, liberal in spirit, and delightfully clear and simple in style. We wish that theologians and philosophers in general would write in Professor Momerie's manner....... Following the chapters on Agnosticism, there are ten other chapters on the book of Ecclesiastes. They form an admirable and scholarly analysis of that strange and melancholy book."—*The Inquirer.*

"We are thankful for so masterly, so comprehensive, and so complete a vindication of the principles of Christian Theism, with its powerful refutation of the main positions of Agnosticism. The book meets a real and widespread need, in a style as trenchant and effective as it is popular."—*Freeman.*

"Dr Momerie's breadth of intellect and sympathy, his clear thinking and well-chastened style, as well as his deep religiousness, which will, no doubt, after a time assume a more positively evangelical form, eminently adapt him to be a teacher to his generation. He has freed himself, by we know not what process, from many of the prejudices of the older schools; but he can search into the very soul of unbelieving sophistry, and the spirit of his exhortation is always ennobling and heavenward."—*Methodist Times.*

"It is long since we have met with a volume of sermons which will so well repay a careful study."—*Ecclesiastical Gazette.*

"The work of a majestic intellect."—*Fifeshire Journal.*

VI.
PREACHING AND HEARING;
AND OTHER SERMONS.

Second Edition. Crown 8vo, 4s. 6d.

"The author, himself one of the most eloquent preachers of the day, is eminently qualified to do justice to his subject. He has brought to it an experience and scholarly proficiency which few men could have done."—*Christian Union.*

"For such preaching as this, and for all the ample learning and wise thought by which it is fortified, the Church of God has every reason to be thankful."—*Literary World.*

"Marked by all the force, acuteness, and eloquence which we have learnt to expect from him, and in addition by a knowledge of men and manners not generally associated with philosophical research........His literary style is another proof, if proof were needed, of the vast resources of the simple Anglo-Saxon."—*Fifeshire Journal.*

"His sermons are unlike any sermons we can call to mind."—*Guardian.*

"If such sermons were often to be heard from the pulpit, preachers would not have to complain of empty pews or inattentive listeners."—*Rock.*

"Their delivery was quite startling."—*Swansea Journal.*

"Those who would know what pulpit boldness in the present day really means should make these sermons their study."—*Christian World.*

"The present volume is more directly popular in style, and amply maintains the reputation of the writer."—*Inquirer.*

VII.

BELIEF IN GOD.

Second Edition. Crown 8vo, 3s.

"One of the most brilliant arguments for the Divine existence."—*Christian World.*

"In some respects Professor Momerie is the ablest preacher of his day. ......He is ever endeavouring to present recondite problems in the simplest, clearest language, and in this he is eminently successful.......It is not too abstruse even for mere smatterers in philosophical discussion. Considering its scope, it is indeed astonishingly lucid."—*Dundee Advertiser.*

"No preacher need be ashamed to face the most scientific sceptic with this little book in his hand."—*Literary World.*

"From the time that Professor Momerie published anonymously the volume on 'The Origin of Evil,' his writings have been devoured with exceptional keenness by intelligent readers. Many were the conjectures as to who the author of that work was, but it was universally allowed that the anonymous writer was destined to leave his mark upon the mind of the country: he was a daring and fresh thinker, and was possessed of rare unravelling power. This little volume bears the impress of his majestic intellect....... It is a model of lucid style, clear and consecutive reasoning, fairness to an honourable opponent, and humility in victory."—*Perthshire Advertiser.*

"'Belief in God' was originally written for the 'Helps to Belief' Series, but the editor, thinking it too abstruse, recommended considerable alterations. We are devoutly thankful the gifted Professor refused to mutilate his work, and withdrew it from the series."—*Nonconformist.*

"His criticism of Herbert Spencer's theory of the Unknowable is very acute."—*Glasgow Herald.*

"It is spread out into only eighty pages, but those eighty pages contain more material for thought than many another volume or series of volumes contain in eight hundred."—*Inquirer.*

VIII.

INSPIRATION;

AND OTHER SERMONS.

Second Edition.   Crown 8vo, 5s.

"Canon Liddon, preaching last Sunday afternoon in St Paul's Cathedral, declared that it would be difficult to maintain the authority of Christ as a teacher of religious truth if the Book of Daniel were written in the second, and not in the sixth century B.C. Statements of this kind are as deplorable as they are unwarranted........ A happier and a wiser method of dealing with the relations of science and criticism to the Scriptures has been adopted by Professor Momerie in his new volume."—*Christian World.*

"The gifted Professor has broken at many points with rigid orthodoxy. He is a Broad Churchman of the Broad Churchmen. But his very breadth and catholicity of view, the unswerving steadfastness of his search after truth, and his gift of powerful expression, make him an ally whom even the narrowest sticklers for the faith without change cannot be blind enough to throw over."—*Fifeshire Journal.*

"The sermons on 'Pessimism' constitute a treatise in themselves."—*Irish Ecclesiastical Gazette.*

"The abilities of Dr Momerie, and his services with respect to those questions in which the spheres of religion and philosophy touch, are well known; and there is much in the present volume that will repay attentive perusal. The treatment of pessimism leaves nothing to be desired."—*Saturday Review.*

"Professor Momerie's latest volume fully bears out his reputation for originality, vigour, and lucidity."—*John Bull.*

"A unique contribution to the literature of the day."—*Lady's Pictorial.*

"Here is a bold note, boldly struck; it is only one of many in the book that deserve the attention of opponents as well as friends, and that only a brave man dared touch."—*Scottish Leader.*

"In the course of this remarkable book he passes in review many of the doctrinal questions which are now agitating the Church, and gives a rational explanation of some of the difficulties that perplex both young and old students of theology."—*Dundee Advertiser.*

"Professor Momerie has approached his work with a mental penetration and spiritual devotion worthy of so distinguished a Biblical scholar. The initial chapter, which discusses 'The Evolution of the Bible,' is a masterly exposition. There is a freshness and potency in the author's thought and reasoning that both charm and convince."—*Christian Union.*

IX.

CHURCH AND CREED.

Second Edition. Crown 8vo, 4s. 6d.

"I cannot say that I am in the habit of reading many sermons. But I did read 'Church and Creed,' and I can recommend them to all those desirous of allying religion with common-sense."—*Truth.*

"Persons who still retain the old-fashioned notion that an ordained clergyman holds, in some sense, a brief for the defence, will be bewildered by this wholesale tearing to pieces of dogmas and creeds; and many more, while admiring much in the sermons themselves, will probably take exception, not so much to what is said as to where it is said. 'Church and Creed,' however, is a remarkable book, and a sign of the times which will be noted with different feelings by various classes of thinkers."—*Life.*

"Original, fearless, reverent criticism."—*Yorkshire Post.*

"Simple yet masterly."—*Lincolnshire Free Press.*

"The discourses, one and all, in the volume before us are indeed works of art."—*Glasgow Herald.*

"His lessons on self-sacrifice are well worth careful attention."—*Ecclesiastical Gazette.*

"Dr Momerie is a law unto himself, and is a great illustration of the freedom of thought allowed in the English pulpit. Take for example the sermon in the present volume, entitled 'The Gods of the Bible,' and see what a new face it puts upon our cherished notions of a uniform deistic belief. The whole of the present volume overflows with similar dry, fearless, decisive, almost caustic enunciations that cut athwart hereditary faiths, and it requires a strong mind to follow the preacher as he advances from one startling proposition to another."—*Irish Ecclesiastical Gazette.*

"It is this cheerful and healthful view of life, combined with a hatred of all bigotry and narrowness, that makes Professor Momerie's sermons the inspiration that crowded congregations find them. The man who can persuade people in these pessimistic days that God meant them to laugh and enjoy the life He has given them, and yet be in the truest sense of the word religious, is doing a service to the age which it greatly needs."—*Literary World.*

"It is to be earnestly hoped that the great Head of the Church will raise up an Athanasius in our midst to combat and refute the errors with which it abounds."—*Newbery House Magazine.*

WILLIAM BLACKWOOD & SONS, EDINBURGH AND LONDON.

And all Booksellers.

CATALOGUE

OF

MESSRS BLACKWOOD & SONS' PUBLICATIONS.

PHILOSOPHICAL CLASSICS FOR ENGLISH READERS.
Edited by WILLIAM KNIGHT, LL.D.,
Professor of Moral Philosophy in the University of St Andrews.

In crown 8vo Volumes, with Portraits, price 3s. 6d.

Now ready—

Descartes, by Professor Mahaffy, Dublin.—Butler, by Rev. W. Lucas Collins, M.A.—Berkeley, by Professor Campbell Fraser, Edinburgh.—Fichte, by Professor Adamson, Owens College, Manchester.—Kant, by Professor Wallace, Oxford.—Hamilton, by Professor Veitch, Glasgow.—Hegel, by Professor Edward Caird, Glasgow.—Leibniz, by J. Theodore Merz.—Vico, by Professor Flint, Edinburgh—Hobbes, by Professor Croom Robertson, London.—Hume, by the Editor.—Spinoza, by the Very Rev. Principal Caird, Glasgow.—Bacon: Part I. The Life by Professor Nichol, Glasgow.—Bacon: Part II. Philosophy, by the same Author.—Locke, by Professor Campbell Fraser, Edinburgh.

Mill, . . . *In preparation.*

FOREIGN CLASSICS FOR ENGLISH READERS.
Edited by Mrs OLIPHANT.

In crown 8vo, 2s. 6d.

Contents of the Series.

Dante, by the Editor.—Voltaire, by General Sir E. B. Hamley, K.C.B.—Pascal, by Principal Tulloch.—Petrarch, by Henry Reeve, C.B.—Goethe, By A. Hayward, Q.C.—Moliere, by the Editor and F. Tarver, M.A.—Montaigne, by Rev. W. L. Collins, M.A.—Rabelais, by Walter Besant, M.A.—Calderon, by E. J. Hasell.—Saint Simon, by Clifton W. Collins, M.A.—Cervantes, by the Editor.—Corneille and Racine, by Henry M. Trollope.—Madame de Sévigné, by Miss Thackeray.—La Fontaine, and other French Fabulists, by Rev. W. Lucas Collins, M.A.—Schiller, by James Sime, M.A., Author of 'Lessing, his Life and Writings.'—Tasso, by E. J. Hasell.—Rousseau, by Henry Grey Graham.—Alfred de Musset, by C. F. Oliphant.

In preparation.
Leopardi. By the Editor.

Now Complete.

ANCIENT CLASSICS FOR ENGLISH READERS.
Edited by the Rev. W. LUCAS COLLINS, M.A.

Complete in 28 Vols. crown 8vo, cloth, price 2s. 6d. each. And may also be had in 14 Volumes, strongly and neatly bound, with calf or vellum back, £3, 10s.

Contents of the Series.

Homer: The Iliad, by the Editor.—Homer: The Odyssey, by the Editor.—Herodotus, by George C. Swayne, M.A.—Xenophon, by Sir Alexander Grant, Bart., LL.D.—Euripides, by W. B. Donne.—Aristophanes, by the Editor.—Plato, by Clifton W. Collins, M.A.—Lucian, by the Editor.—Æschylus, by the Right Rev. the Bishop of Colombo.—Sophocles, by Clifton W. Collins, M.A.—Hesiod and Theognis, by the Rev. J. Davies, M.A.—Greek Anthology, by Lord Neaves.—Virgil, by the Editor.—Horace, by Sir Theodore Martin, K.C.B.—Juvenal, by Edward Walford, M.A.—Plautus and Terence, by the Editor.—The Commentaries of Cæsar, by Anthony Trollope.—Tacitus, by W. B. Donne.—Cicero, by the Editor.—Pliny's Letters, by the Rev. Alfred Church, M.A., and the Rev. W. J. Brodribb, M.A.—Livy, by the Editor.—Ovid, by the Rev. A. Church, M.A.—Catullus, Tibullus, and Propertius, by the Rev. Jas. Davies, M.A.—Demosthenes, by the Rev. W. J. Brodribb, M.A.—Aristotle, by Sir Alexander Grant, Bart., LL.D.—Thucydides, by the Editor.—Lucretius, by W. H. Mallock, M.A.—Pindar, by the Rev. F. D. Morice, M.A.

Saturday Review.—"It is difficult to estimate too highly the value of such a series as this in giving 'English readers' an insight, exact as far as it goes, into those olden times which are so remote, and yet to many of us so close."

CATALOGUE

OF

MESSRS BLACKWOOD & SONS'

PUBLICATIONS.

ALISON. History of Europe. By Sir ARCHIBALD ALISON, Bart., D.C.L.
  1. From the Commencement of the French Revolution to the Battle of Waterloo.
     LIBRARY EDITION, 14 vols., with Portraits. Demy 8vo, £10, 10s.
     ANOTHER EDITION, in 20 vols. crown 8vo, £6.
     PEOPLE'S EDITION, 13 vols. crown 8vo, £2, 11s.
  2. Continuation to the Accession of Louis Napoleon.
     LIBRARY EDITION, 8 vols. 8vo, £6, 7s. 6d.
     PEOPLE'S EDITION, 8 vols. crown 8vo, 34s.
  3. Epitome of Alison's History of Europe. Twenty-ninth Thousand, 7s. 6d.
  4. Atlas to Alison's History of Europe. By A. Keith Johnston.
     LIBRARY EDITION, demy 4to, £3, 3s.
     PEOPLE'S EDITION, 31s. 6d.
  ——— Life of John Duke of Marlborough. With some Account of his Contemporaries, and of the War of the Succession. Third Edition. 2 vols. 8vo. Portraits and Maps, 30s.
  ——— Essays: Historical, Political, and Miscellaneous. 3 vols. demy 8vo, 45s.

ACTA SANCTORUM HIBERNIÆ; Ex Codice Salmanticensi. Nunc primum integre edita opera CAROLI DE SMEDT et JOSEPHI DE BACKER, e Soc. Jesu, Hagiographorum Bollandianorum; Auctore et Sumptus Largiente JOANNE PATRICIO MARCHIONE BOTHAE. In One handsome 4to Volume, bound in half roxburghe, £2, 2s.; In paper wrapper, 31s. 6d.

AIRD. Poetical Works of Thomas Aird. Fifth Edition, with Memoir of the Author by the Rev. JARDINE WALLACE, and Portrait. Crown 8vo, 7s. 6d.

ALLARDYCE. The City of Sunshine. By ALEXANDER ALLARDYCE. Three vols. post 8vo, £1, 5s. 6d.
  ——— Memoir of the Honourable George Keith Elphinstone, K.B., Viscount Keith of Stonehaven, Marischal, Admiral of the Red. 8vo, with Portrait, Illustrations, and Maps, 21s.

ALMOND. Sermons by a Lay Head-master. By HELY HUTCHINSON ALMOND, M.A. Oxon., Head-master of Loretto School. Crown 8vo, 5s.

ANCIENT CLASSICS FOR ENGLISH READERS. Edited by Rev. W. LUCAS COLLINS, M.A. Price 2s. 6d. each. For list of Vols., see page 2.

AYTOUN. Lays of the Scottish Cavaliers, and other Poems. By W. EDMONDSTOUNE AYTOUN, D.C.L., Professor of Rhetoric and Belles-Lettres in the University of Edinburgh. New Edition. Fcap. 8vo, 3s. 6d.
  Another Edition, being the Thirtieth. Fcap. 8vo, cloth extra, 7s. 6d.
  Cheap Edition. Fcap. 8vo. Illustrated Cover. Price 1s. Cloth, 1s. 3d.
  ——— An Illustrated Edition of the Lays of the Scottish Cavaliers. From designs by Sir NOEL PATON. Small 4to, in gilt cloth, 21s.
  ——— Bothwell: a Poem. Third Edition. Fcap. 7s. 6d.
  ——— Poems and Ballads of Goethe. Translated by Professor AYTOUN and Sir THEODORE MARTIN, K.C.B. Third Edition. Fcap., 6s.

LIST OF BOOKS PUBLISHED BY

AYTOUN. Bon Gaultier's Book of Ballads. By the SAME. Fifteenth Edition. With Illustrations by Doyle, Leech, and Crowquill. Fcap. 8vo, 5s.

—— The Ballads of Scotland. Edited by Professor AYTOUN. Fourth Edition. 2 vols. fcap. 8vo, 12s.

—— Memoir of William E. Aytoun, D.C.L. By Sir THEODORE MARTIN, K.C.B. With Portrait. Post 8vo, 12s.

BACH. On Musical Education and Vocal Culture. By ALBERT B. BACH. Fourth Edition. 8vo, 7s. 6d.

—— The Principles of Singing. A Practical Guide for Vocalists and Teachers. With Course of Vocal Exercises. Crown 8vo, 6s.

—— The Art of Singing. With Musical Exercises for Young People. Crown 8vo, 3s.

—— The Art Ballad: Loewe and Schubert. With Music Illustrations. With a Portrait of LOEWE. Third Edition. Small 4to. 5s.

BALLADS AND POEMS. By MEMBERS OF THE GLASGOW BALLAD CLUB. Crown 8vo, 7s. 6d.

BANNATYNE. Handbook of Republican Institutions in the United States of America. Based upon Federal and State Laws, and other reliable sources of information. By DUGALD J. BANNATYNE, Scotch Solicitor, New York; Member of the Faculty of Procurators, Glasgow. Cr. 8vo, 7s. 6d.

BELLAIRS. The Transvaal War, 1880-81. Edited by Lady BELLAIRS. With a Frontispiece and Map. 8vo, 15s.

—— Gossips with Girls and Maidens, Betrothed and Free. New Edition. Crown 8vo. 3s. 6d. Cloth, extra gilt edges, 5s.

BESANT. The Revolt of Man. By WALTER BESANT, M.A. Ninth Edition. Crown 8vo, 3s. 6d.

—— Readings in Rabelais. Crown 8vo, 7s. 6d.

BEVERIDGE. Culross and Tulliallan; or Perthshire on Forth. Its History and Antiquities. With Elucidations of Scottish Life and Character from the Burgh and Kirk-Session Records of that District. By DAVID BEVERIDGE. 2 vols. 8vo, with Illustrations, 42s.

—— Between the Ochils and the Forth; or, From Stirling Bridge to Aberdour. Crown 8vo, 6s.

BLACK. Heligoland and the Islands of the North Sea. By WILLIAM GEORGE BLACK. Crown 8vo, 4s.

BLACKIE. Lays and Legends of Ancient Greece. By JOHN STUART BLACKIE, Emeritus Professor of Greek in the University of Edinburgh. Second Edition. Fcap. 8vo. 5s.

—— The Wisdom of Goethe. Fcap. 8vo. Cloth, extra gilt, 6s.

—— Scottish Song: Its Wealth, Wisdom, and Social Significance. Crown 8vo. With Music. 7s. 6d.

—— A Song of Heroes. Crown 8vo, 6s.

BLACKWOOD'S MAGAZINE, from Commencement in 1817 to February 1892. Nos. 1 to 916, forming 150 Volumes.

—— Index to Blackwood's Magazine. Vols. 1 to 50. 8vo, 15s.

BLACKWOOD. Tales from Blackwood. Price One Shilling each, in Paper Cover. Sold separately at all Railway Bookstalls.
They may also be had bound in cloth, 18s., and in half calf, richly gilt, 30s. Or 12 volumes in 6, roxburghe, 21s., and half red morocco, 28s.

—— Tales from Blackwood. New Series. Complete in Twenty-four Shilling Parts. Handsomely bound in 12 vols., cloth, 30s. In leather back, roxburghe style. 37s. 6d. In half calf, gilt. 52s. 6d. In half morocco, 55s.

—— Tales from Blackwood. Third Series. Complete in 6 vols. Handsomely bound in cloth, 15s.; or in 12 vols. 18s. Bound in roxburghe, 21s. Half calf, 25s. Half morocco, 28s. Also in 12 parts, price 1s. each.

—— Travel, Adventure, and Sport. From 'Blackwood's Magazine.' Uniform with 'Tales from Blackwood.' In Twelve Parts, each price 1s. Or handsomely bound in 6 vols., 15s. Half calf, 25s.

BLACKWOOD. New Uniform Series of Three-and-Sixpenny Novels (Copyright). Crown 8vo, cloth. Now ready:—

BEGGAR MY NEIGHBOUR. By E. D. Gerard.
THE WATERS OF HERCULES. By the Same.
SONS AND DAUGHTERS. By Mrs Oliphant.
FAIR TO SEE. By L. W. M. Lockhart.
THE REVOLT OF MAN. By Walter Besant.
MINE IS THINE. By L. W. M. Lockhart.
ALTIORA PETO. By Laurence Oliphant
DOUBLES AND QUITS. By L. W. M. Lockhart.
LADY BABY. By D. Gerard.
HURRISH. By the Hon. Emily Lawless.
THE BLACKSMITH OF VOE. By Paul Cushing.
THE DILEMMA. By the Author of 'The Battle of Dorking.'
MY TRIVIAL LIFE AND MISFORTUNE. By A Plain Woman.
PICCADILLY. By Laurence Oliphant. With Illustrations.

Others in preparation.

—— Standard Novels. Uniform in size and legibly Printed. Each Novel complete in one volume.

FLORIN SERIES, Illustrated Boards. Or in New Cloth Binding, 2s. 6d.

TOM CRINGLE'S LOG. By Michael Scott.
THE CRUISE OF THE MIDGE. By the Same.
CYRIL THORNTON. By Captain Hamilton.
ANNALS OF THE PARISH. By John Galt.
THE PROVOST, &c. By John Galt.
SIR ANDREW WYLIE. By John Galt.
THE ENTAIL. By John Galt.
MISS MOLLY. By Beatrice May Butt.
REGINALD DALTON. By J. G. Lockhart.
PEN OWEN. By Dean Hook.
ADAM BLAIR. By J. G. Lockhart.
LADY LEE'S WIDOWHOOD. By General Sir E. B. Hamley.
SALEM CHAPEL. By Mrs Oliphant.
THE PERPETUAL CURATE. By Mrs Oliphant.
MISS MARJORIBANKS. By Mrs Oliphant.
JOHN: A Love Story. By Mrs Oliphant.

SHILLING SERIES, Illustrated Cover. Or in New Cloth Binding, 1s. 6d.

THE RECTOR, and THE DOCTOR'S FAMILY. By Mrs Oliphant.
THE LIFE OF MANSIE WAUCH. By D. M. Moir.
PENINSULAR SCENES AND SKETCHES. By F. Hardman.
SIR FRIZZLE PUMPKIN, NIGHTS AT MESS &c.
THE SUBALTERN.
LIFE IN THE FAR WEST. By G. F. Ruxton.
VALERIUS: A Roman Story. By J. G. Lockhart.

BLACKMORE. The Maid of Sker. By R. D. BLACKMORE, Author of 'Lorna Doone,' &c. New Edition. Crown 8vo, 6s.

BLAIR. History of the Catholic Church of Scotland. From the Introduction of Christianity to the Present Day. By ALPHONS BELLESHEIM, D.D., Canon of Aix-la-Chapelle. Translated, with Notes and Additions, by D. OSWALD HUNTER BLAIR, O.S.B., Monk of Fort Augustus. Complete in 4 vols. demy 8vo, with Maps. Price 12s. 6d. each.

BONNAR. Biographical Sketch of George Meikle Kemp, Architect of the Scott Monument, Edinburgh. By THOMAS BONNAR, F.S.A. Scot., Author of 'The Present Art Revival,' 'The Past of Art in Scotland,' 'Suggestions for the Picturesque of Interiors,' &c. With Three Portraits and numerous Illustrations. In One Volume, post 8vo.

BOSCOBEL TRACTS. Relating to the Escape of Charles the Second after the Battle of Worcester, and his subsequent Adventures. Edited by J. HUGHES, Esq., A.M. A New Edition, with additional Notes and Illustrations, including Communications from the Rev. R. H. BARHAM, Author of the 'Ingoldsby Legends.' 8vo, with Engravings, 16s.

BROUGHAM. Memoirs of the Life and Times of Henry Lord Brougham. Written by HIMSELF. 3 vols. 8vo, £2, 8s. The Volumes are sold separately, price 16s. each.

BROWN. The Forester: A Practical Treatise on the Planting, Rearing, and General Management of Forest-trees. By JAMES BROWN, LL.D., Inspector of and Reporter on Woods and Forests. Fifth Edition, revised and enlarged. Royal 8vo, with Engravings, 36s.

BROWN. A Manual of Botany, Anatomical and Physiological. For the Use of Students. By ROBERT BROWN, M.A., Ph.D. Crown 8vo, with numerous Illustrations, 12s. 6d.

BRUCE. In Clover and Heather. Poems by WALLACE BRUCE. New and Enlarged Edition. Crown 8vo, 4s. 6d.
A limited number of Copies of the First Edition, on large hand-made paper, 12s. 6d.

BRYDALL. Art in Scotland; its Origin and Progress. By ROBERT BRYDALL, Master of St George's Art School of Glasgow. 8vo, 12s. 6d.

BUCHAN. Introductory Text-Book of Meteorology. By ALEXANDER BUCHAN, M.A., F.R.S.E., Secretary of the Scottish Meteorological Society, &c. Crown 8vo, with 8 Coloured Charts and Engravings, 4s. 6d.

BUCHANAN. The Shire Highlands (East Central Africa). By JOHN BUCHANAN, Planter at Zomba. Crown 8vo, 5s.

BURBIDGE. Domestic Floriculture, Window Gardening, and Floral Decorations. Being practical directions for the Propagation, Culture, and Arrangement of Plants and Flowers as Domestic Ornaments. By F. W. BURBIDGE. Second Edition. Crown 8vo, with numerous Illustrations, 7s. 6d.

—— Cultivated Plants: Their Propagation and Improvement. Including Natural and Artificial Hybridisation, Raising from Seed, Cuttings, and Layers, Grafting and Budding, as applied to the Families and Genera in Cultivation. Crown 8vo, with numerous Illustrations, 12s. 6d.

BURTON. The History of Scotland: From Agricola's Invasion to the Extinction of the last Jacobite Insurrection. By JOHN HILL BURTON, D.C.L., Historiographer-Royal for Scotland. New and Enlarged Edition. 8 vols., and Index. Crown 8vo, £3, 3s.

—— History of the British Empire during the Reign of Queen Anne. In 3 vols. 8vo. 36s.

—— The Scot Abroad. Third Edition. Crown 8vo, 10s. 6d.

—— The Book-Hunter. New Edition. With Portrait. Crown 8vo, 7s. 6d.

BUTE. The Roman Breviary: Reformed by Order of the Holy Œcumenical Council of Trent; Published by Order of Pope St Pius V.; and Revised by Clement VIII. and Urban VIII.; together with the Offices since granted. Translated out of Latin into English by JOHN, Marquess of Bute, K.T. In 2 vols, crown 8vo. cloth boards, edges uncut. £2, 2s.

—— The Altus of St Columba. With a Prose Paraphrase and Notes. In paper cover, 2s. 6d.

BUTLER. Pompeii: Descriptive and Picturesque. By W. BUTLER. Post 8vo, 5s.

BUTT. Miss Molly. By BEATRICE MAY BUTT. Cheap Edition, 2s.

—— Eugenie. Crown 8vo, 6s. 6d.

—— Elizabeth, and Other Sketches. Crown 8vo, 6s.

—— Novels. New and Uniform Edition. Crown 8vo, each 2s. 6d. Delicia. *Now ready.*

CAIRD. Sermons. By JOHN CAIRD, D.D., Principal of the University of Glasgow. Sixteenth Thousand. Fcap. 8vo, 5s.

—— Religion in Common Life. A Sermon preached in Crathie Church, October 14, 1855, before Her Majesty the Queen and Prince Albert. Published by Her Majesty's Command. Cheap Edition, 3d.

CALDER. Chaucer's Canterbury Pilgrimage. Epitomised by WILLIAM CALDER. With Photogravure of the Pilgrimage Company, and other Illustrations, Glossary, &c. Crown 8vo, 4s.

CAMPBELL. Critical Studies in St Luke's Gospel: Its Demonology and Ebionitism. By COLIN CAMPBELL, B.D., Minister of the Parish of Dundee, formerly Scholar and Fellow of Glasgow University. Author of the 'Three First Gospels in Greek, arranged in parallel columns. Post 8vo, 7s. 6d.

CAMPBELL. Sermons Preached before the Queen at Balmoral. By the Rev. A. A. CAMPBELL, Minister of Crathie. Published by Command of Her Majesty. Crown 8vo, 4s. 6d.

CAMPBELL. Records of Argyll. Legends, Traditions, and Recollections of Argyllshire Highlanders, collected chiefly from the Gaelic. With Notes on the Antiquity of the Dress, Clan Colours or Tartans of the Highlanders. By LORD ARCHIBALD CAMPBELL. Illustrated with Nineteen full-page Etchings. 4to, printed on hand-made paper, £3, 3s.

CANTON. A Lost Epic, and other Poems. By WILLIAM CANTON. Crown 8vo, 5s.

CARRICK. Koumiss; or, Fermented Mare's Milk: and its Uses in the Treatment and Cure of Pulmonary Consumption, and other Wasting Diseases. With an Appendix on the best Methods of Fermenting Cow's Milk. By GEORGE L. CARRICK, M.D., L.R.C.S.E. and L.R.C.P.E., Physician to the British Embassy, St Petersburg, &c. Crown 8vo, 10s. 6d.

CARSTAIRS. British Work in India. By R. CARSTAIRS. Cr. 8vo, 6s.

CAUVIN. A Treasury of the English and German Languages. Compiled from the best Authors and Lexicographers in both Languages. By JOSEPH CAUVIN, LL.D. and Ph.D., of the University of Göttingen, &c. Crown 8vo, 7s. 6d.

CAVE-BROWN. Lambeth Palace and its Associations. By J. CAVE-BROWN, M.A., Vicar of Detling, Kent, and for many years Curate of Lambeth Parish Church. With an Introduction by the Archbishop of Canterbury. Second Edition, containing an additional Chapter on Medieval Life in the Old Palaces. 8vo, with Illustrations, 21s.

CHARTERIS. Canonicity; or, Early Testimonies to the Existence and Use of the Books of the New Testament. Based on Kirchhoffer's 'Quellensammlung.' Edited by A. H. CHARTERIS, D.D., Professor of Biblical Criticism in the University of Edinburgh. 8vo, 18s.

CHRISTISON. Life of Sir Robert Christison, Bart., M.D., D.C.L. Oxon., Professor of Medical Jurisprudence in the University of Edinburgh. Edited by his Sons. In two vols. 8vo. Vol. I.—Autobiography. 16s. Vol. II.—Memoirs. 16s.

CHRONICLES OF WESTERLY: A Provincial Sketch. By the Author of 'Culmshire Folk,' 'John Orlebar,' &c. 3 vols. crown 8vo, 25s. 6d.

CHURCH SERVICE SOCIETY. A Book of Common Order: Being Forms of Worship issued by the Church Service Society. Sixth Edition. Crown, 8vo, 6s. Also in 2 vols, crown 8vo, 6s. 6d.

CLOUSTON. Popular Tales and Fictions: their Migrations and Transformations. By W. A. CLOUSTON, Editor of 'Arabian Poetry for English Readers,' &c. 2 vols. post 8vo, roxburghe binding, 25s.

COCHRAN. A Handy Text-Book of Military Law. Compiled chiefly to assist Officers preparing for Examination; also for all Officers of the Regular and Auxiliary Forces. Comprising also a Synopsis of part of the Army Act. By Major F. COCHRAN, Hampshire Regiment Garrison Instructor, North British District. Crown 8vo, 7s. 6d.

COLQUHOUN. The Moor and the Loch. Containing Minute Instructions in all Highland Sports, with Wanderings over Crag and Corrie, Flood and Fell. By JOHN COLQUHOUN. Seventh Edition. With Illustrations. 8vo, 21s.

COTTERILL. Suggested Reforms in Public Schools. By C. C. COTTERILL, M.A. Crown 8vo, 3s. 6d.

CRANSTOUN. The Elegies of Albius Tibullus. Translated into English Verse, with Life of the Poet, and Illustrative Notes. By JAMES CRANSTOUN, LL.D., Author of a Translation of 'Catullus.' Crown 8vo, 6s. 6d.

—— The Elegies of Sextus Propertius. Translated into English Verse, with Life of the Poet, and Illustrative Notes. Crown 8vo, 7s. 6d.

CRAWFORD. Saracinesca. By F. MARION CRAWFORD, Author of 'Mr Isaacs,' 'Dr Claudius,' 'Zoroaster,' &c. &c. Fifth Ed. Crown 8vo, 6s.

CRAWFORD. The Doctrine of Holy Scripture respecting the Atonement. By the late THOMAS J. CRAWFORD, D.D., Professor of Divinity in the University of Edinburgh. Fifth Edition. 8vo, 12s.

—— The Fatherhood of God, Considered in its General and Special Aspects. Third Edition, Revised and Enlarged. 8vo, 9s.

—— The Preaching of the Cross, and other Sermons. 8vo, 7s. 6d.

—— The Mysteries of Christianity. Crown 8vo, 7s. 6d.

CRAWFORD. An Atonement of East London, and other Poems. By HOWARD CRAWFORD, M.A. Crown 8vo, 5s.

CUSHING. The Blacksmith of Voe. By PAUL CUSHING, Author of 'The Bull i' th' Thorn.' Cheap Edition. Crown 8vo, 3s. 6d.

—— Cut with his own Diamond. A Novel. 3 vols. cr. 8vo, 25s. 6d.

DAVIES. Norfolk Broads and Rivers; or, The Waterways, Lagoons, and Decoys of East Anglia. By G. CHRISTOPHER DAVIES. Illustrated with Seven full-page Plates. New and Cheaper Edition. Crown 8vo, 6s.

——— Our Home in Aveyron. Sketches of Peasant Life in Aveyron and the Lot. By G. CHRISTOPHER DAVIES and Mrs BROUGHALL. Illustrated with full-page Illustrations. 8vo, 15s. Cheap Edition, 7s. 6d.

DAYNE. Tribute to Satan. A Novel. By J. BELFORD DAYNE, Author of 'In the Name of the Tzar.' Crown 8vo, 2s. 6d.

DE LA WARR. An Eastern Cruise in the 'Edeline.' By the Countess DE LA WARR. In Illustrated Cover. 2s.

DESCARTES. The Method, Meditations, and Principles of Philosophy of Descartes. Translated from the Original French and Latin. With a New Introductory Essay, Historical and Critical, on the Cartesian Philosophy. By Professor VEITCH, LL.D., Glasgow University. Ninth Edition. 6s. 6d.

DICKSON. Gleanings from Japan. By W. G. DICKSON, Author of 'Japan: Being a Sketch of its History, Government, and Officers of the Empire.' With Illustrations. 8vo, 16s.

DOGS, OUR DOMESTICATED: Their Treatment in reference to Food, Diseases, Habits, Punishment, Accomplishments. By 'MAGENTA.' Crown 8vo, 2s. 6d.

DOMESTIC EXPERIMENT, A. By the Author of 'Ideala: A Study from Life.' Crown 8vo, 6s.

DR HERMIONE. By the Author of 'Lady Bluebeard,' 'Zit and Xoe.' Crown 8vo, 6s.

DU CANE. The Odyssey of Homer, Books I.-XII. Translated into English Verse. By Sir CHARLES DU CANE, K.C.M.G. 8vo, 10s. 6d.

DUDGEON. History of the Edinburgh or Queen's Regiment Light Infantry Militia, now 3rd Battalion The Royal Scots; with an Account of the Origin and Progress of the Militia, and a Brief Sketch of the old Royal Scots. By Major R. C. DUDGEON, Adjutant 3rd Battalion The Royal Scots. Post 8vo, with Illustrations. 10s. 6d.

DUNCAN. Manual of the General Acts of Parliament relating to the Salmon Fisheries of Scotland from 1828 to 1882. By J. BARKER DUNCAN. Crown 8vo, 5s.

DUNSMORE. Manual of the Law of Scotland as to the Relations between Agricultural Tenants and their Landlords, Servants, Merchants, and Bowers. By W. DUNSMORE. 8vo, 7s. 6d.

DUPRÈ. Thoughts on Art, and Autobiographical Memoirs of Giovanni Duprè. Translated from the Italian by E. M. PERUZZI, with the permission of the Author. New Edition. With an Introduction by W. W. STORY. Crown 8vo, 10s. 6d.

ELIOT. George Eliot's Life, Related in her Letters and Journals. Arranged and Edited by her husband, J. W. CROSS. With Portrait and other Illustrations. Third Edition. 3 vols. post 8vo, 42s.

——— George Eliot's Life. (Cabinet Edition.) With Portrait and other Illustrations. 3 vols. crown 8vo, 15s.

——— George Eliot's Life. With Portrait and other Illustrations. New Edition, in one volume. Crown 8vo, 7s. 6d.

——— Works of George Eliot (Cabinet Edition). Handsomely printed in a new type, 21 volumes, crown 8vo, price £5, 5s. The Volumes are also sold separately, price 5s. each, viz.:—
Romola. 2 vols.—Silas Marner, The Lifted Veil, Brother Jacob. 1 vol.—Adam Bede. 2 vols.—Scenes of Clerical Life. 2 vols.—The Mill on the Floss. 2 vols.—Felix Holt. 2 vols.—Middlemarch. 3 vols.—Daniel Deronda. 3 vols.—The Spanish Gypsy. 1 vol.—Jubal, and other Poems, Old and New. 1 vol.—Theophrastus Such. 1 vol.—Essays. 1 vol.

——— Novels by GEORGE ELIOT. Cheap Edition. Adam Bede. Illustrated. 3s. 6d., cloth.—The Mill on the Floss. Illustrated. 3s. 6d., cloth.—Scenes of Clerical Life. Illustrated. 3s., cloth.—Silas Marner: the Weaver of Raveloe. Illustrated. 2s. 6d., cloth.—Felix Holt, the Radical. Illustrated. 3s. 6d., cloth.—Romola. With Vignette. 3s. 6d., cloth.

——— Middlemarch. Crown 8vo, 7s. 6d.

ELIOT. Daniel Deronda. Crown 8vo, 7s. 6d.
——— Essays. New Edition. Crown 8vo, 5s.
——— Impressions of Theophrastus Such. New Ed. Cr. 8vo, 5s.
——— The Spanish Gypsy. New Edition. Crown 8vo, 5s.
——— The Legend of Jubal, and other Poems, Old and New. New Edition. Crown 8vo, 5s.
——— Wise, Witty, and Tender Sayings, in Prose and Verse. Selected from the Works of GEORGE ELIOT. Eighth Edition. Fcap. 8vo, 6s.
——— The George Eliot Birthday Book. Printed on fine paper, with red border, and handsomely bound in cloth, gilt. Fcap. 8vo, cloth, 3s. 6d. And in French morocco or Russia, 5s.

ESSAYS ON SOCIAL SUBJECTS. Originally published in the 'Saturday Review.' New Ed. First & Second Series. 2 vols. cr. 8vo, 6s. each.

EWALD. The Crown and its Advisers; or, Queen, Ministers, Lords and Commons. By ALEXANDER CHARLES EWALD, F.S.A. Crown 8vo, 5s.

FAITHS OF THE WORLD, The. A Concise History of the Great Religions Systems of the World. By various Authors. Crown 8vo, 5s.

FARRER. A Tour in Greece in 1880. By RICHARD RIDLEY FARRER. With Twenty-seven full-page Illustrations by LORD WINDSOR. Royal 8vo, with a Map, 21s.

FERRIER. Philosophical Works of the late James F. Ferrier, B.A. Oxon., Professor of Moral Philosophy and Political Economy, St Andrews. New Edition. Edited by Sir ALEX. GRANT, Bart., D.C.L., and Professor LUSHINGTON. 3 vols. crown 8vo, 34s. 6d.

——— Institutes of Metaphysic. Third Edition. 10s. 6d.
——— Lectures on the Early Greek Philosophy. 3d Ed. 10s. 6d.
——— Philosophical Remains, including the Lectures on Early Greek Philosophy. 2 vols., 24s.

FITZROY. Dogma and the Church of England. By A. I. FITZROY. Post 8vo, 7s. 6d.

FLINT. The Philosophy of History in Europe. By ROBERT FLINT, D.D., LL.D., Professor of Divinity, University of Edinburgh. 2 vols. 8vo. [New Edition in preparation.
——— Theism. Being the Baird Lecture for 1876. Eighth Edition. Crown 8vo, 7s. 6d.
——— Anti-Theistic Theories. Being the Baird Lecture for 1877. Fourth Edition. Crown 8vo, 10s. 6d.
——— Agnosticism. Being the Croall Lectures for 1887-88. [In the press.

FORBES. Insulinde: Experiences of a Naturalist's Wife in the Eastern Archipelago. By Mrs H. O. FORBES. Crown 8vo, with a Map. 4s. 6d.

FOREIGN CLASSICS FOR ENGLISH READERS. Edited by Mrs OLIPHANT. Price 2s. 6d. For List of Volumes published, see page 2.

FOSTER. The Fallen City, and Other Poems. By WILL FOSTER. Crown 8vo, 6s.

FRANCILLON. Gods and Heroes; or, The Kingdom of Jupiter. By R. E. FRANCILLON. With 8 Illustrations. Crown 8vo, 5s.

FULLARTON. Merlin: A Dramatic Poem. By RALPH MACLEOD FULLARTON. Crown 8vo, 5s.

GALT. Novels by JOHN GALT. Fcap. 8vo, boards, 2s.; cloth, 2s. 6d. Annals of the Parish.—The Provost.—Sir Andrew Wylie.—The Entail.

GENERAL ASSEMBLY OF THE CHURCH OF SCOTLAND.
——— Prayers for Social and Family Worship. Prepared by a Special Committee of the General Assembly of the Church of Scotland. Entirely New Edition, Revised and Enlarged. Fcap. 8vo, red edges, 2s.
——— Prayers for Family Worship. A Selection from the complete book. Fcap. 8vo, red edges, price 1s.

GENERAL ASSEMBLY OF THE CHURCH OF SCOTLAND.
—— Scottish Hymnal, with Appendix Incorporated. Published for Use in Churches by Authority of the General Assembly. 1. Large type, cloth, red edges, 2s. 6d.; French morocco, 4s. 2. Bourgeois type, limp cloth, 1s.; French morocco, 2s. 3. Nonpareil type, cloth, red edges, 6d.; French morocco, 1s. 4d. 4. Paper covers, 3d. 5. Sunday-School Edition, paper covers, 1d. No. 1, bound with the Psalms and Paraphrases, French morocco, 8s. No. 2, bound with the Psalms and Paraphrases, cloth, 2s.; French morocco, 3s.

GERARD. Reata: What's in a Name. By E. D. GERARD. New Edition. Crown 8vo, 6s.
—— Beggar my Neighbour. Cheap Edition. Crown 8vo, 3s. 6d.
—— The Waters of Hercules. Cheap Edition. Crown 8vo, 3s. 6d.
GERARD. The Land beyond the Forest. Facts, Figures, and Fancies from Transylvania. By E. GERARD. In Two Volumes. With Maps and Illustrations. 25s.
—— Bis: Some Tales Retold. Crown 8vo, 6s.
—— A Secret Mission. 2 vols. crown 8vo, 17s.
GERARD. Lady Baby. By DOROTHEA GERARD, Author of 'Orthodox.' Cheap Edition. Crown 8vo, 3s. 6d.
—— Recha. Second Edition. Crown 8vo, 6s.
GERARD. Stonyhurst Latin Grammar. By Rev. JOHN GERARD.
[*New Edition in preparation.*
GILL. Free Trade: an Inquiry into the Nature of its Operation. By RICHARD GILL. Crown 8vo, 7s. 6d.
—— Free Trade under Protection. Crown 8vo, 7s. 6d.
GOETHE'S FAUST. Translated into English Verse by Sir THEODORE MARTIN, K.C.B. Part I. Second Edition, post 8vo, 6s. Ninth Edition, fcap., 3s. 6d. Part II. Second Edition, revised. Fcap. 8vo, 6s.
GOETHE. Poems and Ballads of Goethe. Translated by Professor AYTOUN and Sir THEODORE MARTIN, K.C.B. Third Edition, fcap. 8vo, 6s.
GOODALL. Juxta Crucem. Studies of the Love that is over us. By the late Rev. CHARLES GOODALL, B.D., Minister of Barr. With a Memoir by Rev. Dr Strong, Glasgow, and Portrait. Crown 8vo, 6s.
GORDON CUMMING. Two Happy Years in Ceylon. By C. F. GORDON CUMMING. With 15 full-page Illustrations and a Map. Second Edition. 2 vols. 8vo, 30s.
—— At Home in Fiji. Fourth Edition, post 8vo. With Illustrations and Map. 7s. 6d.
—— A Lady's Cruise in a French Man-of-War. New and Cheaper Edition. 8vo. With Illustrations and Map. 12s. 6d.
—— Fire-Fountains. The Kingdom of Hawaii: Its Volcanoes, and the History of its Missions. With Map and Illustrations. 2 vols. 8vo, 25s.
—— Wanderings in China. New and Cheaper Edition. 8vo, with Illustrations, 10s.
—— Granite Crags: The Yō-semitè Region of California. Illustrated with 8 Engravings. New and Cheaper Edition. 8vo, 8s. 6d
GRAHAM. The Life and Work of Syed Ahmed Khan, C.S.I. By Lieut.-Colonel G. F. I. GRAHAM, B.S.C. 8vo, 14s.
GRAHAM. Manual of the Elections (Scot.) (Corrupt and Illegal Practices) Act, 1890. With Analysis, Relative Act of Sederunt, Appendix containing the Corrupt Practices Acts of 1883 and 1885, and Copious Index. By J. EDWARD GRAHAM, Advocate. 8vo, 4s. 6d.
GRANT. Bush-Life in Queensland. By A. C. GRANT. New Edition. Crown 8vo, 6s.
GRIFFITHS. Locked Up. By Major ARTHUR GRIFFITHS, Author of 'The Wrong Road,' 'Chronicles of Newgate,' &c. With Illustrations by C. J. STANILAND, R.I. Crown 8vo, 2s. 6d.
GUTHRIE-SMITH. Crispus: A Drama. By H. GUTHRIE-SMITH. In one volume. Fcap. 4to, 5s.

HAINES. Unless! A Romance. By RANDOLPH HAINES. Crown 8vo, 6s.

HALDANE. Subtropical Cultivations and Climates. A Handy Book for Planters, Colonists, and Settlers. By R. C. HALDANE. Post 8vo, 9s.

HALLETT. A Thousand Miles on an Elephant in the Shan States. By HOLT S. HALLETT, M. Iust. C.E., F.R.G.S., M.R.A.S., Hon. Member Manchester and Tyneside Geographical Societies. 8vo, with Maps and numerous Illustrations, 21s.

HAMERTON. Wenderholme: A Story of Lancashire and Yorkshire Life. By PHILIP GILBERT HAMERTON, Author of 'A Painter's Camp.' A New Edition. Crown 8vo, 6s.

HAMILTON. Lectures on Metaphysics. By Sir WILLIAM HAMILTON, Bart., Professor of Logic and Metaphysics in the University of Edinburgh. Edited by the Rev. H. L. MANSEL, B.D., LL.D., Dean of St Paul's; and JOHN VEITCH, M.A., LL.D., Professor of Logic and Rhetoric, Glasgow. Seventh Edition. 2 vols. 8vo, 24s.

—— Lectures on Logic. Edited by the SAME. Third Edition. 2 vols., 24s.

—— Discussions on Philosophy and Literature, Education and University Reform. Third Edition, 8vo, 21s.

—— Memoir of Sir William Hamilton, Bart., Professor of Logic and Metaphysics in the University of Edinburgh. By Professor VEITCH, of the University of Glasgow. 8vo, with Portrait, 18s.

—— Sir William Hamilton: The Man and his Philosophy. Two Lectures delivered before the Edinburgh Philosophical Institution, January and February 1883. By the SAME. Crown 8vo, 2s.

HAMLEY. The Operations of War Explained and Illustrated. By General Sir EDWARD BRUCE HAMLEY, K.C.B., K.C.M.G., M.P. Fifth Edition, revised throughout. 4to, with numerous Illustrations, 30s.

—— National Defence; Articles and Speeches. Post 8vo, 6s.

—— Shakespeare's Funeral, and other Papers. Post 8vo, 7s. 6d.

—— Thomas Carlyle: An Essay. Second Ed. Cr. 8vo, 2s. 6d.

—— On Outposts. Second Edition. 8vo, 2s.

—— Wellington's Career; A Military and Political Summary. Crown 8vo, 2s.

—— Lady Lee's Widowhood. Crown 8vo, 2s. 6d.

—— Our Poor Relations. A Philozoic Essay. With Illustrations, chiefly by Ernest Griset. Crown 8vo, cloth gilt, 3s. 6d.

HAMLEY. Guilty, or Not Guilty? A Tale. By Major-General W. G. HAMLEY, late of the Royal Engineers. New Edition. Crown 8vo, 3s. 6d.

HARRISON. The Scot in Ulster. The Story of the Scottish Settlement in Ulster. By JOHN HARRISON, Author of 'Oure Tounis Colledge.' Crown 8vo, 2s. 6d.

HASELL. Bible Partings. By E. J. HASELL. Crown 8vo, 6s.

—— Short Family Prayers. Cloth, 1s.

HAY. The Works of the Right Rev. Dr George Hay, Bishop of Edinburgh. Edited under the Supervision of the Right Rev. Bishop STRAIN. With Memoir and Portrait of the Author. 5 vols. crown 8vo, bound in extra cloth, £1, 1s. The following Volumes may be had separately—viz.: The Devout Christian Instructed in the Law of Christ from the Written Word. 2 vols., 8s.—The Pious Christian Instructed in the Nature and Practice of the Principal Exercises of Piety. 1 vol., 3s.

HEATLEY. The Horse-Owner's Safeguard. A Handy Medical Guide for every Man who owns a Horse. By G. S. HEATLEY, M.R.C.V.S. Crown 8vo, 5s.

—— The Stock-Owner's Guide. A Handy Medical Treatise for every Man who owns an Ox or a Cow. Crown 8vo, 4s. 6d.

HEDDERWICK. Lays of Middle Age; and other Poems. By JAMES HEDDERWICK, LL.D. Price 3s. 6d.

HEDDERWICK. Backward Glances; or, Some Personal Recollections. With a Portrait. Post 8vo, 7s. 6d.

HEMANS. The Poetical Works of Mrs Hemans. Copyright Editions.—Royal 8vo, 5s.—The Same, with Engravings, cloth, gilt edges, 7s. 6d.—Six Vols. in Three, fcap., 12s. 6d.

SELECT POEMS OF MRS HEMANS. Fcap., cloth, gilt edges, 3s.

HERKLESS. Cardinal Beaton Priest and Politician. By JOHN HERKLESS, Minister of Tannadice. With a Portrait. Post 8vo, 7s. 6d.

HOME PRAYERS. By Ministers of the Church of Scotland and Members of the Church Service Society. Second Edition. Fcap. 8vo, 3s.

HOMER. The Odyssey. Translated into English Verse in the Spenserian Stanza. By PHILIP STANHOPE WORSLEY. Third Edition, 2 vols. fcap., 12s.

—— The Iliad. Translated by P. S. WORSLEY and Professor CONINGTON. 2 vols. crown 8vo, 21s.

HUTCHINSON. Hints on the Game of Golf. By HORACE G. HUTCHINSON. Sixth Edition, Enlarged. Fcap. 8vo, cloth, 1s.

IDDESLEIGH. Lectures and Essays. By the late EARL OF IDDESLEIGH, G.C.B., D.C.L., &c. 8vo, 16s.

—— Life, Letters, and Diaries of Sir Stafford Northcote, First Earl of Iddesleigh. By ANDREW LANG. With Three Portraits and a View of Pynes. Third Edition. 2 vols. Post 8vo, 31s. 6d.

POPULAR EDITION. In one volume. With two Plates. Post 8vo, 7s. 6d.

INDEX GEOGRAPHICUS: Being a List, alphabetically arranged, of the Principal Places on the Globe, with the Countries and Subdivisions of the Countries in which they are situated, and their Latitudes and Longitudes. Imperial 8vo, pp. 676, 21s.

JEAN JAMBON. Our Trip to Blunderland; or, Grand Excursion to Blundertown and Back. By JEAN JAMBON. With Sixty Illustrations designed by CHARLES DOYLE, engraved by DALZIEL. Fourth Thousand. Cloth, gilt edges, 6s. 6d. Cheap Edition, cloth, 3s. 6d. Boards, 2s. 6d.

JENNINGS. Mr Gladstone: A Study. By LOUIS J. JENNINGS, M.P., Author of 'Republican Government in the United States,' 'The Croker Memoirs,' &c. Popular Edition. Crown 8vo, 1s.

JERNINGHAM. Reminiscences of an Attaché. By HUBERT E. H. JERNINGHAM. Second Edition. Crown 8vo, 5s.

—— Diane de Breteuille. A Love Story. Crown 8vo, 2s. 6d.

JOHNSTON. The Chemistry of Common Life. By Professor J. F. W. JOHNSTON. New Edition, Revised, and brought down to date. By ARTHUR HERBERT CHURCH, M.A. Oxon.; Author of 'Food: its Sources, Constituents, and Uses,' &c. With Maps and 102 Engravings. Cr. 8vo, 7s. 6d.

—— Elements of Agricultural Chemistry and Geology. Revised, and brought down to date. By Sir CHARLES A. CAMERON, M.D., F.R.C.S.I., &c. Sixteenth Edition. Fcap. 8vo, 6s. 6d.

—— Catechism of Agricultural Chemistry and Geology. Revised by Sir C. A. CAMERON. With numerous Illustrations.
[*New Edition in preparation.*

JOHNSTON. Patrick Hamilton: a Tragedy of the Reformation in Scotland, 1528. By T. P. JOHNSTON. Crown 8vo, with Two Etchings. 5s.

KEBBEL. The Old and the New: English Country Life. The Country Clergy—The Country Gentlemen—The Farmers—The Peasantry—The Eighteenth Century. By T. E. KEBBEL, M.A., Author of 'Agricultural Labourers,' 'Essays in History and Politics,' 'Life of Lord Beaconsfield.' Crown 8vo, 5s.

KING. The Metamorphoses of Ovid. Translated in English Blank Verse. By HENRY KING, M.A., Fellow of Wadham College, Oxford, and of the Inner Temple, Barrister-at-Law. Crown 8vo, 10s. 6d.

KINGLAKE. History of the Invasion of the Crimea. By A. W. KINGLAKE. Cabinet Edition, revised. With an Index to the Complete Work. Illustrated with Maps and Plans. Complete in 9 Vols., crown 8vo, at 6s. each.

KINGLAKE. History of the Invasion of the Crimea. Demy 8vo.
Vol. VI. Winter Troubles. With a Map, 16s. Vols. VII. and VIII. From the Morrow of Inkerman to the Death of Lord Raglan. With an Index to the Whole Work. With Maps and Plans. 28s.

——— Eothen. A New Edition, uniform with the Cabinet Edition of the 'History of the Invasion of the Crimea,' price 6s.

KNEIPP. My Water-Cure. As Tested through more than Thirty Years, and Described for the Healing of Diseases and the Preservation of Health. By SEBASTIAN KNEIPP, Parish Priest of Wörishofen (Bavaria). With a Portrait and other Illustrations. Only Authorised English Translation. Translated from the Thirtieth German Edition by A. de F. Crown 8vo, 5s.

KNOLLYS. The Elements of Field-Artillery. Designed for the Use of Infantry and Cavalry Officers. By HENRY KNOLLYS, Captain Royal Artillery; Author of 'From Sedan to Saarbrück,' Editor of 'Incidents in the Sepoy War,' &c. With Engravings. Crown 8vo, 7s. 6d.

LAMINGTON. In the Days of the Dandies. By the late Lord LAMINGTON. Crown 8vo. Illustrated cover, 1s.; cloth, 1s. 6d.

LAWLESS. Hurrish: a Study. By the Hon. EMILY LAWLESS, Author of 'A Chelsea Householder,' &c. Fourth Edition, crown 8vo, 3s. 6d.

LAWSON. Spain of To-day: A Descriptive, Industrial, and Financial Survey of the Peninsula, with a full account of the Rio Tinto Mines. By W. R. LAWSON. Crown 8vo, 3s 6d.

LEES. A Handbook of the Sheriff and Justice of Peace Small Debt Courts. 8vo, 7s. 6d.

LIGHTFOOT. Studies in Philosophy. By the Rev. J. LIGHTFOOT, M.A., D.Sc., Vicar of Cross Stone, Todmorden. Crown 8vo, 4s. 6d.

LOCKHART. Novels by LAURENCE W. M. LOCKHART. See Blackwoods' New Series of Three-and-Sixpenny Novels on page 5.

LORIMER. The Institutes of Law: A Treatise of the Principles of Jurisprudence as determined by Nature. By the late JAMES LORIMER, Professor of Public Law and of the Law of Nature and Nations in the University of Edinburgh. New Edition, revised and much enlarged. 8vo, 18s.

——— The Institutes of the Law of Nations. A Treatise of the Jural Relation of Separate Political Communities. In 2 vols. 8vo. Volume I., price 16s. Volume II., price 20s.

LOVE. Scottish Church Music. Its Composers and Sources. With Musical Illustrations. By JAMES LOVE. In 1 vol. post 8vo, 7s. 6d.

M'COMBIE. Cattle and Cattle-Breeders. By WILLIAM M'COMBIE, Tillyfour. New Edition, enlarged, with Memoir of the Author. By JAMES MACDONALD, of the 'Farming World.' Crown 8vo, 3s. 6d.

MACRAE. A Handbook of Deer-Stalking. By ALEXANDER MACRAE, late Forester to Lord Henry Bentinck. With Introduction by HORATIO ROSS, Esq. Fcap. 8vo, with two Photographs from Life. 3s. 6d.

M'CRIE. Works of the Rev. Thomas M'Crie, D.D. Uniform Edition. Four vols. crown 8vo, 24s.

——— Life of John Knox. Containing Illustrations of the History of the Reformation in Scotland. Crown 8vo, 6s. Another Edition, 3s. 6d.

——— Life of Andrew Melville. Containing Illustrations of the Ecclesiastical and Literary History of Scotland in the Sixteenth and Seventeenth Centuries. Crown 8vo, 6s.

——— History of the Progress and Suppression of the Reformation in Italy in the Sixteenth Century. Crown 8vo, 4s.

——— History of the Progress and Suppression of the Reformation in Spain in the Sixteenth Century. Crown 8vo, 3s. 6d.

——— Lectures on the Book of Esther. Fcap. 8vo, 5s.

MACDONALD. A Manual of the Criminal Law (Scotland) Procedure Act, 1887. By NORMAN DORAN MACDONALD. Revised by the LORD JUSTICE-CLERK. 8vo, cloth, 10s. 6d.

MACGREGOR. Life and Opinions of Major-General Sir Charles MacGregor, K.C.B., C.S.I., C.I.E, Quartermaster-General of India. From his Letters and Diaries. Edited by LADY MACGREGOR. With Portraits and Maps to illustrate Campaigns in which he was engaged. 2 vols. 8vo, 35s.

M'INTOSH. The Book of the Garden. By CHARLES M'INTOSH, formerly Curator of the Royal Gardens of his Majesty the King of the Belgians, and lately of those of his Grace the Duke of Buccleuch, K.G., at Dalkeith Palace. 2 vols. royal 8vo, with 1350 Engravings. £4, 7s. 6d. Vol. I. On the Formation of Gardens and Construction of Garden Edifices. £2, 10s. Vol. II. Practical Gardening. £1, 17s. 6d.

MACINTYRE. Hindu-Koh: Wanderings and Wild Sports on and beyond the Himalayas. By Major-General DONALD MACINTYRE, V.C., late Prince of Wales' Own Goorkhas, F.R.G.S. *Dedicated to H.R.H. The Prince of Wales.* New and Cheaper Edition, revised, with numerous Illustrations, post 8vo, 7s. 6d.

MACKAY. A Sketch of the History of Fife and Kinross. A Study of Scottish History and Character. By Æ. J. G. MACKAY, Sheriff of these Counties. Crown 8vo, 6s.

MACKAY. A Manual of Modern Geography; Mathematical, Physical, and Political. By the Rev. ALEXANDER MACKAY, LL.D., F.R.G.S. 11th Thousand, revised to the present time. Crown 8vo, pp. 688. 7s. 6d.

—— Elements of Modern Geography. 55th Thousand, revised to the present time. Crown 8vo, pp. 300, 3s.

—— The Intermediate Geography. Intended as an Intermediate Book between the Author's 'Outlines of Geography' and 'Elements of Geography.' Sixteenth Edition, revised. Crown 8vo, pp. 238, 2s.

—— Outlines of Modern Geography. 188th Thousand, revised to the present time. 18mo, pp. 118, 1s.

—— First Steps in Geography. 105th Thousand. 18mo, pp. 56. Sewed, 4d.; cloth, 6d.

—— Elements of Physiography and Physical Geography. With Express Reference to the Instructions issued by the Science and Art Department. 30th Thousand, revised. Crown 8vo, 1s. 6d.

—— Facts and Dates; or, the Leading Events in Sacred and Profane History, and the Principal Facts in the various Physical Sciences. For Schools and Private Reference. New Edition. Crown 8vo, 3s. 6d.

MACKAY. An Old Scots Brigade. Being the History of Mackay's Regiment, now incorporated with the Royal Scots. With an Appendix containing many Original Documents connected with the History of the Regiment. By JOHN MACKAY (late) OF HERRIESDALE. Crown 8vo, 5s.

MACKENZIE. Studies in Roman Law. With Comparative Views of the Laws of France, England, and Scotland. By LORD MACKENZIE, one of the Judges of the Court of Session in Scotland. Sixth Edition, Edited by JOHN KIRKPATRICK, Esq., M.A., LL.B., Advocate, Professor of History in the University of Edinburgh. 8vo, 12s.

M'KERLIE. Galloway: Ancient and Modern. An Account of the Historic Celtic District. By P. H. M'KERLIE, F.S.A. Scot., F.R.G.S., &c. Author of 'Lands and their Owners in Galloway.' Crown 8vo, 7s. 6d.

M'PHERSON. Summer Sundays in a Strathmore Parish. By J. GORDON M'PHERSON, Ph.D., F.R.S.E., Minister of Ruthven. Crown 8vo, 5s.

—— Golf and Golfers. Past and Present. With an Introduction by the Right Hon. A. J. BALFOUR, and a Portrait of the Author. Fcap. 8vo, 1s. 6d.

MAIN. Three Hundred English Sonnets. Chosen and Edited by DAVID M. MAIN. Fcap. 8vo, 6s.

MAIR. A Digest of Laws and Decisions, Ecclesiastical and Civil, relating to the Constitution, Practice, and Affairs of the Church of Scotland. With Notes and Forms of Procedure. By the Rev. WILLIAM MAIR, D.D., Minister of the Parish of Earlston. Crown 8vo. With Supplements, 8s.

MARMORNE. The Story is told by ADOLPHUS SEGRAVE, the youngest of three Brothers. Third Edition. Crown 8vo, 6s.

MARSHALL. French Home Life. By FREDERIC MARSHALL, Author of 'Claire Brandon.' Second Edition. 5s.

MARSHALL. It Happened Yesterday. A Novel. Crown 8vo, 6s.

MARSHMAN. History of India. From the Earliest Period to the Close of the India Company's Government; with an Epitome of Subsequent Events. By JOHN CLARK MARSHMAN, C.S.I. Abridged from the Author's larger work. Second Edition, revised. Crown 8vo, with Map, 6s. 6d.

MARTIN. Goethe's Faust. Part I. Translated by Sir THEODORE MARTIN, K.C.B. Second Ed., crown 8vo, 6s. Ninth Ed., fcap. 8vo, 3s. 6d.

—— Goethe's Faust. Part II. Translated into English Verse. Second Edition, revised. Fcap. 8vo, 6s.

—— The Works of Horace. Translated into English Verse, with Life and Notes. 2 vols. New Edition, crown 8vo, 21s.

—— Poems and Ballads of Heinrich Heine. Done into English Verse. Second Edition. Printed on *papier vergé*, crown 8vo, 8s.

—— The Song of the Bell, and other Translations from Schiller, Goethe, Uhland, and Others. Crown 8vo, 7s. 6d.

—— Catullus. With Life and Notes. Second Ed., post 8vo, 7s. 6d.

—— Aladdin : A Dramatic Poem. By ADAM OEHLENSCHLAEGER. Fcap. 8vo, 5s.

—— Correggio : A Tragedy. By OEHLENSCHLAEGER. With Notes. Fcap. 8vo, 3s.

—— King Rene's Daughter : A Danish Lyrical Drama. By HENRIK HERTZ. Second Edition, fcap., 2s. 6d.

MARTIN. On some of Shakespeare's Female Characters. In a Series of Letters. By HELENA FAUCIT, LADY MARTIN. Dedicated by permission to Her Most Gracious Majesty the Queen. New Edition, enlarged. 8vo, with Portrait by Lane, 7s. 6d.

MATHESON. Can the Old Faith Live with the New? or the Problem of Evolution and Revelation. By the Rev. GEORGE MATHESON, D.D. Third Edition. Crown 8vo, 7s. 6d.

—— The Psalmist and the Scientist; or, Modern Value of the Religious Sentiment. New and Cheaper Edition. Crown 8vo, 5s.

—— Spiritual Development of St Paul. 3d Edition. Cr. 8vo, 5s.

—— Sacred Songs. New and Cheaper Edition. Cr. 8vo, 2s. 6d.

MAURICE. The Balance of Military Power in Europe. An Examination of the War Resources of Great Britain and the Continental States. By Colonel MAURICE, R.A., Professor of Military Art and History at the Royal Staff College. Crown 8vo, with a Map. 6s.

MEREDYTH. The Brief for the Government, 1886-92. A Handbook for Conservative and Unionist Writers, Speakers, &c. Second Edition. By W. H. MEREDYTH. Crown 8vo, 2s. 6d.

MICHEL. A Critical Inquiry into the Scottish Language. With the view of Illustrating the Rise and Progress of Civilisation in Scotland. By FRANCISQUE-MICHEL, F.S.A. Lond. and Scot., Correspondant de l'Institut de France, &c. 4to, printed on hand-made paper, and bound in Roxburghe, 66s.

MICHIE. The Larch : Being a Practical Treatise on its Culture and General Management. By CHRISTOPHER Y. MICHIE, Forester, Cullen House. Crown 8vo, with Illustrations. New and Cheaper Edition, enlarged, 5s.

—— The Practice of Forestry. Cr. 8vo, with Illustrations. 6s.

MIDDLETON. The Story of Alastair Bhan Comyn ; or, The Tragedy of Dunphail. A Tale of Tradition and Romance. By the Lady MIDDLETON. Square 8vo 10s. Cheaper Edition, 5s.

MILLER. Landscape Geology. A Plea for the Study of Geology by Landscape Painters. By HUGH MILLER, of H.M. Geological Survey. Cr.8vo, 3s.

MILNE. The Problem of the Churchless and Poor in our Large Towns. With special reference to the Home Mission Work of the Church of Scotland. By the Rev. ROBT. MILNE, M.A., D.D., Ardler. New and Cheaper Edition. Crown 8vo, 1s.

MILNE-HOME. Mamma's Black Nurse Stories. West Indian Folk-lore. By MARY PAMELA MILNE-HOME. With six full-page tinted Illustrations. Small 4to, 5s.

MINTO. A Manual of English Prose Literature, Biographical and Critical: designed mainly to show Characteristics of Style. By W. MINTO, M.A., Professor of Logic in the University of Aberdeen. Third Edition, revised. Crown 8vo, 7s. 6d.

―――― Characteristics of English Poets, from Chaucer to Shirley. New Edition, revised. Crown 8vo, 7s. 6d.

MOIR. Life of Mansie Wauch, Tailor in Dalkeith. By D. M. MOIR. With 8 Illustrations on Steel, by the late GEORGE CRUIKSHANK. Crown 8vo, 3s. 6d. Another Edition, fcap. 8vo, 1s. 6d.

MOMERIE. Defects of Modern Christianity, and other Sermons. By ALFRED WILLIAMS MOMERIE, M.A., D.Sc., LL.D. 4th Edition. Cr. 8vo, 5s.

―――― The Basis of Religion. Being an Examination of Natural Religion. Third Edition. Crown 8vo, 2s. 6d.

―――― The Origin of Evil, and other Sermons. Seventh Edition, enlarged. Crown 8vo, 5s.

―――― Personality. The Beginning and End of Metaphysics, and a Necessary Assumption in all Positive Philosophy. Fourth Ed. Cr. 8vo, 3s.

―――― Agnosticism. Third Edition, Revised. Crown 8vo, 5s.

―――― Preaching and Hearing; and other Sermons. Third Edition, Enlarged. Crown 8vo, 5s.

―――― Belief in God. Third Edition. Crown 8vo, 3s.

―――― Inspiration; and other Sermons. Second Ed. Cr. 8vo, 5s.

―――― Church and Creed. Second Edition. Crown 8vo, 4s. 6d.

MONTAGUE. Campaigning in South Africa. Reminiscences of an Officer in 1879. By Captain W. E. MONTAGUE, 94th Regiment, Author of 'Claude Meadowleigh,' &c. 8vo, 10s. 6d.

MONTALEMBERT. Memoir of Count de Montalembert. A Chapter of Recent French History. By Mrs OLIPHANT, Author of the 'Life of Edward Irving,' &c. 2 vols. crown 8vo, £1, 4s.

MORISON. Sordello. An Outline Analysis of Mr Browning's Poem. By JEANIE MORISON, Author of 'The Purpose of the Ages,' 'Ane Booke of Ballades,' &c. Crown 8vo, 3s.

―――― Selections from Poems. Crown 8vo, 4s. 6d.

―――― There as Here. Crown 8vo, 3s.
*** A limited impression on handmade paper, bound in vellum, 7s. 6d.

―――― "Of Fifine at the Fair," "Christmas Eve and Easter Day," and other of Mr Browning's Poems. Crown 8vo, 3s.

MOZLEY. Essays from 'Blackwood.' By the late ANNE MOZLEY, Author of 'Essays on Social Subjects'; Editor of 'The Letters and Correspondence of Cardinal Newman,' 'Letters of the Rev. J. B. Mozley,' &c. With a Memoir by her Sister, FANNY MOZLEY. Post 8vo, 7s. 6d.

MUNRO. On Valuation of Property. By WILLIAM MUNRO, M.A., Her Majesty's Assessor of Railways and Canals for Scotland. Second Edition. Revised and enlarged. 8vo, 3s. 6d.

MURDOCH. Manual of the Law of Insolvency and Bankruptcy: Comprehending a Summary of the Law of Insolvency, Notour Bankruptcy, Composition-contracts, Trust-deeds, Cessios, and Sequestrations; and the Winding-up of Joint-Stock Companies in Scotland; with Annotations on the various Insolvency and Bankruptcy Statutes; and with Forms of Procedure applicable to these Subjects. By JAMES MURDOCH, Member of the Faculty of Procurators in Glasgow. Fifth Edition, Revised and Enlarged, 8vo, £1, 10s.

MY TRIVIAL LIFE AND MISFORTUNE: A Gossip with no Plot in Particular. By A PLAIN WOMAN. Cheap Ed., crown 8vo, 3s. 6d.

By the SAME AUTHOR.

POOR NELLIE. New Edition. Crown 8vo, 6s.

NAPIER. The Construction of the Wonderful Canon of Logarithms. By JOHN NAPIER of Merchiston. Translated, with Notes, and a Catalogue of Napier's Works, by WILLIAM RAE MACDONALD. Small 4to, 15s. *A few large-paper copies on Whatman paper*, 30s.

NEAVES. Songs and Verses, Social and Scientific. By an Old Contributor to 'Maga.' By the Hon. Lord NEAVES. Fifth Ed., fcap. 8vo, 4s.

—— The Greek Anthology. Being Vol. XX. of 'Ancient Classics for English Readers.' Crown 8vo, 2s. 6d.

NICHOLSON. A Manual of Zoology, for the Use of Students. With a General Introduction on the Principles of Zoology. By HENRY ALLEYNE NICHOLSON, M.D., D.Sc., F.L.S., F.G.S., Regius Professor of Natural History in the University of Aberdeen. Seventh Edition, rewritten and enlarged. Post 8vo, pp. 956, with 555 Engravings on Wood, 18s.

—— Text-Book of Zoology, for the Use of Schools. Fourth Edition, enlarged. Crown 8vo, with 188 Engravings on Wood, 7s. 6d.

—— Introductory Text-Book of Zoology, for the Use of Junior Classes. Sixth Edition, revised and enlarged, with 166 Engravings, 3s.

—— Outlines of Natural History, for Beginners; being Descriptions of a Progressive Series of Zoological Types. Third Edition, with Engravings, 1s. 6d.

—— A Manual of Palæontology, for the Use of Students. With a General Introduction on the Principles of Palæontology. By Professor H. ALLEYNE NICHOLSON and RICHARD LYDEKKER, B.A. Third Edition. Rewritten and greatly enlarged. 2 vols. 8vo, with Engravings, £3, 3s.

—— The Ancient Life-History of the Earth. An Outline of the Principles and Leading Facts of Palæontological Science. Crown 8vo, with 276 Engravings, 10s. 6d.

—— On the "Tabulate Corals" of the Palæozoic Period, with Critical Descriptions of Illustrative Species. Illustrated with 15 Lithograph Plates and numerous Engravings. Super-royal 8vo, 21s.

—— Synopsis of the Classification of the Animal Kingdom. 8vo, with 106 Illustrations, 6s.

—— On the Structure and Affinities of the Genus Monticulipora and its Sub-Genera, with Critical Descriptions of Illustrative Species. Illustrated with numerous Engravings on wood and lithographed Plates. Super-royal 8vo, 18s.

NICHOLSON. Communion with Heaven, and other Sermons. By the late MAXWELL NICHOLSON, D.D., Minister of St Stephen's, Edinburgh. Crown 8vo, 5s. 6d.

—— Rest in Jesus. Sixth Edition. Fcap. 8vo, 4s. 6d.

NICHOLSON. A Treatise on Money, and Essays on Present Monetary Problems. By JOSEPH SHIELD NICHOLSON, M.A., D.Sc., Professor of Commercial and Political Economy and Mercantile Law in the University of Edinburgh. 8vo, 10s. 6d.

—— Thoth. A Romance. Third Edition. Crown 8vo, 4s. 6d.

—— A Dreamer of Dreams. A Modern Romance. Second Edition. Crown 8vo, 6s.

NICOLSON AND MURE. A Handbook to the Local Government (Scotland) Act, 1889. With Introduction, Explanatory Notes, and Index. By J. BADENACH NICOLSON, Advocate, Counsel to the Scotch Education Department, and W. J. MURE, Advocate, Legal Secretary to the Lord Advocate for Scotland. Ninth Reprint. 8vo, 5s.

OLIPHANT. Masollam: a Problem of the Period. A Novel. By LAURENCE OLIPHANT. 3 vols. post 8vo, 25s. 6d

—— Scientific Religion; or, Higher Possibilities of Life and Practice through the Operation of Natural Forces. Second Edition. 8vo, 16s.

—— Altiora Peto. By LAURENCE OLIPHANT. Cheap Edition. Crown 8vo, boards, 2s. 6d.; cloth, 3s. 6d. Illustrated Edition. Crown 8vo, cloth, 6s.

—— Piccadilly: A Fragment of Contemporary Biography. With Illustrations by Richard Doyle. New Edition, 3s. 6d. Cheap Edition, boards, 2s. 6d.

—— Traits and Travesties; Social and Political. Post 8vo, 10s. 6d.

OLIPHANT. The Land of Gilead. With Excursions in the Lebanon. With Illustrations and Maps. Demy 8vo, 21s.
——— Haifa: Life in Modern Palestine. 2d Edition. 8vo, 7s. 6d.
——— Episodes in a Life of Adventure; or, Moss from a Rolling Rolling Stone. Fifth Edition. Post 8vo, 6s.
——— Memoir of the Life of Laurence Oliphant, and of Alice Oliphant, his Wife. By Mrs M. O. W. OLIPHANT. Seventh Edition. In 2 vols. post 8vo, with Portraits. 21s.
OLIPHANT. Katie Stewart. By Mrs OLIPHANT. 2s. 6d.
——— Two Stories of the Seen and the Unseen. The Open Door —Old Lady Mary. Paper Covers, 1s.
——— Sons and Daughters. Crown 8vo, 3s. 6d.
OLIPHANT. Notes of a Pilgrimage to Jerusalem and the Holy Land. By F. R. OLIPHANT. Crown 8vo, 3s. 6d.
ON SURREY HILLS. By "A SON OF THE MARSHES." Second Edition. Crown 8vo, 6s.

BY THE SAME AUTHOR.

Annals of a Fishing Village. Edited by J. A. OWEN. Crown 8vo, with Illustrations, 7s. 6d.
OSSIAN. The Poems of Ossian in the Original Gaelic. With a Literal Translation into English, and a Dissertation on the Authenticity of the Poems. By the Rev. ARCHIBALD CLERK. 2 vols. Imperial 8vo, £1. 11s. 6d.
OSWALD. By Fell and Fjord; or, Scenes and Studies in Iceland. By E. J. OSWALD. Post 8vo, with Illustrations. 7s. 6d.
PAGE. Introductory Text-Book of Geology. By DAVID PAGE, LL.D., Professor of Geology in the Durham University of Physical Science Newcastle, and Professor LAPWORTH of Mason Science College, Birmingham. With Engravings and Glossarial Index. Twelfth Edition. Revised and Enlarged. 3s. 6d.
——— Advanced Text-Book of Geology, Descriptive and Industrial. With Engravings, and Glossary of Scientific Terms. Sixth Edition, revised and enlarged, 7s. 6d.
——— Introductory Text-Book of Physical Geography. With Sketch-Maps and Illustrations. Edited by Professor LAPWORTH, LL.D., F.G.S., &c., Mason Science College, Birmingham. 12th Edition. 2s. 6d.
——— Advanced Text-Book of Physical Geography. Third Edition, Revised and Enlarged by Prof. LAPWORTH. With Engravings. 5s.
PATON. Spindrift. By Sir J. NOEL PATON. Fcap., cloth, 5s.
——— Poems by a Painter. Fcap., cloth, 5s.
PATON. Body and Soul. A Romance in Transcendental Pathology. By FREDERICK NOEL PATON. Third Edition. Crown 8vo, 1s.
PATRICK. The Apology of Origen in Reply to Celsus. A Chapter in the History of Apologetics. By Rev. J. PATRICK, B.D. In 1 vol. crown 8vo. [In the press.
PATTERSON. Essays in History and Art. By R. HOGARTH PATTERSON. 8vo, 12s.
——— The New Golden Age, and Influence of the Precious Metals upon the World. 2 vols. 8vo, 31s. 6d.
PAUL. History of the Royal Company of Archers, the Queen's Body-Guard for Scotland. By JAMES BALFOUR PAUL, Advocate of the Scottish Bar. Crown 4to, with Portraits and other Illustrations. £2, 2s.
PEILE. Lawn Tennis as a Game of Skill. With latest revised Laws as played by the Best Clubs. By Captain S. C. F. PEILE, B.S.C. Cheaper Edition, fcap. cloth, 1s.
PETTIGREW. The Handy Book of Bees, and their Profitable Management. By A. PETTIGREW. Fifth Edition, Enlarged, with Engravings. Crown 8vo, 3s. 6d.
PHILIP. The Function of Labour in the Production of Wealth. By ALEXANDER PHILIP, LL.B., Edinburgh. Crown 8vo, 3s. 6d.

PHILOSOPHICAL CLASSICS FOR ENGLISH READERS.
Edited by WILLIAM KNIGHT, LL.D., Professor of Moral Philosophy, University of St Andrews. In crown 8vo volumes, with portraits, price 3s. 6d.
[For list of Volumes published, see page 2.

POLLOK. The Course of Time : A Poem. By ROBERT POLLOK, A.M. Small fcap. 8vo, cloth gilt, 2s. 6d. Cottage Edition, 32mo, 8d. The Same, cloth, gilt edges, 1s. 6d. Another Edition, with Illustrations by Birket Foster and others, fcap., cloth, 3s. 6d., or with edges gilt, 4s.

PORT ROYAL LOGIC. Translated from the French ; with Introduction, Notes, and Appendix. By THOMAS SPENCER BAYNES, LL.D., Professor in the University of St Andrews. Tenth Edition, 12mo, 4s.

POTTS AND DARNELL. Aditus Faciliores : An easy Latin Construing Book, with Complete Vocabulary. By the late A. W. POTTS, M.A., LL.D., and the Rev. C. DARNELL, M.A., Head-Master of Cargilfield Preparatory School, Edinburgh. Tenth Edition, fcap. 8vo, 3s. 6d.

——— Aditus Faciliores Graeci. An easy Greek Construing Book, with Complete Vocabulary. Fourth Edition, fcap. 8vo, 3s.

POTTS. School Sermons. By the late ALEXANDER WM. POTTS, LL.D., First Head-Master of Fettes College. With a Memoir and Portrait. Crown 8vo, 7s. 6d.

PRINGLE. The Live-Stock of the Farm. By ROBERT O. PRINGLE. Third Edition. Revised and Edited by JAMES MACDONALD. Cr. 8vo, 7s. 6d.

PUBLIC GENERAL STATUTES AFFECTING SCOTLAND from 1707 to 1847, with Chronological Table and Index. 3 vols. large 8vo, £3, 3s.

PUBLIC GENERAL STATUTES AFFECTING SCOTLAND, COLLECTION OF. Published Annnally with General Index.

RADICAL CURE FOR IRELAND, The. A Letter to the People of England and Scotland concerning a new Plantation. With 2 Maps. 8vo, 7s. 6d.

RAMSAY. Rough Recollections of Military Service and Society. By Lieut.-Col. BALCARRES D. WARDLAW RAMSAY. Two vols. post 8vo, 21s.

RAMSAY. Scotland and Scotsmen in the Eighteenth Century. Edited from the MSS. of JOHN RAMSAY, Esq. of Ochtertyre, by ALEXANDER ALLARDYCE, Author of 'Memoir of Admiral Lord Keith, K.B.,' &c. 2 vols. 8vo, 31s. 6d.

RANKIN. A Handbook of the Church of Scotland. By JAMES RANKIN, D.D., Minister of Muthill; Author of 'Character Studies in the Old Testament,' &c. An entirely New and much Enlarged Edition. Crown 8vo, with 2 Maps, 7s. 6d.

——— The Creed in Scotland. An Exposition of the Apostles' Creed With Extracts from Archbishop Hamilton's Catechism of 1552, John Calvin's Catechism of 1556, and a Catena of Ancient Latin and other Hymns. Post 8vo, 7s. 6d.

——— First Communion Lessons. Twenty-third Edition. Paper Cover, 2d.

RECORDS OF THE TERCENTENARY FESTIVAL OF THE UNIVERSITY OF EDINBURGH. Celebrated in April 1884. Published under the Sanction of the Senatus Academicus. Large 4to, £2, 12s. 6d.

ROBERTSON. The Early Religion of Israel. As set forth by Biblical Writers and Modern Critical Historians. Being the Baird Lecture for 1888-89. By JAMES ROBERTSON, D.D., Professor of Oriental Languages in the University of Glasgow. Crown 8vo, 10s. 6d.

ROBERTSON. Orellana, and other Poems. By J. LOGIE ROBERTSON, M.A. Fcap. 8vo. Printed on hand-made paper. 6s.

ROBERTSON. Our Holiday Among the Hills. By JAMES and JANET LOGIE ROBERTSON. Fcap. 8vo, 3s. 6d.

ROSCOE. Rambles with a Fishing-rod. By E. S. ROSCOE. Crown 8vo, 4s. 6d.

ROSS. Old Scottish Regimental Colours. By ANDREW ROSS, S.S.C., Hon. Secretary Old Scottish Regimental Colours Committee. Dedicated by Special Permission to Her Majesty the Queen. Folio. £2, 12s. 6d.

RUSSELL. The Haigs of Bemersyde. A Family History. By JOHN RUSSELL. Large 8vo, with Illustrations. 21s.

LIST OF BOOKS PUBLISHED BY

RUSSELL. Fragments from Many Tables. Being the Recollections of some Wise and Witty Men and Women. By GEO. RUSSELL. Cr. 8vo, 4s. 6d.

RUTLAND. Notes of an Irish Tour in 1846. By the DUKE OF RUTLAND, G.C.B. (Lord JOHN MANNERS). New Edition. Crown 8vo, 2s. 6d.

—— Correspondence between the Right Honble. William Pitt and Charles Duke of Rutland, Lord Lieutenant of Ireland, 1781-1787. With Introductory Note by John Duke of Rutland. 8vo, 7s. 6d.

RUTLAND. Gems of German Poetry. Translated by the DUCHESS OF RUTLAND (Lady JOHN MANNERS). [*New Edition in preparation.*

—— Impressions of Bad-Homburg. Comprising a Short Account of the Women's Associations of Germany under the Red Cross. Crown 8vo, 1s. 6d.

—— Some Personal Recollections of the Later Years of the Earl of Beaconsfield, K.G. Sixth Edition, 6d.

—— Employment of Women in the Public Service. 6d.

—— Some of the Advantages of Easily Accessible Reading and Recreation Rooms, and Free Libraries. With Remarks on Starting and Maintaining Them. Second Edition, crown 8vo, 1s.

—— A Sequel to Rich Men's Dwellings, and other Occasional Papers. Crown 8vo, 2s. 6d.

—— Encouraging Experiences of Reading and Recreation Rooms, Aims of Guilds, Nottingham Social Guild, Existing Institutions, &c., &c. Crown 8vo, 1s.

SCHILLER. Wallenstein. A Dramatic Poem. By FREDERICK VON SCHILLER. Translated by C. G. A. LOCKHART. Fcap. 8vo, 7s. 6d.

SCOTCH LOCH FISHING. By "Black Palmer." Crown 8vo, interleaved with blank pages, 4s.

SCOUGAL. Prisons and their Inmates; or, Scenes from a Silent World. By FRANCIS SCOUGAL. Crown 8vo, boards, 2s.

SELLAR. Manual of the Education Acts for Scotland. By the late ALEXANDER CRAIG SELLAR, M.P. Eighth Edition. Revised and in great part rewritten by J. EDWARD GRAHAM, B.A. Oxon., Advocate. With Rules for the conduct of Elections, with Notes and Cases. With a Supplement, being the Acts of 1889 in so far as affecting the Education Acts. 8vo, 12s. 6d.

[SUPPLEMENT TO SELLAR'S MANUAL OF THE EDUCATION ACTS. 8vo, 2s.]

SETH. Scottish Philosophy. A Comparison of the Scottish and German Answers to Hume. Balfour Philosophical Lectures, University of Edinburgh. By ANDREW SETH, M.A., Professor of Logic and Metaphysics in Edinburgh University. Second Edition. Crown 8vo, 5s.

—— Hegelianism and Personality. Balfour Philosophical Lectures. Second Series. Crown 8vo, 5s.

SETH. Freedom as Ethical Postulate. By JAMES SETH, M.A., George Munro Professor of Philosophy, Dalhousie College, Halifax, Canada. 8vo, 1s.

SHADWELL. The Life of Colin Campbell, Lord Clyde. Illustrated by Extracts from his Diary and Correspondence. By Lieutenant-General SHADWELL, C.B. 2 vols. 8vo. With Portrait, Maps, and Plans. 36s.

SHAND. Half a Century; or, Changes in Men and Manners. By ALEX. INNES SHAND, Author of 'Against Time,' &c. Second Edition, 8vo, 12s. 6d.

—— Letters from the West of Ireland. Reprinted from the 'Times.' Crown 8vo, 5s.

—— Kilcarra. A Novel. 3 vols. crown 8vo, 25s. 6d.

SHARPE. Letters from and to Charles Kirkpatrick Sharpe. Edited by ALEXANDER ALLARDYCE, Author of 'Memoir of Admiral Lord Keith, K.B.,' &c. With a Memoir by the Rev. W. K. R. BEDFORD. In two vols. 8vo. Illustrated with Etchings and other Engravings. £2, 12s. 6d.

SIM. Margaret Sim's Cookery. With an Introduction by L. B. WALFORD, Author of 'Mr Smith : A Part of His Life,' &c. Crown 8vo, 5s.

SKELTON. Maitland of Lethington; and the Scotland of Mary Stuart. A History. By JOHN SKELTON, C.B., LL.D., Author of 'The Essays of Shirley.' Demy 8vo. 2 vols., 28s.
—— The Handbook of Public Health. A Complete Edition of the Public Health and other Sanitary Acts relating to Scotland. Annotated, and with the Rules, Instructions, and Decisions of the Board of Supervision brought up to date with relative forms. 8vo, with Supplement, 8s. 6d.
—— Supplement to Skelton's Handbook. The Administration of the Public Health Act in Counties. 8vo, cloth, 1s. 6d.
—— The Local Government (Scotland) Act in Relation to Public Health. A Handy Guide for County and District Councillors, Medical Officers, Sanitary Inspectors, and Members of Parochial Boards. Second Edition. With a new Preface on appointment of Sanitary Officers. Crown 8vo, 2s.
SMITH. For God and Humanity. A Romance of Mount Carmel. By HASKETT SMITH, Author of 'The Divine Epiphany,' &c. 3 vols. post 8vo, 25s. 6d.
SMITH. Thorndale; or, The Conflict of Opinions. By WILLIAM SMITH, Author of 'A Discourse on Ethics,' &c. New Edition. Cr. 8vo, 10s. 6d.
—— Gravenhurst; or, Thoughts on Good and Evil. Second Edition, with Memoir of the Author. Crown 8vo, 8s.
—— The Story of William and Lucy Smith. Edited by GEORGE MERRIAM. Large post 8vo, 12s. 6d.
SMITH. Memoir of the Families of M'Combie and Thoms, originally M'Intosh and M'Thomas. Compiled from History and Tradition. By WILLIAM M'COMBIE SMITH. With Illustrations. 8vo, 7s. 6d.
SMITH. Greek Testament Lessons for Colleges, Schools, and Private Students, consisting chiefly of the Sermon on the Mount and the Parables of our Lord. With Notes and Essays. By the Rev. J. HUNTER SMITH, M.A., King Edward's School, Birmingham. Crown 8vo, 6s.
SMITH. Writings by the Way. By JOHN CAMPBELL SMITH, M.A., Sheriff-Substitute. Crown 8vo, 9s.
SMITH. The Secretary for Scotland. Being a Statement of the Powers and Duties of the new Scottish Office. With a Short Historical Introduction and numerous references to important Administrative Documents. By W. C. SMITH, LL.B., Advocate. 8vo, 6s.
SORLEY. The Ethics of Naturalism. Being the Shaw Fellowship Lectures, 1884. By W. R. SORLEY, M.A., Fellow of Trinity College, Cambridge, Professor of Logic and Philosophy in University College of South Wales. Crown 8vo, 6s.
SPEEDY. Sport in the Highlands and Lowlands of Scotland with Rod and Gun. By TOM SPEEDY. Second Edition, Revised and Enlarged. With Illustrations by Lieut.-Gen. Hope Crealocke, C.B., C.M.G., and others. 8vo, 15s.
SPROTT. The Worship and Offices of the Church of Scotland. By GEORGE W. SPROTT, D.D., Minister of North Berwick. Crown 8vo, 6s.
STAFFORD. How I Spent my Twentieth Year. Being a Record of a Tour Round the World, 1886-87. By the MARCHIONESS OF STAFFORD. With Illustrations. Third Edition, crown 8vo, 8s. 6d.
STARFORTH. Villa Residences and Farm Architecture: A Series of Designs. By JOHN STARFORTH, Architect. 102 Engravings. Second Edition, medium 4to, £2, 17s. 6d.
STATISTICAL ACCOUNT OF SCOTLAND. Complete, with Index, 15 vols. 8vo, £16, 16s.
Each County sold separately, with Title, Index, and Map, neatly bound in cloth.
STEPHENS' BOOK OF THE FARM; detailing the Labours of the Farmer, Farm-Steward, Ploughman, Shepherd, Hedger, Farm-Labourer, Field-Worker, and Cattleman. Illustrated with numerous Portraits of Animals and Engravings of Implements, and Plans of Farm Buildings. Fourth Edition. Revised, and in great part rewritten by JAMES MACDONALD, of the 'Farming World,' &c., &c. Assisted by many of the leading agricultural authorities of the day. Complete in Six Divisional Volumes, bound in cloth, each 10s. 6d., or handsomely bound, in 3 volumes, with leather back and gilt top, £3, 3s.
—— The Book of Farm Implements and Machines. By J. SLIGHT and R. SCOTT BURN, Engineers. Edited by HENRY STEPHENS. Large 8vo, £2, 2s.

STEVENSON. British Fungi. (Hymenomycetes.) By Rev. JOHN STEVENSON, Author of 'Mycologia Scotia,' Hon. Sec. Cryptogamic Society of Scotland. 2 vols. post 8vo, with Illustrations, price 12s. 6d. each.
Vol. I. AGARICUS—BOLBITIUS. Vol. II. CORTINARIUS—DACRYMYCES.

STEWART. Advice to Purchasers of Horses. By JOHN STEWART, V.S. New Edition. 2s. 6d.

——— Stable Economy. A Treatise on the Management of Horses in relation to Stabling, Grooming, Feeding, Watering, and Working. Seventh Edition, fcap. 8vo, 6s. 6d.

STEWART. A Hebrew Grammar, with the Pronunciation, Syllabic Division and Tone of the Words, and Quantity of the Vowels. By Rev. DUNCAN STEWART, D.D. Fourth Edition. 8vo, 3s. 6d.

STEWART. Boethius: An Essay. By HUGH FRASER STEWART, M.A., Trinity College, Cambridge. Crown 8vo, 7s. 6d.

STODDART. Angling Songs. By THOMAS TOD STODDART. New Edition, with a Memoir by ANNA M. STODDART. Crown 8vo, 7s. 6d.

STORMONTH. Etymological and Pronouncing Dictionary of the English Language. Including a very Copious Selection of Scientific Terms. For Use in Schools and Colleges, and as a Book of General Reference. By the Rev. JAMES STORMONTH. The Pronunciation carefully Revised by the Rev. P. H. PHELP, M.A. Cantab. Tenth Edition, Revised throughout. Crown 8vo, pp. 800. 7s. 6d.

——— Dictionary of the English Language, Pronouncing, Etymological, and Explanatory. Revised by the Rev. P. H. PHELP. Library Edition. Imperial 8vo, handsomely bound in half morocco, 31s. 6d.

——— The School Etymological Dictionary and Word-Book. Fourth Edition. Fcap. 8vo, pp. 254. 2s.

STORY. Nero; A Historical Play. By W. W. STORY, Author of 'Roba di Roma.' Fcap. 8vo, 6s.

——— Vallombrosa. Post 8vo, 5s.

——— Poems. 2 vols. fcap., 7s. 6d.

——— Fiammetta. A Summer Idyl. Crown 8vo, 7s. 6d.

——— Conversations in a Studio. 2 vols. crown 8vo, 12s. 6d.

——— Excursions in Art and Letters. Crown 8vo, 7s. 6d.

STRICKLAND. Life of Agnes Strickland. By her SISTER. Post 8vo, with Portrait engraved on Steel, 12s. 6d.

STURGIS. John-a-Dreams. A Tale. By JULIAN STURGIS. New Edition, crown 8vo, 3s. 6d.

——— Little Comedies, Old and New. Crown 8vo, 7s. 6d.

SUTHERLAND. Handbook of Hardy Herbaceous and Alpine Flowers, for general Garden Decoration. Containing Descriptions of upwards of 1000 Species of Ornamental Hardy Perennial and Alpine Plants; along with Concise and Plain Instructions for their Propagation and Culture. By WILLIAM SUTHERLAND, Landscape Gardener; formerly Manager of the Herbaceous Department at Kew. Crown 8vo, 7s. 6d.

TAYLOR. The Story of My Life. By the late Colonel MEADOWS TAYLOR, Author of 'The Confessions of a Thug,' &c. &c. Edited by his Daughter. New and cheaper Edition, being the Fourth. Crown 8vo, 6s

TELLET. Pastor and Prelate. A Story of Clerical Life. By ROY TELLET, Author of 'The Outcasts,' &c. 3 vols. crown 8vo, 25s. 6d.

THOLUCK. Hours of Christian Devotion. Translated from the German of A. Tholuck, D.D., Professor of Theology in the University of Halle. By the Rev. ROBERT MENZIES, D.D. With a Preface written for this Translation by the Author. Second Edition, crown 8vo, 7s. 6d.

THOMSON. Handy Book of the Flower-Garden: being Practical Directions for the Propagation, Culture, and Arrangement of Plants in Flower-Gardens all the year round. With Engraved Plans. By DAVID THOMSON, Gardener to His Grace the Duke of Buccleuch, K.T., at Drumlanrig Fourth and Cheaper Edition, crown 8vo, 5s.

THOMSON. The Handy Book of Fruit-Culture under Glass: being a series of Elaborate Practical Treatises on the Cultivation and Forcing of Pines, Vines, Peaches, Figs, Melons, Strawberries, and Cucumbers. With Engravings of Hothouses, &c. Second Ed. Cr. 8vo, 7s. 6d.

THOMSON. A Practical Treatise on the Cultivation of the Grape Vine. By WILLIAM THOMSON, Tweed Vineyards. Tenth Edition, 8vo, 5s.

THOMSON. Cookery for the Sick and Convalescent. With Directions for the Preparation of Poultices, Fomentations, &c. By BARBARA THOMSON. Fcap. 8vo, 1s. 6d.

THORNTON. Opposites. A Series of Essays on the Unpopular Sides of Popular Questions. By LEWIS THORNTON. 8vo, 12s. 6d.

TOM CRINGLE'S LOG. A New Edition, with Illustrations. Crown 8vo, cloth gilt, 5s. Cheap Edition, 2s.

TRANSACTIONS OF THE HIGHLAND AND AGRICULTURAL SOCIETY OF SCOTLAND. Published annually, price 5s.

TULLOCH. Rational Theology and Christian Philosophy in England in the Seventeenth Century. By JOHN TULLOCH, D.D., Principal of St Mary's College in the University of St Andrews; and one of her Majesty's Chaplains in Ordinary in Scotland. Second Edition. 2 vols. 8vo, 16s.

—— Modern Theories in Philosophy and Religion. 8vo, 15s.

—— Luther, and other Leaders of the Reformation. Third Edition, enlarged. Crown 8vo, 3s. 6d.

—— Memoir of Principal Tulloch, D.D., LL.D. By Mrs OLIPHANT, Author of 'Life of Edward Irving.' Third and Cheaper Edition. 8vo, with Portrait. 7s. 6d.

TWEEDIE. The Arabian Horse: his Country and People. With Portraits of Typical or Famous Arabians, and numerous other Illustrations; also a Map of the Country of the Arabian Horse, and a descriptive Glossary of Arabic words and proper names. By Colonel W. TWEEDIE, C.S.I., Bengal Staff Corps, H.B.M.'s Consul-General, Baghdad. [In the press.

VEITCH. Institutes of Logic. By JOHN VEITCH, LL.D., Professor of Logic and Rhetoric in the University of Glasgow. Post 8vo, 12s. 6d.

—— The Feeling for Nature in Scottish Poetry. From the Earliest Times to the Present Day. 2 vols. fcap. 8vo, in roxburghe binding. 15s.

—— Merlin and Other Poems. Fcap. 8vo. 4s. 6d.

—— Knowing and Being. Essays in Philosophy. First Series. Crown 8vo, 5s.

VIRGIL. The Æneid of Virgil. Translated in English Blank Verse by G. K. RICKARDS, M.A., and Lord RAVENSWORTH. 2 vols. fcap. 8vo, 10s.

WALFORD. Four Biographies from 'Blackwood': Jane Taylor, Hannah More, Elizabeth Fry, Mary Somerville. By L. B. WALFORD. Crown 8vo, 5s.

WARREN'S (SAMUEL) WORKS :—
Diary of a Late Physician. Cloth, 2s. 6d.; boards, 2s.
Ten Thousand A-Year. Cloth, 3s. 6d.; boards, 2s. 6d.
Now and Then. The Lily and the Bee. Intellectual and Moral Development of the Present Age. 4s. 6d.
Essays: Critical, Imaginative, and Juridical. 5s.

WARREN. The Five Books of the Psalms. With Marginal Notes. By Rev. SAMUEL L. WARREN, Rector of Esher, Surrey; late Fellow, Dean, and Divinity Lecturer, Wadham College, Oxford. Crown 8vo, 5s.

WEBSTER. The Angler and the Loop-Rod. By DAVID WEBSTER. Crown 8vo, with Illustrations, 7s. 6d.

WELLINGTON. Wellington Prize Essays on "the System of Field Manœuvres best adapted for enabling our Troops to meet a Continental Army." Edited by General Sir EDWARD BRUCE HAMLEY, K.C.B., K.C.M.G. 8vo, 12s. 6d.

WENLEY. Socrates and Christ: A Study in the Philosophy of Religion. By R. M. WENLEY, M.A., Lecturer on Mental and Moral Philosophy in Queen Margaret College, Glasgow; Examiner in Philosophy in the University of Glasgow. Crown 8vo, 6s.

WERNER. A Visit to Stanley's Rear-Guard at Major Barttelot's Camp on the Aruhwimi. With an Account of River-Life on the Congo. By J. R. WERNER, F.R.G.S., Engineer, late in the Service of the Etat Independant du Congo. With Maps, Portraits, and other Illustrations. 8vo. 16s.

WESTMINSTER ASSEMBLY. Minutes of the Westminster Assembly, while engaged in preparing their Directory for Church Government, Confession of Faith, and Catechisms (November 1644 to March 1649). Edited by the Rev. Professor ALEX. T. MITCHELL, of St Andrews, and the Rev. JOHN STRUTHERS, LL.D. With a Historical and Critical Introduction by Professor Mitchell. 8vo, 15s.

WHITE. The Eighteen Christian Centuries. By the Rev. JAMES WHITE. Seventh Edition, post 8vo, with Index. 6s.

———— History of France, from the Earliest Times. Sixth Thousand, post 8vo, with Index, 6s.

WHITE. Archæological Sketches in Scotland—Kintyre and Knapdale. By Colonel T. P. WHITE, R.E., of the Ordnance Survey. With numerous Illustrations. 2 vols. folio, £4, 4s. Vol. I., Kintyre, sold separately, £2, 2s.

———— The Ordnance Survey of the United Kingdom. A Popular Account. Crown 8vo, 5s.

WICKS. Golden Lives. The Story of a Woman's Courage. By FREDERICK WICKS. Cheap Edition, with 120 Illustrations. Illustrated Boards. 8vo, 2s. 6d.

WILLIAMSON. Poems of Nature and Life. By DAVID R. WILLIAMSON, Minister of Kirkmaiden. Fcap. 8vo, 3s.

WILLS AND GREENE. Drawing-room Dramas for Children. By W. G. WILLS and the Hon. Mrs GREENE. Crown 8vo, 6s.

WILSON. Works of Professor Wilson. Edited by his Son-in-Law, Professor FERRIER. 12 vols. crown 8vo, £2, 8s.

———— Christopher in his Sporting-Jacket. 2 vols., 8s.

———— Isle of Palms, City of the Plague, and other Poems. 4s.

———— Lights and Shadows of Scottish Life, and other Tales. 4s.

———— Essays, Critical and Imaginative. 4 vols., 16s.

———— The Noctes Ambrosianæ. 4 vols., 16s.

———— Homer and his Translators, and the Greek Drama. Crown 8vo, 4s.

WINGATE. Lily Neil. A Poem. By DAVID WINGATE. Crown 8vo, 4s. 6d.

WORDSWORTH. The Historical Plays of Shakspeare. With Introductions and Notes. By CHARLES WORDSWORTH, D.C.L., Bishop of S. Andrews. 3 vols. post 8vo, cloth, each price 7s. 6d., or handsomely bound in half-calf, each price 9s. 9d.

WORSLEY. Poems and Translations. By PHILIP STANHOPE WORSLEY, M.A. Edited by EDWARD WORSLEY. 2d Ed., enlarged. Fcap. 8vo, 6s.

YATE. England and Russia Face to Face in Asia. A Record of Travel with the Afghan Boundary Commission. By Captain A. C. YATE, Bombay Staff Corps. 8vo, with Maps and Illustrations, 21s.

YATE. Northern Afghanistan; or, Letters from the Afghan Boundary Commission. By Major C. E. YATE, C.S.I., C.M.G. Bombay Staff Corps, F.R.G.S. 8vo, with Maps. 18s.

YOUNG. A Story of Active Service in Foreign Lands. Compiled from letters sent home from South Africa, India, and China, 1856-1882. By Surgeon-General A. GRAHAM YOUNG, Author of 'Crimean Cracks.' Crown 8vo, Illustrated, 7s. 6d.

YULE. Fortification: for the Use of Officers in the Army, and Readers of Military History. By Col. YULE, Bengal Engineers. 8vo, with numerous Illustrations, 10s. 6d.

www.ingramcontent.com/pod-product-compliance
Lightning Source LLC
Chambersburg PA
CBHW051242300426
44114CB00011B/854